GOLDEN WATTLE

COOKERY BOOK

ORIGINAL AUTHORS:

Margaret A. Wylie

Mabel E. Yewers

Margaret H. Reeves

Doris S. Gray

Marie A. McKinnon

Officers of the Education Department,
Western Australia

Angus&Robertson
An imprint of HarperCollins*Publishers*

First Edition	1926	Second	1928
Third	1930	Fourth	1931
Fifth	1935	Sixth	1937
Seventh	1939	Eighth	1942
Ninth	1946	Tenth	1949
Eleventh	1950	Twelfth	1952
Thirteenth	1954	Fourteenth	1956
Fifteenth	1958	Sixteenth	1960
Seventeenth	1963	Eighteenth	1966
Nineteenth	1968	Twentieth	1969
Twenty First	1973	Twenty Second	1975
Twenty Third	1976	Twenty Fourth	1977
Twenty Fifth	1980	Twenty Sixth	1982
Twenty Seventh	1984	Twenty Eighth	1989
Twenty Ninth	1992	Thirtieth	1999
Thirty First	2000	Thirty Second	2001
Thirty Third	2002		

Introduction

The Author gratefully acknowledges the kindness of Professor E.J. Underwood, C.B.E., F.A.A., F.R.S., Chairman, National Committee for Nutritional Sciences, Australian Academy of Science, for the valuable contribution of Chapter on Food Values and The Best Use of Food.

The Book was originally compiled with the following objects in view:—

1. To place before young students a record of methods of cookery taught at school; supplementing lessons given from foundation recipes, and generally increasing their knowledge of the subject.

2. To enable girls who have left school to maintain their interest in cookery, and to have in their possession a book of dependable recipes which may stimulate a desire to venture further in the culinary art.

3. To give, in a concise and simple form, information on food values and the cooking of food.

4. To set before those taking up life in rural districts of the State simple directions for bread-making, jam and jelly making and fruit preserving, which will secure success at the outset.

INDEX

A

B

C

E

F

G

H

I

J

K

L

M

M

P

Q

R

S

S

T

V

W

Y

Z

FOOD VALUES AND THE BEST USE OF FOOD

By Professor E.J. Underwood, C.B.E., F.A.A., F.R.S.,
Chairman, National Committee for Nutritional Sciences,
Australian Academy of Science.

The Functions of Food in the Body

Foods have the following functions to perform in the body:—

(i)   To supply fuel or energy (calories) for internal and external bodily movements, for growth and for the maintenance of body temperature.

(ii) To build up and repair the "wear and tear" of body tissues, especially the muscles and bones during growth.

(iii) To regulate the body processes and promote healthy tissues, and organs.

The Composition of Foods

In order satisfactorily to fulfil all these functions foods must supply adequate amounts of a range of chemical compounds called *nutrients,* in a palatable and digestible form.

Most foods contain hundreds of different chemical compounds but fortunately these can be reduced to a few broad classes of substances which, between them, supply all the requirements of the body. These are:—

(i)   Carbohydrates, e.g. sugars and starches.

(ii) Fats and oils.

(i) and (ii) are the chief sources of fuel or energy in most diets.

(iii) Proteins, e.g. meat, fish and egg; cheese and milk and certain legume seeds like peas, beans and lentils.

Proteins are the body-building and flesh-forming constituents of the diet.

(iv) Minerals, e.g. calcium (lime) and phosphorus, and iron, iodine, zinc and chromium.

These are concerned with the building of bones and teeth and blood and with the maintenance of healthy body fluids and glands.

(v)   Vitamins, e.g. Vitamin A, Vitamin B1 and Vitamin C.

Vitamins

These vitamins are present in most foods in minute amounts and are necessary for the regulation of body processes, the promotion of growth and health and the proper utilisation of the rest of the food nutrients.

It is essential to realise that a satisfactory diet must first of all supply enough fuel or energy because this is the body's primary need. It must also supply enough proteins and minerals for growth and repair. However rich in vitamins, a diet will *not* be satisfactory unless it first of all meets these requirements. Nevertheless, the vitamins are in practice of great importance for the following reasons:

(a)   They are more likely to be lacking from our modern diets *without our being aware of it* than other dietary essentials, because the body has no way of telling us immediately of a shortage. Lack of energy foods causes *hunger* and weakness and loss of weight fairly quickly and our intake of energy is quickly raised to meet any temporary lack. No such obvious signs of vitamin lack show up, except over long periods of time. That is why vitamin deficiencies are sometimes described as "hidden hungers".

(b)   There is a rapidly increasing consumption of refined and processed foods and of prepared or 'convenience' foods which have frequently but not necessarily lost some of their vitamin content during treatment. An extreme example of this is refined white sugar which is pure carbohydrate supplying nothing but energy.

(c)   More and more people are living away from the land where the food is grown. This means that much of our food has to be stored, transported and preserved in various ways, which usually results in some loss of vitamin content. This applies particularly to green vegetables which in the days and sometimes weeks which usually elapse between picking and eating lose a high proportion of their Vitamin C content. Vitamin C is necessary for the maintenance of healthy gums and blood vessels and for resistance to infection.

The answer to the problem of satisfactory supply of vitamins should not lie in the purchase of vitamin tablets from the pharmacist, though this may be necessary at times on medical advice. It lies in the consumption of a good well-balanced diet as described below.

The Values of Common Foods

Most of the common articles of food can be grouped according to their main usefulness in the diet as follows:

(i)   *Breads and cereals*—Very valuable sources of fuel or energy and fair sources of protein but very poor sources of calcium (unless fortified) and of vitamins A, D and C.

(ii) *Sugars and fats*—very good sources of energy, especially fats and oils, but very poor sources of protein, minerals and the 'B' vitamins.

(iii) *Meats (including fish and poultry)*—rich in protein and sometimes in fat—moderate sources of vitamins and minerals except for liver and kidney which can be high in these nutrients.

(iv) *Fruits & Vegetables*—important sources of most minerals and vitamins but generally poor sources of energy and protein, with the exception of tubers such as potatoes.

(v)   *Milk*—very important as a source of energy, protein, vitamins and minerals, particularly for growing children and pregnant and nursing women.

In the above simple classification eggs may be regarded as coming between meat and milk.

Characteristics of a Good Diet

A diet which meets modern health standards must supply a proper balance of these types of food, in daily amounts which will not lead to overweight. Most Australians consume more energy (calories) than they need. Since fats and oils are the most concentrated sources of energy, a reduction in the intake of foods rich in fat, such as pastries, is recommended to all 'waist-watchers'. Medical opinion favours the use of vegetable oils in cooking and polyunsaturated margarine as a means of reducing the risk of cardiovascular disease.

No hard and fast rules can be laid down as to quantities as these will obviously vary with the age and the physical activity of the individual and with the cost and the availability of the various food items. A really satisfactory diet should aim to include something like the following:

Milk—Children 1 pint daily.

Butter or polyunsaturated Margarine—1 oz. per day.

Cheese—At least twice per week.

Egg—About four weekly or one per day.

Meat—One serving daily.

Potatoes—One serving daily

Fruit—Two pieces of *fresh* fruit daily.

Vegetables—Two servings—one of green, leafy and one of 'other' daily.

Bread & Cereals—Two servings daily, but with sweet biscuits and cakes reduced to an absolute minimum. Sugar should also be reduced to a minimum as Australian households are among the highest consumers of this very refined food in the world.

Kitchen Economics

Stale Bread—

(a)   A loaf may be freshened by wrapping in waxed paper, or alfoil and baking in slow oven for 20 minutes. A covered roaster or two pie dishes may be used. Cakes and scones for 10 to 15 minutes.

(b)   Pieces may be used for puddings, stuffing, dried rusks and breadcrumbs.

Stale Scones—Cut in halves, spread with butter and grated cheese. Toast.

Stale Cake—Use for milk puddings, trifle, jelly.

Dry Cheese—May be grated and used for cheese flavoured savouries, scones, salads, soups, sauces.

Lemon and Orange Peel—May be used for flavouring jams, stews. Could be candied.

Herbs—Tie in bundles, hang till dry, powder and bottle.

Bacon Rinds—May be used for flavouring soups or rendered for fat.

Scraps of Fat—Render for dripping.

Sour Milk—Scones using plain flour and bi-carbonate of soda, and can be added to stews.

Cooked Foods (Cold)—Meat, Fish, Vegetables, Rice, Sauces and Gravy. See Re-heating (page 74).

Vegetable Water—Use in soups, gravies, sauces.

Jam and Chutney—Scrapings from jars may be kept for curry.

Meat and Fish Bones—Use for Stock (see page 28)

Spiced Vinegars (Beetroot or Onion)—Keep for further use. Re-boil each time.

Homely Measurements

Spoons

One spoonful is two level spoonsful.
Half a spoonful is one level spoonful.
Quarter spoonful is one level spoonful halved lengthways of spoon.

When measuring, level off ingredients with a knife.

Abbreviations

Tablespoon . . . . tbsp.
Dessertspoon . . . . dsp.
Teaspoon . . . . tsp.

Weight of One Level Tablespoonful

Butter or Margarine . . . . 21 grams (¾ ounce)
Cornflour . . . . 7 grams (¼ ounce)
Cocoa . . . . 7 grams (¼ ounce)
Flour . . . . 9 grams (1/3 ounce)
Honey, Golden Syrup or Treacle . . . . 28 grams (1 ounce)
Rice . . . . 28 grams (1 ounce)
Sugar . . . . 14 grams (½ ounce)

Cup Measurements

Use a graded measuring cup for accuracy.

Flour 3 cups of unsifted . . . . 454 grams (1 pound)
Sugar 2 cups of sugar . . . . 454 grams (1 pound)
Liquid 2½ cups . . . . 568 millilitres or grams (1 pint)

Abbreviations

Metric	Imperial Measure
Measures of Length	
Millimetre . . . . mm.	Inch . . . . . . .in.
Centimetre . . . . .cm.	
Dry and Liquid Measure	
Millilitre . . . . ml.	Pint . . . . pt.
Centilitre . . . . .cl.	Quart . . . . . qt.
Decilitre . . . . .dl.	Gallon . . . . .gal.
Litre . . . . .l.	

Measures of Weight

Milligram . . . . mg	Ounce . . . . . oz.
Centigram . . . . cg.	Pound . . . . . .lb.
Decigram . . . . dg.	
Gram . . . . g.	
Kilogram . . . . kg.	

Terms Used For Cookery

Baste—To keep surface of food moist by spooning liquid or melted fat over during cooking (e.g. roasting meat, poaching or frying eggs).

Blanch—To whiten. Cover food with cold water, bring slowly to boil, strain.

Almonds—Cover with boiling water, stand until skin peels easily.

Blended Flour—Add milk or water gradually to flour making a smooth liquid paste.

Bouquet Garni—A bunch of herbs tied in muslin (see page 28)

Caramel—A colouring liquid made from browned sugar (page 261) used for colouring soups, gravies, etc.

Casserole—An oven ware vessel with lid used for oven stewing and braising.

Croutons—Bread cut in 1 centimetre cubes and fried.

Fillets—Pieces of fish freed from the bone. Under cuts of meat.

Forcemeat or Stuffing—Seasoning for meat and fish etc. (see page 77).

Fricassee—A white stew.

Garnish—Trimming or decoration.

Glaze—To brush over with beaten egg, milk or syrup.

Knead—To fold and press the outside edges into the middle (dough of bread, pastry, etc.).

Mask—To cover food with a thick sauce.

Puree—Pulped fruit or vegetables rubbed through a sieve.

Saute—To cook without browning in a little butter or fat. Keep lid on saucepan.

Seasoned Flour—Flour mixed with salt and pepper.

Sippets—Small triangles of dry toast.

Temperatures—Oven . . . see page 148.
Water—boiling 212° Fahr.—100° Celsius.
Water—simmering 185° Fahr.—87° Celsius.
Water—tepid (luke warm) 80° Fahr. 38° Celsius.

RAISING AGENTS

Raising Agent No. 1

A *combination* of an *alkali* with *acid,* mainly used in cake, biscuit and pudding recipes.

1. Raising agents, when moistened, form a gas—carbon dioxide—which expands when heated. This action makes mixture rise.

2. A raising agent is a combination of an alkali, usually bi-carbonate of soda with an acid which may be one of the following:—

cream of tartar	dried fruits
sour milk	golden syrup or
lemon juice	treacle
vinegar	cold tea

3. Baking powder is a combination of an alkali and an acid.
4. Self-raising flour contains a raising agent.
5. Raising agents should be measured accurately.

Raising Agent No. 2

Yeast—see notes on Bread Making (page 191)

Raising Agent No. 3

Air—introduced by *beating* ingredients, particularly eggs—e.g. batters, sponge cakes, souffles, meringue, cold sweets containing gelatine, ice cream.

Folding and *enclosing* air—e.g. pastries, particularly puff, rough puff or flaky.

BREAKFAST COOKERY

TEA—

1. Use freshly boiled water.
2. Heat teapot with boiling water.
3. Empty teapot, put in tea, allowing 1 teaspoon for each person and 1 teaspoon extra.
4. Pour on boiling water.
5. Allow to brew 3 to 5 minutes.
6. Too much brewing draws out tannic acid.

COCOA—

1. Allow ½ teaspoon cocoa and ½ teaspoon sugar to each cup of milk or milk and water.
2. Blend cocoa and sugar with a little boiling water.
3. Pour mixture into hot milk or milk and water. Bring to boil.

COFFEE—

1. Allow 4 rounded dessertspoons of ground coffee to 3 cups of water.
2. Place coffee in a fire proof jug or saucepan, pour on boiling water. Allow to stand for a few minutes. Keep hot but do not boil. Strain.
3. Serve black with sliced lemon and sugar or with cream or hot milk and sugar (if liked).

PORRIDGE (1st) METHOD

INGREDIENTS—

2 tablespoons wheatmeal.   2 cups water (hot).
½ teaspoon salt.

METHOD—

1. Mix meal to a paste with a little cold water.
2. Stir in hot water and salt.
3. Stir over heat until boiling. Simmer 15 minutes.

PORRIDGE (2nd) METHOD

INGREDIENTS—

 2 tablespoons oat meal, or   ½ teaspoon salt.
   rolled oats.   2 cups hot water.

METHOD—

1. Add salt to water. Stir water while you sift in the meal gradually.
2. Bring to boil. Simmer gently for 10 minutes.

Note 1—When using a double saucepan, increase the time for cooking.

Note 2—For early breakfast, soak meal overnight or make porridge the night before. Cover container firmly then place in a hay box or wrap container in old blanket.

BACON — FRIED—

1. Cut rind off bacon rashers.
2. Fry bacon slowly in its own fat until clear.
3. If bacon is very lean, melt a little fat in frying pan before cooking.
4. Serve on a hot dish.

Note—If bacon is very salty, put into cold water and just bring to boil before frying.

BACON — GRILLED—

1. Cut off bacon rind.
2. Make a roll of each piece of bacon, thread rolls on a skewer.
3. Grill for 2 or 3 minutes.

EGG — BOILED—

No. 1 Method—

1. Have sufficient boiling water to cover egg.
2. Slip the egg in gently.
3. Boil from 2½ to 3½ minutes.

No. 2 Method—

1. Put egg into saucepan with enough boiling water to cover. Put lid on.
2. Draw to side of stove. Leave 5 minutes.

EGG — FRIED—

1. Melt fat in frying pan.
2. Test egg by breaking into a cup.
3. Slip egg into hot fat, tilting the pan.
4. Fry gently until set. Baste.
5. Lift egg with slice. Drain well.
6. Serve on a hot dish with bacon.
7. Avoid overheated fat.

EGG — SCRAMBLED—

1. Beat egg well.
2. Add 1 tablespoon milk, pepper, ¼ teaspoon salt.
3. Melt 1 teaspoon butter or dripping in pan.
4. Pour mixture into pan. Cook gently until thickened.
5. Serve on buttered toast.

EGG — POACHED—

1. Prepare toast.
2. Have ready a frying pan containing sufficient boiling water to cover eggs. Add a level teaspoon of salt and tablespoon of vinegar to 3 cups water.
3. Break egg into a cup, draw pan off strong heat, gently drop in egg.
4. Keep water hot, but not boiling, until egg is set. Baste if necessary.
5. Lift out with egg slice, drain off water, serve on hot buttered toast.

Note—A mould (e.g. a scone cutter) placed in pan prevents egg white from spreading.

OMELET

INGREDIENTS—

2 eggs.
2 dessertspoons milk or
  water.
1 teaspoon chopped parsley.

¼ teaspoon salt.
Pepper.
1 teaspoon butter.

Omelet—Continued

METHOD—
1. Separate yolks and whites.
2. Beat whites stiffly, adding salt.
3. Mix yolks, milk, pepper, parsley.
4. Add to whites gradually.
5. Melt butter in pan, pour in mixture.
6. Cook till light brown, taking care to loosen edge.
7. Lightly toast top. Fold in two.
8. Garnish with parsley, serve at once.

SAVOURY OMELET—

May be made by adding finely chopped ham, brains, chicken or tomato.

SWEET OMELET—

Omit seasoning, add 1 dessertspoon sugar, pinch salt. 1 tablespoon jam (in the mixture or as a garnish).

VEGETABLES — RE-HEATED—

1. Mash or chop vegetable, season to taste.
2. Heat fat in pan, add vegetables, cover with a plate. When plate is quite hot the vegetables are ready.

APPLES — FRIED—

1. Peel and core apples and cut in thick slices.
2. Fry in hot fat until brown and tender.
3. Serve with bacon.
4. Bananas may be cooked in the same way.

TOMATOES — FRIED—

1. Cut tomatoes across in halves.
2. Fry in hot fat till brown and tender.
3. Sprinkle with salt, pepper and a little sugar.
4. Serve with fried bacon or toast.

BRAINS — FRIED—

1. Soak brains in salted water for ½ an hour.
2. Remove skin, dry well, dip in egg and breadcrumbs.
3. Fry in hot fat until brown.
4. Serve with bacon (fried or grilled).

MUSHROOMS — FRIED—

1. Remove skin from mushrooms; wash thoroughly until all grit is removed; dry well.
2. Fry in butter or clarified fat until tender.
3. Serve mushrooms hot, with butter, pepper and salt.

LAMB'S FRY AND BACON

INGREDIENTS—

1 Lamb's Fry.
240 grams bacon (8 oz).
2 tablespoons flour.

1 teaspoon salt.
Pepper.
Parsley.

METHOD—

1. Cut liver into slices, wash in salted water, dry well.
2. Mix flour, pepper and salt.
3. Dip liver into flour, then put into a pan of hot fat.
4. Brown on both sides, cooking gently for 5 to 7 minutes.
5. Place on a hot dish.
6. Make gravy, (serve with liver).
7. Garnish with grilled bacon and parsley.

GRILLED KIDNEYS—

INGREDIENTS—

Kidneys.
Salt and pepper.

Grilled bacon rolls.

METHOD—

1. Skin and wash kidneys. Dry.
2. Cut kidneys in halves lengthwise and place on greased griller, cut side towards heat. Grill gently on both sides 5 to 7 minutes.
3. Serve on hot dish, garnish with grilled bacon rolls.

DEVILLED KIDNEYS—

INGREDIENTS—

Kidneys.
Thin slices of onion.
Pinch of cayenne.

Salt and pepper, chopped
    parsley.
Water to moisten.

METHOD—

1. Skin kidneys, wash and cut finely.
2. Add minced onion, parsley, salt, pepper, cayenne and water.
3. Melt little dripping in saucepan and add mixture. Cook gently
    over slow heat.
4. Serve on buttered toast.

ECONOMICAL SAUSAGE ROLLS

INGREDIENTS—

Equal quantities of sausage
    meat and mashed potatoes.
1 egg
Flour.

1 Tablespoon tomato or
    Worcester sauce.
Salt and pepper to taste.

METHOD—

1. Mix meat and potatoes together.
2. Add salt, pepper, sauce and beaten egg. Mix well.
3. Turn mixture onto floured board. Knead and roll out.
4. Cut into pieces and shape.
5. Roll in flour and fry in hot fat until golden brown.
6. Drain on kitchen paper and serve hot.

TOMATO CREAM

INGREDIENTS—

4 tomatoes (large).
1 tablespoon butter or
    bacon fat.
1 teaspoon sugar.

2 eggs.
2 teaspoons cornflour.
Pinch cayenne.
1 level teaspoon salt.

Tomato Cream—Continued

METHOD—

1. Put tomatoes into boiling water to loosen skins. Peel and cut up roughly.
2. Melt butter in saucepan, add tomatoes, sugar, salt, cayenne.
3. Cook gently until tomatoes pulp.
4. Allow to cool a little, add well beaten eggs and cornflour blended with a little cold water gradually.
5. Stir over heat until mixture thickens.
6. Serve on hot toast.

Note—Vermicilli may be used instead of eggs.

AMERICAN DRY HASH

METHOD—

1. Fry a thinly sliced onion in a little fat.
2. Cut some cold, cooked mutton into small pieces, dip in seasoned flour and fry with onions until brown.
3. Skin 2 or 3 tomatoes, cut up, add to the meat and cook until soft and pulpy.
4. Serve hot.

STOCK and SOUP

STOCK is the liquid in which meat, bones and vegetables have been cooked.

It is the foundation of soups and may also be used for gravies and sauces.

Stock should be brought slowly to the boil, then allowed to simmer for a long time in order to extract all the nourishment from the ingredients.

Skim stock while cooking.

Strain off liquid and allow to cool so that the fat will harden.

Remove all fat from stock before using. Strain.

The same bones may be used again with fresh vegetables and water; this is called "second stock", and may be used for rich soups and purees.

FISH STOCK for fish soups is made by boiling fish bones and heads.

A Bouquet Garni (used for flavouring stock and soups) is a bunch of herbs, consisting of the following:—

1 blade mace.	4 cloves.
1 sprig thyme.	1 bay leaf.
1 sprig marjoram.	Strip lemon rind.
6 peppercorns.	Tie all together in muslin.

STOCK

INGREDIENTS—

1 kilogram and 500 grams bones (3lb 5oz).	Parsley stalks.
1 onion.	1 teaspoon salt.
1 carrot.	1 stick celery.
1 turnip.	A bouquet garni.
1 parsnip.	Sufficient cold water to cover bones.

METHOD—

1. Wash bones thoroughly.
2. Put into saucepan with cold water and salt. Stand ½ hour or longer.
3. Bring slowly to boil.
4. Peel vegetables and cut up roughly.
5. When liquid boils remove scum, add vegetables and bouquet garni.
6. Simmer for 4 hours.
7. Strain off liquid; when cold, remove fat.

SOUP MAKING

Soup is a nourishing and stimulating food. It contains the goodness from meat and vegetables in very fine particles. These particles are easily absorbed by the tiny blood vessels which line the walls of the stomach.

Taken at the beginning of a dinner, soup acts as a stimulant to the digestive system, thus preparing it for the solid food to follow. Clear soups are most suitable for this purpose. When soup is the principal part of the meal it should be rich. Broths and thick soups are most suitable in this case.

Soup also assists in supplying water to the body.

Soup is of three classes:—(1) Broths. (2) Thick soup (Puree). (3) Clear Soup (Consomme).

Good soup is made from a foundation of stock. Water may be used instead of stock for broths and purees.

Soups must simmer. Boiling destroys nourishing properties. The saucepan used for stocks and soups must have a tight fitting lid to keep in flavours which are volatile.

SCOTCH BROTH

INGREDIENTS—

500 grams neck mutton
(1 lb 2 oz).
1 carrot.
1 onion.
1 turnip.

2 sticks celery.
1½ teaspoons salt.
2 tablespoons rice or barley.
2¼ litres cold water
(2 quarts).

METHOD—

1. Cut meat into small pieces, remove any fat.
2. Put meat, bones, water, salt and well washed rice or barley into a saucepan. Let stand 15 minutes.
3. Bring slowly to boil.
4. Peel vegetables, cut into small dice.
5. When liquid boils, remove scum, add vegetables.
6. Simmer for 2 to 3 hours.
7. Remove bones and any fat; leave pieces of meat in soup.
8. Sprinkle with chopped parsley just before serving.

TOMATO SOUP

INGREDIENTS—

1 kilogram tomatoes
  (2 lb 3 oz).
1 onion.
½ litre stock or water
  (2¼ cups).
1 teaspoon salt.
Pinch cayenne.
Pinch nutmeg.

1 slice lean bacon or rinds.
1 tablespoon butter.
1 tablespoon sago or 1½ tablespoons flour (blended).
1 teaspoon sugar.
1¼ cups milk or 2 tablespoons
  evaporated milk.

METHOD—

1. Cut up tomatoes and onions roughly.
2. Melt fat in saucepan, add vegetables and bacon. Cook gently
   with lid on pan (Saute) for 10 minutes. Do not brown.
3. Add stock, seasoning, sugar; simmer till tender.
4. Remove bacon, rub vegetables through sieve.
5. Return soup to saucepan. When boiling, add sago or flour.
   Cook till sago is clear. For flour thickening boil 3
   minutes.
6. Draw pan off stove.
7. Add heated milk just before serving. Do not allow soup to
   boil.
8. Serve with croutons.

PEA SOUP

INGREDIENTS—

240 grams split peas (8 oz).
1 carrot.
1 onion.
2 sticks celery.
1¾ litres stock or water
  (3 pints).

Ham bones or bacon rind.
1 teaspoon salt.
1 teaspoon dried mint or
  1 tablespoon fresh mint.
1 tablespoon flour.
Croutons.

METHOD—

1. Wash peas and soak overnight or soak them in hot water with a pinch of bi-carb. of soda for ½ hour.
2. Peel vegetables and cut up roughly.
3. Put peas, vegetables, salt, pepper, ham bones and water in a saucepan. Simmer for 3 hours.
4. Remove bones, turn soup into a sieve and rub through peas and vegetables.
5. Return to saucepan.
6. Mix flour to a smooth paste with a little cold water, stir into soup, boil 3 minutes.
7. Sprinkle with chopped mint.
8. Serve with croutons of fried bread.

LENTIL SOUP

Make in the same way as Pea Soup, substituting lentils for peas.

MULLIGATAWNY SOUP

INGREDIENTS—

2¼ litres stock or water
  (2 quarts).
1 tablespoon curry powder.
1 teaspoon salt.
Pepper.
1 dessertspoon lemon juice
  or vinegar.
1 tablespoon butter or
  substitute.

2 tablespoons flour.
1 onion.
1 leek.
1 carrot.
½ turnip.
1 apple.
1 rasher of lean bacon.
1 dessertspoon sugar.

Mulligatawny Soup — Continued.

METHOD—

1. Cut up bacon.
2. Peel and slice vegetables and apple.
3. Melt fat in saucepan; fry onion till golden brown.
4. Add apple, vegetables, bacon, curry powder, stir over heat for five minutes.
5. Add stock, salt, pepper, sugar.
6. Simmer for 1 hour, then strain, rub through sieve.
7. Thicken with blended flour.
8. Add lemon juice or vinegar just before serving.
9. Serve with boiled rice.

BROWN VEGETABLE SOUP

INGREDIENTS—

1 litre stock (1¾ pints).   1 tablespoon flour.
1 carrot.   Bacon rinds.
1 onion.   ½ teaspoon salt.
1 turnip.   Pepper.
1 stick celery.   1 tablespoon dripping.
1 tomato.

METHOD—

1. Peel and slice vegetables.
2. Melt good dripping in a saucepan; add vegetables fry till brown.
3. Add stock, bacon rind, salt and pepper.
4. Simmer for 1 hour.
5. Strain through a sieve, rubbing through vegetable pulp.
6. Return liquid to saucepan and thicken with blended flour.
7. A little caramel may be used if necessary for further browning.
8. Serve with croutons of fried bread.

OX TAIL SOUP

INGREDIENTS—

1 ox tail.   1 tablespoon clarified fat.
2¼ litres water (2 quarts).   2 tablespoons flour.
1 carrot.   6 cloves.
1 turnip.   1 dessertspoon salt.
1 onion.   Pepper.
½ head celery.

Ox Tail Soup—Continued

METHOD—

1. Cut ox tail into joints—roll them in flour.
2. Peel and slice vegetables.
3. Melt fat in saucepan, fry meat, fry vegetables till brown.
4. Put all ingredients except flour in pan.
5. Simmer from 4 to 5 hours. Stand overnight.
6. Remove fat, strain, rub vegetables through sieve.
7. Thicken soup with blended flour.
8. Serve with croutons of fried bread.

KANGAROO TAIL SOUP

Make in the same way as Ox Tail Soup, using sago or tapioca for
   thickening.

VERMICELLI SOUP

INGREDIENTS—

1 litre good clear stock   Pepper.
   (1¾ pints).   Salt to taste.
2 tablespoons vermicelli.   Caramel.

METHOD—

1. Wash vermicelli. Strain stock.
2. Put all ingredients, except caramel, on to cook.
3. Simmer for ½ hour. Skim if necessary.
4. Add sufficient caramel to make soup light brown.

JULIENNE SOUP

INGREDIENTS—

1 litre good clear stock   1 tablespoon chopped chives.
   (1¾ pints).   Pepper.
1 carrot.   Salt to taste.
1 turnip.   Caramel colouring if
Little celery.   required.

METHOD—

1. Peel vegetable—cut into match strips.
2. Put all ingredients on to cook in stock.
3. Simmer for ½ hour or until tender.
4. Serve hot garnished with finely shredded lettuce.

GREEN PEA SOUP

INGREDIENTS—

500 grams green peas
  (1lb 2oz).
1 small onion.
1 sprig parsley.
1 sprig mint.
1 teaspoon salt.
1 teaspoon sugar.

Pepper.
1 level tablespoon butter
  or substitute.
1 litre stock (1¾ pints).
¾ cup milk.
1 tablespoon flour.

METHOD—

1. Shell peas, wash. Fresh pods may be included.
2. Peel and slice onion.
3. Melt fat in saucepan, add all vegetables.
4. Put lid on pan, cook gently for 10 minutes shaking pan frequently.
5. Add stock, parsley, mint, salt and pepper.
6. Simmer for ½ hour or till tender. Remove mint and parsley.
7. Rub vegetables through sieve.
8. Thicken soup with blended flour.
9. Draw off stove, add milk just before serving. Re-heat.
10. Serve with croutons and freshly chopped mint or parsley.

OYSTER SOUP

INGREDIENTS—

1 litre fish stock
  (1¾ pints).
2 doz. or 1 tin oysters.
1 level tablespoon butter.
1½ tablespoons flour.
1 cup milk.

1 blade mace or sprinkle of
  nutmeg.
One teaspoon grated lemon
  rind (yellow only).
Salt to taste.
Pinch cayenne pepper.

METHOD—

1. Melt butter in saucepan, add flour, stir till smooth.
2. Add stock gradually, also liquor from oysters.
3. Add salt, pepper, lemon rind and mace.
4. Bring soup slowly to boil, stirring occasionally.
5. Remove soup from stove, remove mace.
6. Add milk gradually, then oysters. Reheat.
7. Serve soup garnished with finely chopped parsley.

WHITE VEGETABLE SOUP

INGREDIENTS—

1 litre stock (1¾ pints).	Pepper.
1 carrot.	1 tablespoon chopped parsley.
1 onion.	1 dessertspoon good fat.
1 stick celery.	1½ tablespoons flour.
1 turnip.	1 cup milk.
Salt to taste.	

METHOD—

1. Melt fat in saucepan, add flour, mix till smooth; do not brown.
2. Add stock, gradually stirring till blended with flour. Bring to boil stirring frequently.
3. Add pepper and salt.
4. Peel vegetables, cut onion in rings and other vegetables in match strips.
5. Add onion to stock, simmer 15 minutes.
6. Add other vegetables, simmer for 15 minutes longer.
7. Vegetables must be tender, but not broken.
8. Draw pan to one side, add milk gradually.
9. Sprinkle with chopped parsley just before serving.

GIBLET BROTH

INGREDIENTS—

2 sets giblets.	1 teaspoon salt.
1 small onion.	1 litre water (1¾ pints).
Blade mace or sprinkle of nutmeg.	6 cloves.
	1½ tablespoons sago or rice.
Stick of celery.	

METHOD—

1. Prepare and wash giblets and cut in small pieces.
2. Put into saucepan with water, cloves, salt, mace, and chopped vegetable. Bring slowly to the boil.
3. Simmer for 2 hours, then strain.
4. Put rice or sago in saucepan, add liquid gradually.
5. Boil for 15 minutes, add pepper to taste.

POTATO SOUP

INGREDIENTS—

500 grams potatoes (1 lb 2 oz).
2 sticks celery.
1 onion.
1 teaspoon salt.
Pepper.
1 litre stock (1¾ pints).

1 cup milk.
1 level tablespoon butter or substitute.
1 tablespoon flour.
1 tablespoon chopped parsley or capers.

METHOD—

1. Peel vegetables, cut up roughly.
2. Melt butter in saucepan, add vegetables, put lid on pan, cook without browning for 5 minutes.
3. Add stock, salt, pepper; simmer for 1½ hours.
4. Strain and rub vegetables through sieve.
5. Return to saucepan, thicken with blended flour. Reheat.
6. Draw to one side, add milk just before serving.
7. Add parsley or capers.
8. Serve with croutons.

FISH SOUP

Use recipe for Oyster Soup omitting oysters (page 34). Pieces of cooked fish (flaked) may be added.

MUSHROOM SOUP

INGREDIENTS—

240 grams mushrooms (8 ozs).
1 litre chicken or mutton stock (1¾ pints)
½ small white onion.

Salt and pepper to taste.
1 tablespoon butter.
2 tablespoons flour.
1 cup milk or ½ cup cream.

METHOD—

1. Wash, peel and cut up mushrooms. Cut up onion.
2. Cook mushrooms and onions till tender. Rub through strainer or leave whole.
3. Melt butter in saucepan, add flour. Stir in stock etc. gradually.
4. Stir over heat to boiling point.
5. Add milk or cream just before serving.

FISH

1. Fish contains a little albumen and fibrin and a great quantity of gelatine (nitrogenous or flesh forming substances); varying amounts of oil (heat and energy givers); much mineral salts (phosphates of lime, soda and potash) which assist in purifying the blood.

2. It is easily digested and nutritious, but owing to the lack of carbohydrates in its composition, fish should be served with starchy foods to maintain the proper proportion between the flesh forming and heat giving substances.

3. The carbohydrates served with fish are bread, potatoes and the starchy matter in the white sauce.

4. White fish (being free from oil) are the most delicate and easily digested. Whiting, flounder, schnapper etc. are white fish.

5. The oily fish (mullet, herring, tailer) are more nutritious, but not so digestible as white fish.

POINTS TO CONSIDER WHEN CHOOSING

1. Eyes bright.
2. Gills red and plentiful supply of scales.
3. Flesh firm to touch.
4. No unpleasant smell.
5. Choose fish in season.

TO CLEAN

1. Remove scales and fins. Trim tail. Remove inside. Take out eyes.

2. Wash in salt water. Dry thoroughly. (Do not leave in water or fibre will be softened, and may break in cooking.)

RULES FOR FILLETING FISH

1. To fillet is to cut flesh from bones in suitable pieces.
2. Remove fins.
3. Cut flesh to bones below head, about tail and along back bone.
4. Carefully slice away fillet. Remove small bones.
5. Remove fillet on other side in same way.
6. To remove skin lay fillet on board, skin down, tail towards you. Loosen skin at tail.
7. Take firm hold of skin with salted fingers, press back of knife on skin and gently draw skin away from flesh.
8. Wash and dry fillet.

BOILED FISH (Large)

1. Scale, clean, wash and dry fish, leaving on head. Remove eyes.
2. To keep shape, tie fish in thin cloth.
3. Put into boiling water adding ½ teaspoon salt, 1 tablespoon vinegar to each quart of water.
4. Simmer till tender allowing 10 minutes to **500** grams (1lb 2oz) for big fish or 7 minutes for smaller fish.
5. When cooked lift to hot dish.
6. Garnish with slices of lemon.
7. Serve with parsley or egg sauce.

Note—To give a well flavoured fish stock, celery, carrot and bouquet garni should be added.

STEAMED FISH

1. Fish may be steamed whole or in fillets. Prepare in usual way.
2. Sprinkle with salt, pepper and lemon juice.
3. Wrap in greased paper.
4. Steam until tender (10 to 30 minutes), according to size.
5. Serve on hot dish. Mask with white sauce.
6. Garnish with lemon and chopped parsley or hard boiled egg.

BAKED FISH

1. Clean, wash and dry fish. Remove eyes.
2. Cut off fins. Trim tail. Rub fish with lemon juice.
3. Make stuffing (page 77). Stuff and sew fish.
4. Lay on well greased baking tin with some butter or good dripping.
5. Cover with well greased paper.
6. Bake in moderate oven 20 to 30 minutes. Test with skewer.
7. Serve on hot dish, with gravy from dish.
8. Garnish with slice of lemon and parsley.

FRIED FISH

1. Clean fish, wash, dry. Trim.
2. Dip in seasoned flour or batter.
3. Fry in hot fat.
4. Drain on kitchen paper.
5. Serve on hot dish; garnish with lemon and parsley.

Note—Fish may be dipped in egg and bread crumbs and deep fried.

GRILLED FISH

1. Clean fish, wash and dry.
2. Heat the griller and grease.
3. Whole fish should be cut across to allow heat to penetrate.
4. Grill gently on both sides until cooked through.
5. Serve with butter and finely chopped parsley or a heated mixture of butter, grated rind and juice of one orange.

FISH CROQUETTES

INGREDIENTS—

240 grams cooked fish (8 oz).
240 grams cooked potatoes (8 oz).
Salt and pepper.
1 teaspoon chopped parsley.

1 tablespoon milk, if necessary.
1 or 2 eggs.
Bread crumbs.
Flour.

METHOD—

1. Remove bone and skin. Break up fish.
2. Mash and warm potatoes. Add to fish with parsley, pepper, salt. Mix well. Add 1 tablespoon beaten egg.
3. Divide into even pieces. Mould into shape, using very little flour.
4. Dip in beaten egg and breadcrumbs.
5. Fry in deep fat. Drain.
6. Serve on paper d'oyley. Garnish with lemon and parsley.

Note—When tinned fish is used, drain off liquid.

KEDGEREE

INGREDIENTS—

240 grams cooked fish (cold) (8 oz).
1 small cup cooked rice.
½ tablespoon butter.

1 teaspoon curry powder.
1 egg (hard boiled).
Salt and pepper.
Finely chopped parsley.

METHOD—

1. Break fish into pieces, remove bones.
2. Melt butter in saucepan. Add rice, fish, curry powder and chopped white of egg.
3. Make all very hot. Pile in centre of dish. Press into shape.
4. Grate yolk of egg over top.
5. Garnish with chopped parsley and lemon.

Note—Tinned salmon makes an attractive kedgeree.

FISH CUSTARD

INGREDIENTS—

240 grams fish (raw or cooked)   2 eggs.
(8 oz).   1 level teaspoon salt.
2 cups milk.   Butter.

METHOD—

1. Flake or slice fish thinly, place in a buttered oven dish.
   Sprinkle half of salt on fish.
2. Beat eggs, add salt (remainder) and milk. Pour onto fish. Add
   a little butter.
3. Stand dish in baking dish of water, bake slowly until set,
   about 30 minutes.

FISH CUSTARD, SAVOURY

INGREDIENTS—

500 grams Hake or other fish   1 level tablespoon curry
(1 lb 2 oz).   powder.
1 cup cornflakes.   1 large onion.
2 eggs.   1 dessertspoon sugar.
1 cup milk.   Salt and pepper.
2 tablespoons vinegar.

METHOD—

1. Steam fish till nearly cooked.
2. Peel and chop onion, fry in a little butter or good fat till
   tender.
3. Flake fish, add onion, cornflakes, liquid from fish, vinegar,
   curry powder, sugar, salt and pepper and one egg, beaten
   well.
4. Put mixture into a greased oven dish and cook in a moderate
   oven till firm.
5. Beat other egg, add milk and seasoning, pour over mixture,
   bake slowly till set, about 30 minutes.

FISH OMELET

INGREDIENTS—

3 or 4 eggs.   1 tablespoon cream or
240 grams salted fish (8 oz).   evaporated milk.
1 tablespoon grated cheese   Salt and pepper.
(strong flavour).

Fish Omelet—Continued

METHOD—
1. Cook fish, drain then flake.
2. Mix egg yolks with cream, cheese, salt and pepper. Stir into fish.
3. Beat egg whites stiffly, fold into fish mixture.
4. Pour into a well heated and buttered frying pan. Cook slowly until set and brown underneath. Lightly toast top surface, roll or fold, serve immediately.

SOUSED FISH

1. Clean and trim some small fish.
2. Place in a pie dish with butter, vinegar or lemon juice and seasoning. Cover.
3. Bake in moderately hot oven until tender.
4. Serve hot or cold, garnished with lemon.

CRAYFISH MORNAY

INGREDIENTS—

2 Crayfish.
White sauce (melted butter) (page 125).
120 grams grated cheese (4oz).
1 dessertspoon of butter.

2 tablespoons of fine fresh bread crumbs.
Salt, pepper, cayenne, level teaspoon of mustard.
Juice of lemon.

METHOD—
1. Remove shells from crayfish. Cut meat into neat pieces.
2. Make sauce, remove from stove. Add ¾ of cheese, seasoning, lemon juice and mixed mustard.
3. Put prepared crayfish into pyrex. Add sauce and top with bread crumbs, butter and remainder of cheese—sprinkle with a little salt and cayenne.
4. Bake in moderate oven ½ hour or until nicely browned.
5. Serve hot.

CRAYFISH OR LOBSTER MAYONNAISE

INGREDIENTS—

1 Lobster.
Mayonnaise.
1 hard boiled egg.

Lettuce.
Garnish—parsley, lemon, yolk
and white of egg.

MAYONNAISE—

2 yolks of eggs.
½ cup good oil.
1 dessertspoon of white
vinegar.
1 dessertspoon of tarragon
vinegar.
½ teaspoon made mustard.

1 teaspoon of chilli
vinegar.
½ teaspoon salt.
1 teaspoon of lemon juice.
1 teaspoon of sugar.
Pinch of cayenne.

METHOD—

1. Put yolk of egg in basin. Add mustard, salt, cayenne and
   sugar. Mix well with wooden spoon.
2. Keep stirring with right hand, with left add oil drop at a time
   until sauce is quite thick.
3. Add vinegar gradually stirring all the time.
4. Do not add ingredients too quickly or sauce will curdle and
   keep basin cool while working.

To Serve—

1. Remove claws. Cut crayfish lengthwise.
2. Remove flesh. Remove waste matter, clean out shell halves.
3. Cut up flesh, arrange in shell pieces, cover with mayonnaise.
4. Garnish with chopped white of egg and egg yolk rubbed
   through strainer.
5. Arrange filled shells on a bed of lettuce leaves. Garnish with
   claws, slices of lemon and sprigs of parsley.
6. Serve cold.

SHERRIED FISH DRESSING

INGREDIENTS—

1 cup mayonnaise.
1 teaspoon Chilli sauce.
3 tablespoons sherry.

½ teaspoon Worcestershire
Sauce.
Salt and pepper to taste.

METHOD—

Combine all ingredients, mix well, then chill.
An excellent dressing for any fish, particularly crab, prawns,
crayfish.

MEAT

FOOD VALUE OF MEAT

1. Meat provides proteins, the body building food stuffs.

2. Fat of meat provides fat, the energy and warmth giving food.

3. Meat is an expensive item in the diet, and one in which economy might be practised, providing fish, eggs, milk or cheese are used to supplement the supply of animal protein.

4. Expensive cuts of meat are no more nutritive than the cheap cuts.

5. Great care should be taken in the cooking of meat to preserve nutriment.

CHOICE OF MEAT

BEEF.—The flesh should be firm and elastic to the touch, juicy and finely grained and of a good red colour. The fat should be firm and creamy.

MUTTON.—The flesh firm and of a good colour, the fat white and very firm.

PORK.—The flesh should be of a pink colour and the fat white. The skin should be smooth.

VEAL.—The flesh should be firm and dry and of a pink, silky appearance.

JOINTS AND THEIR ACCOMPANIMENTS

BAKED MUTTON.—Baked vegetables, brown gravy and red currant jelly, green vegetable.

BAKED LAMB.—Baked vegetables, mint sauce and brown gravy. Green peas.

ROAST BEEF.—Yorkshire pudding, baked potatoes, greens, horse-radish sauce and thin, brown gravy.

ROAST VEAL.—Forecemeat, slices of lemon, brown gravy, green vegetable and boiled ham or bacon.

ROAST PORK.—Sage and onion seasoning, baked vegetable, gravy and apple sauce, greens.

CORNED BEEF.—Carrots, turnips, cabbage, suet dumplings.

BOILED MUTTON.—Root vegetable, onion, parsley or caper sauce.

CUTS OF MEAT — HOW TO COOK

BAKING—
Mutton—Leg, loin, shoulder saddle, flap.
Beef—Sirloin, ribs, wing rib, topside.
Veal—Shoulder, fillet leg, loin.
Pork—Leg and loin.

GRILLING—
Mutton and Lamb—Short loin, loin and rib chops.
Beefsteak fillet, rump, T-bone and porterhouse.
Bacon, Sheep's kidneys and small birds.

FRYING—
Cutlets, sausages, liver, kidneys, brains, bacon, fillet of pork and
veal, pork chops and rump steak.

BOILING—
Fresh Meats—
Mutton—leg, neck, shoulder, tongues.
Beef—brisket.

Corned Meats—
Mutton—leg, tongue.
Beef—silver side, brisket, tongue, aitch bone.
Pork—hand, leg, belly, cheek, trotters.

STEWING—
Beef—Skirt, buttock, topside, blade-bone and chuck steaks,
tripe, ox kidney, ox tail.
Mutton—Breast, neck, best end forequarter, flaps, kidneys and
brains.

FOR SOUPS—
Shin of beef, knuckles and shanks of mutton bones.
Scrag end of neck.
Sheep's head and knuckles of veal.

BEEF SECTIONS

1. Rump.
2. Steak piece.
3. Sirloin
4. } Ribs.
5.
6. Shin.
7. Sticking piece.
8. Head.
9. Round.
10. Buttock.
11. Leg.
12. Flank.
13. Brisket.
14. Shoulder.
15. Clod.

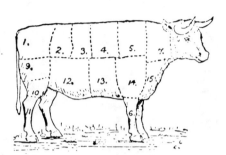

MUTTON SECTIONS

1. Loin (chump end).
2. Loin (best end).
3. Ribs (cutlets).
4. Neck—
    (a) Best end.
    (b) Scrag end.
5. Head.
6. Neck.
7. Leg.
8. Breast.
9. Shoulder.
10. Shank.
11. Trotter.

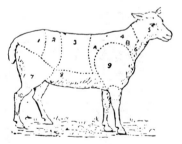

THE CARE OF MEAT

Its preservation in household refrigerators

FRESH: store uncovered or loosely covered in refrigerator.
FROZEN: store closely wrapped in freezer compartment.
COOKED: store closely covered in refrigerator.
CURED: store wrapped in refrigerator.

LAMB
and Hogget

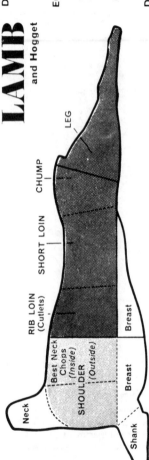

DEMANDED CUTS
Cutlets, Short Loin and Chump Chops, Leg Roast

ECONOMIC CUTS
Best Neck, Forequarter and Leg Chops, Shanks and Breast, Shoulder and Forequarter Roasts

Neck

Best Neck Chops (*Inside*)

SHOULDER (*Outside*)

Shank

Breast

Breast

RIB LOIN (Cutlets)

SHORT LOIN

CHUMP

LEG

BEEF

DEMANDED CUTS
Sirloin, "T" Bone, Fillet, Rump and Topside Steaks, Sirloin Roast, Wing Rib Roast, Corned Silverside, Rolled Rib Roasts

ECONOMIC CUTS
Round Steak, Cross Cut Blade, Bladebone, Chuck, Skirt Steaks, Gravy Beef, Corner Topside, Bolar Blade Roasts, Brisket (fresh or corned)

Mince Steak

Chuck Steak (*Inside*)

BLADE BONE STEAK (*Outside*)

RIBS OF BEEF (Sold Rolled)

RIB STEAK

WING RIB

SET OF RIBS Flank of Ribs

Flank of Wing Rib

SIRLOIN *Porterhouse or T-Bone Steak*

FILLET STEAK (*Inside*)

TOPSIDE STEAK (*Inside*)

Flank of Sirloin

RUMP STEAK (Outside)

Thin Flank

SILVERSIDE (*Outside*)

Leg of Beef

ROUND STEAK (*Thick Flank*)

Brisket

Shin of Beef

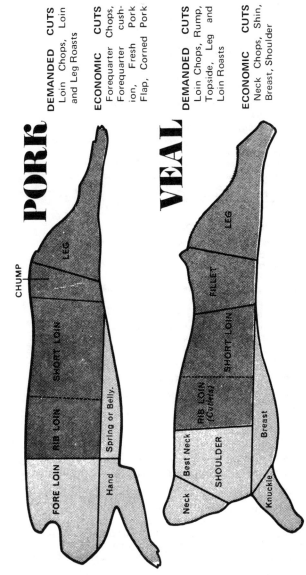

PORK

DEMANDED CUTS
Loin Chops, Loin and Leg Roasts

ECONOMIC CUTS
Forequarter Chops, Forequarter cushion, Fresh Pork Flap, Corned Pork

(Pork diagram labels: FORE LOIN, RIB LOIN, SHORT LOIN, CHUMP, LEG, Hand, Spring or Belly)

VEAL

DEMANDED CUTS
Loin Chops, Rump, Topside, Leg and Loin Roasts

ECONOMIC CUTS
Neck Chops, Shin, Breast, Shoulder

(Veal diagram labels: Neck, Best Neck, SHOULDER, RIB LOIN (Cutlets), SHORT LOIN, FILLET, LEG, Knuckle, Breast)

THE ▮ DEMANDED AND ▯ ECONOMICAL CUTS

These may vary in different parts of Australia and throughout the year, according to the season.

CARVING

SIRLOIN OF BEEF—

1. When serving, place thickest end at left hand side of carver with undercut underneath.
2. Raise joint and turn over, bringing undercut to front.
3. Cut undercut first across towards bone in fairly thick slices—downwards.
4. Carve upper part in long slices, parallel with ribs.
5. Insert knife between bone and meat to detach slices.

Note—The round of beef is cut in thin slices.

LEG OF MUTTON, LAMB OR PORK—

1. Place small end to left hand side of carver, with thickest part to far side of dish.
2. Insert fork in thickest part.
3. Raise joint slightly towards you.
4. Cut slices of medium thicknesses down through thickest part down to bone.
5. Slip knife along underneath slices, detaching them from each other working towards thin end of joint.
6. Serve a small piece of fat with each portion.

LOIN OF MUTTON, LAMB OR PORK—

1. Place on dish with thick part towards outside.
2. Insert knife between bones and cut right through separating cutlets.

FORE QUARTER OF LAMB—

1. Raise shoulder from ribs and breast inserting fork in most fleshy part.
2. Cut round shoulder. Raise and cut it away without removing much meat from underneath. This part may be put aside and used cold unless required for the meal.
3. Cut under portion across separating ribs from breast.
4. Divide ribs from each other—from back to front.
5. Cut breast in slices.

SHOULDER OF MUTTON—

1. Serve skin side uppermost on dish.
2. Insert fork in fleshy part.
3. Raise joint slightly. Cut slices downwards to bone from furthest edge to centre, in slightly curved cuts.
4. Carve in straight line from centre to right edge downwards to bone. Serve a piece of crisp fat with each portion—from front edge.
5. Turn joint, take slices off under side.

HAM—

1. Place on dish in same way as leg of mutton.
2. With a thin sharp knife make an incision through thickest part from back edge downwards to bone.
3. Cut thin slices towards both ends of bone.

Note—A ham is often cut in thin slices beginning from the knuckle end and working up towards thicker part. This is a more economical method.

POULTRY—

1. Place on dish with legs to left hand side of carver.
2. Insert fork deeply across breast bone.
3. Remove wing on side nearest cutting the skin and shaving off a thin slice of breast towards wing joint.
4. Separate joint from carcase with point of knife.
5. Cut meat from breast (side nearest first), in neat slices along length of bird. Do not remove fork but finish carving before serving.
6. Turn bird round—proceed on second side in same way as first.

RULES FOR BAKING

BAKING IS COOKING BY DRY HEAT—

1. Wipe, weigh and trim meat. Do not remove fat.
2. Allow 20 minutes cooking to 500 grams (1lb 2oz) and 20 minutes over or a little longer for thick joints.
3. Stand meat in baking tin with 2 tablespoons of dripping.
4. Place in moderate oven for the first 10 minutes to set outside albumen. This keeps in red juices.
5. Cook at even temperature for remaining time. Turn occasionally.
6. Salt meat half an hour before taking up.
7. Allow 1 to 1½ hours for baking potatoes.
8. Pour off the fat. Make gravy.

Note—Pork requires more cooking than other meats. Allow 30 minutes to 500 grams (1 lb 2 oz) and 30 minutes over.

RULES FOR BOILING

Boiling is cooking in sufficient water to cover food—

1. Wipe, weigh and trim meat.
2. Allow 25 minutes to 500 grams (1 lb 2 oz) and 25 minutes over.
3. Put meat into hot water. Simmer.
4. Add salt ½ hour before taking up.
5. Root vegetables may be cooked with meat. Allow one to one and a half hours for cooking.
6. Boiled meats are served with parsley, onion or caper sauce.

SALTED MEAT — (Pickled Pork, Corned Beef, Corned Mutton)—

1. Allow 30 minutes to 500 grams (1 lb 2 oz) and 30 minutes over.
2. Put into warm water with 1 tablespoon of lemon juice or vinegar. Bring slowly to boil and skim.
3. Simmer until cooked.
4. If possible allow meat to get cold in the water.
5. Serve with root vegetables which may be cooked with meat. The addition of bouquet garni (page 28) improves salted meats.
6. If lean, add 2 tablespoons of dripping to water.

RULES FOR STEAMING MEAT

Steaming is cooking in steam from boiling water—

1. Steaming is suitable for small cuts of meat—mutton, beef, pork.
2. Allow 30 minutes to 500 grams (1 lb 2 oz) and 30 minutes over for steaming fresh meat. Salt meat longer time.
3. Roll meat in greased paper. Put into steamer over saucepan of boiling water.
4. Keep water boiling all the time.
5. Vegetable may be steamed with meat. Allow 1½ hours.
6. Serve with parsley, onion or caper sauce.

STEAMED MEAT

Suitable for a small meal—

1. Take a leg chop or similar small cut of meat and root vegetable for one person.
2. Put ingredients with a little water in steaming basin or jam tin. Cover with greased paper.
3. Stand container in boiling water with water coming half way up basin.
4. Steam 1 hour or longer if necessary.
5. Serve with parsley sauce made with flour, powdered milk and liquid in container.

RULES OF BRAISING

1. Braising is a combination of pot roasting and stewing and is particularly suitable for small joints, rabbits, stuffed steak.
2. It is an economical method of cooking, and gives a good flavour even to joints that might otherwise be lacking in flavour.
3. Use a saucepan with a tight fitting lid.
4. Heat sufficient fat to cover bottom of pan.
5. Dip meat in seasoned flour. Brown. Add sliced vegetables. Brown.
6. Add a little water and seasoning.
7. Cook gently for 2 to 3 hours.
8. Serve on hot dish with vegetable and gravy.

Note—A pot roast may be cooked in the same way, omitting water and sliced vegetables. Whole vegetables, such as potatoes, may be cooked with joint.

RULES FOR FRYING

Frying is cooking in fuming fat or oil—

1. Frying is a method of cooking which should only be used occasionally to add variety to the diet.
2. There are two methods—
   (a) Shallow frying.
   (b) Deep frying.

RULES FOR SHALLOW FRYING

Shallow frying is cooking in a small quantity of fat. It is a suitable method for eggs, bacon, omelets, tomatoes, liver, cutlets, sausages, etc.

METHOD—

1. The fat should have a blue fume (not smoke) rising.
2. Brown the article evenly on both sides. Cook meat gently.
3. Turn articles with a knife. Do not prod with fork.
4. Drain fried food on kitchen paper.
5. Serve on a hot dish. Garnish.
6. Keep frying fat in a special basin.

RULES FOR DEEP FRYING

1. Deep frying is cooking in sufficient fat to cover the article to be fried. It is suitable for small pieces of fish, rissoles, fish croquettes, dough nuts, fritters, etc. Food cooked by this method is preferable to that cooked by shallow frying, as, owing to the great heat of the fat, the pores of food are immediately sealed, thus preventing the absorption of fat and loss of flavour.
2. Food fried in this way should be protected by a covering of egg and breadcrumbs, flour, oatmeal or batter.

METHOD—

1. Have saucepan ½ full of fat.
2. Heat fat till a faint blue fume rises from it and surface is quite still.
3. Heat fry basket. Place article in it and lower gently into fat.
4. Cook until golden brown (3 to 5 minutes).
5. Drain food on crumpled kitchen paper.
6. Serve on paper d'oyley on hot dish, garnish neatly.
7. Remove fat from fire immediately. Strain. It is then ready for future use.

Note—Fuming fat is apt to catch fire if exposed to a draught. Water or steam must not be near fuming fat.

RULES FOR GRILLING

Grilling is cooking by dry heat—

1. Grilling is cooking by exposure to red hot coals or griller (gas or electric).

2. It is a method suitable only for small and best cuts of meat (rump steak, fillet steak, short loin and rib chops, small birds, bacon, sheep's kidney (split)).

3. The meat should be from 2½ to 4 cms (1 to 1½ inches) thick.

4. Have a clear smokeless fire, or hot griller.

5. Trim meat and remove skin, brush with melted fat.

6. Grill steak in as large a piece as possible.

7. Warm grid iron and grease bars to prevent meat sticking to grid iron.

8. Expose meat to heat for 2 minutes on each side at first. Turn frequently while cooking.

9. Time varies with thickness, 8 to 12 minutes.

10. Kidneys should be split and the cut side grilled first.

11. Serve hot with butter and parsley.

STEWING

Stewing is cooking in a small quantity of liquid for a long time—

1. It is a nourishing and economical method of cooking, because—

    (a) The cheaper cuts of meat may be used.

    (b) There is no waste, the goodness extracted from the meat is served in the gravy.

    (c) Very little firing or attention is necessary.

    (d) Vegetables may be cooked with the meat.

Stewing—Continued

2. Meat for stews should be cut in suitable pieces, barely covered with cold water, seasoned with salt and pepper and brought slowly to simmering point. Simmer 2 to 3 hours.

3. Beef requires longer cooking than mutton.

4. There are 3 classes of stews—brown, white and Irish.

5. Brown stews are chiefly made from beef; white stews from mutton, tripe, rabbit, veal, etc.

6. In brown stews, the onions and meat are fried first to improve the flavour and appearance of the dish. White stews are more easily digested than brown stews.

7. Onions thinly sliced are added to all stews; other vegetables may also be used.

8. Stews may be cooked in a double saucepan, thus obviating the need for constant attention. A double saucepan is easily improvised by standing a basin or billy can in a saucepan of water. "A stew boiled is a stew spoiled."

9. Stews may be thickened with flour, rice, or other starchy material.

ROAST BEEF

METHOD—

1. Replace wooden skewers with steel ones.
2. Follow rules for baking meat.
3. Make gravy.
4. Serve with horse-radish sauce.
5. Beef may be garnished with grated horse-radish or baked potatoes or water cress.

GRAVY—

1. Pour off fat, leaving brown sediment in pan.
2. Sprinkle with salt and pepper. Add boiling stock or water. Stir well.
3. Strain into gravy boat.

ROAST LAMB OR MUTTON

METHOD—

1. Prepare joint. The shoulder and loin may be boned and stuffed.
2. Follow rules for baking meat.
3. Serve mint sauce with lamb and red currant jelly with mutton or stuffed joints.

GRAVY—

1. Pour off nearly all fat. Heat remainder until fuming.
2. Sprinkle in flour, pepper and salt. Brown well, scraping tit bits from sides of tin with spoon.
3. Add cold water or stock gradually. Smooth out lumps. Bring to boil. Strain.

ROAST PORK

METHOD—

1. Score the pork all over by cutting the rind through in narrow bands with a sharp knife or razor.
2. Grease rind with oil or melted dripping.
3. Place in a baking tin with some fat.
4. Allow 30 minutes cooking for each 500 grams (1 lb 2 oz) and 30 minutes extra.
5. Place in hot oven until rind is crisp and then cook gently the remainder of time.
6. Baste.
7. Serve on hot dish with brown gravy and apple sauce as accompaniments.

Note—Pork may be boned and stuffed with sage and onion stuffing.

ROAST VEAL

METHOD—

1. Choose nice piece of fillet of veal.
2. Stuff with veal stuffing (page 77).
3. Place in baking tin with plenty of dripping.
4. Allow 25 minutes cooking for each 500 grams (1 lb 2 oz) and 25 minutes over.
5. Place in moderate oven.
6. Cook gently after first 15 minutes.
7. Baste and turn.
8. Serve on hot dish with brown gravy.

IRISH STEW

INGREDIENTS—

500 grams neck chops or best
    end of neck mutton
    (1 lb 2 oz).
1 kilogram potatoes (old)
    (2 lbs 3 oz).

2 onions.
1 cup water.
1½ teaspoons salt.
¼ teaspoon pepper.

METHOD—

1. Trim meat and cut into pieces convenient for serving.
2. Peel and slice onion and ½ the potatoes.
3. Arrange meat and vegetables in layers with seasoning.
4. Add sufficient water to come half way up meat and
   vegetables. Place whole potatoes on top.
5. Simmer 2 hours, stirring frequently.
6. Serve in hot dish with meat in centre and potatoes around
   edge.
Note 1—The successful thickening of this stew depends on the
   breaking down of the potatoes.
Note 2—This stew may be placed in a casserole and baked in
   oven.

HARICOT MUTTON

INGREDIENTS—

500 grams leg chops
    (1 lb 2 oz).
1 onion.
1 carrot.
Salt and pepper.

1 tablespoon dripping.
1 heaped tablespoon flour.
2 cups cold water.
1 dessertspoon chopped
    parsley.

METHOD—

1. Trim meat, removing thick fat.
2. Peel and slice vegetables.
3. Roll meat in seasoned flour.
4. Heat fat, fry onions and remove to plate.
5. Brown meat on both sides and lift out.
6. Brown remainder of flour. Mix to a smooth paste with water.
7. Add meat and vegetables and simmer 2 hours.
8. Serve on hot dish. Sprinkle with chopped parsley.

STEWED TRIPE AND ONIONS

INGREDIENTS—

500 grams tripe (1 lb 2 oz).
2 onions (white).
1 cup water.
1¼ cups milk.
1 teaspoon salt.

1 dessertspoon of chopped
  parsley.
Pepper to taste.
1 tablespoon flour.
1 teaspoon butter.

METHOD—

1. Place in a saucepan, cover with water, bring to boil slowly;
   pour off water.
2. Scrape tripe and cut into neat squares.
3. Add water, salt, pepper and prepared onion.
4. Simmer 1 hour, or until tender.
5. Blend flour with milk. Add and bring to boil.
6. Add butter and chopped parsley.
7. Serve on a hot dish.

Note—When using brown onions blanch or cook tripe and onion
   separately.

FRICASSEE OF RABBIT

INGREDIENTS—

1 rabbit.
2 rashers bacon or bacon
  rinds.
1 large white onion.
1 cup milk.

1 dessertspoon chopped
  parsley.
1½ tablespoons flour.
Salt and pepper to taste.

METHOD—

1. Soak rabbit in salted water for ½ hour. Dry and cut in joints.
2. Peel and slice onion thinly.
3. Place onion and rabbit in pan, barely cover with water.
4. Simmer gently 2 hours. Add bacon when meat is half cooked.
5. Thicken stew with flour blended with milk. Bring to boil.
6. Serve rabbit on hot dish, garnished with chopped parsley and
   bacon.

STUFFED RABBIT

INGREDIENTS—

Rabbit.
Stuffing.

2 slices fat bacon.

METHOD—

1. Soak rabbit in salted water for ½ hour. Drain and dry. Trim and remove kidneys, etc.
2. Make stuffing, using 1 cup breadcrumbs, 1 tablespoon butter, dripping or chopped suet. ½ teaspoon marjoram or thyme, 1 tablespoon chopped parsley, 1 slice chopped bacon, grated rind of ½ lemon, ¾ teaspoon salt, pepper. *Method*—Rub butter into breadcrumbs. Add other ingredients. Mix well.
3. Fill rabbit with stuffing. Fold in halves, bring back legs up to front legs and push into rabbit, tie into good shape. Dust with seasoned flour.
4. Lay slice of bacon on top.
5. Put fat (1 tablespoon) into saucepan. Melt. Put in rabbit. Gently brown on both sides.
6. Add 1 cup of water and simmer for 1 hour.
7. Serve on hot dish with gravy.
8. Garnish with bacon.

Note—Rabbit may be wrapped in thick greased paper and baked in oven.

ROMAN STEW

INGREDIENTS—

500 grams steak (1 lb 2 oz).
1 onion.
2 tomatoes.
1 or 2 sticks chopped celery.
1½ cups stock or water.

1 teaspoon vinegar or lemon juice.
1 rasher lean bacon.
1 tablespoon flour.
Macaroni.

METHOD—

1. Cut meat into 2½ cm (1 in.) cubes, peel and slice vegetables; cut bacon in 5 cm (2 in.) pieces. Ingredients may be browned.
2. Place all in saucepan with stock.
3. Simmer 2 to 3 hours.
4. Thicken with blended flour, boil 3 minutes.
5. Serve on a hot dish with macaroni.

CURRY AND RICE

INGREDIENTS—

500 grams steak (1 lb 2 oz).	1 dessertspoon jam.
1 onion.	1 teaspoon of lemon juice.
1 apple.	1 tablespoon flour.
1 banana.	Salt and pepper.
1 tablespoon sultanas.	1 dessertspoon sugar.
1 tablespoon fat.	2½ cups water or stock.
1 level tablespoon of curry powder.	¼ teaspoon ground ginger (optional).

METHOD—
1. Prepare vegetables and fruit, cut into slices.
2. Fry vegetables and fruit in fat in saucepan.
3. Lift out on to plate.
4. Cut meat into small cubes, toss in seasoned flour. Fry till brown.
5. Add to meat curry powder and remainder of flour.
   Brown. Add lemon juice, ginger, sultanas, sugar, jam.
6. Add vegetables, fruit and liquid. Simmer 2 hours.
7. Serve on hot dish, garnished with a border of rice.
8. Accompaniments—Wedges of lemon, sliced cucumber, sliced banana, toasted coconut, peanuts, chutney.

Note—Cooked meat may be used instead of steak, but do not fry meat. Sausages and chops may be curried in the same way. Fat should be removed.

TOMATO MINCE

INGREDIENTS—

500 grams minced steak (raw) (1 lb 2 oz).	Cold water (soup tin filled).
1 onion.	Salt and pepper to taste.
1 large tin tomato soup.	4 tablespoons macaroni.

METHOD—

1. Peel and chop onion, fry till brown. Add meat, fry a little.
2. Add tomato soup, water, salt and pepper, simmer for one hour or until meat is tender.
3. Add macaroni, simmer till macaroni is cooked (about 20 minutes).

CASSEROLE

INGREDIENTS—

500 grams steak (1 lb 2 oz).	1 carrot.
1 small onion.	½ tablespoon flour.
1¼ cups stock or water.	1 teaspoon salt.
1 stick of celery.	Pepper.
1 tomato.	2 slices bacon.
Pinch of all spice.	

METHOD—

1. Cut meat in pieces. Dip in seasoned flour.
2. Peel and slice vegetables.
3. Place bacon in casserole, ½ vegetables, then steak and remainder of vegetables with bacon on top.
4. Add stock or water.
5. Cover with lid. Place in slow oven. Cook for 2 hours.

Note—Chops, rabbits, chicken and other vegetables are delicious cooked in this way. Potatoes may be cooked with the meat (allow 1 hour).

SAVOURY STEW

INGREDIENTS—

500 grams forequarter chops or steak (1 lb 2 oz).	1 teaspoon salt.
1 onion.	½ teaspoon sugar.
2 tomatoes.	Pepper.
	½ cup of water or wine.

METHOD—

1. Cut meat into sizes for serving.
2. Peel and slice onion.
3. Slice tomatoes.
4. Place ingredients in casserole or saucepan.
5. Cover and cook gently for 1½ to 2 hours.
6. Serve with mashed potatoes.

BROWN STEW

INGREDIENTS—

500 grams stewing steak (1 lb 2 oz).	2 cups water.
1 onion.	1 heaped tablespoon flour.
1 carrot.	1 teaspoon salt.
1 stick celery.	¼ teaspoon pepper.
	1 tablespoon dripping.

Brown Stew—Continued

METHOD—

1. Slice onion and carrot.
2. Mix flour, salt and pepper.
3. Cut meat into neat pieces. Dip in seasoned flour.
4. Melt fat in saucepan. Brown onions then meat.
5. Add remainder of flour. Brown.
6. Add water.
7. Simmer gently for 2 hours.
8. Add carrot 1 hour before serving.
9. Serve on hot dish. Garnish with carrot.

FRICASSEE OF CHOPS

INGREDIENTS—

500 grams neck chops
  (1 lb 2 oz).
1 onion.
Grated lemon rind.
1 cup water.
Chopped parsley.

1 cup milk.
1 heaped tablespoon
  flour.
1 teaspoon salt.
Pepper to taste.

METHOD—

1. Trim chops, removing fat.
2. Put meat, sliced onion, seasoning and water into a saucepan
   and simmer 1½ hours.
3. Blend flour with milk. Stir into fricassee. Bring to boil.
4. Add chopped parsley and serve on hot dish.

STEWED OX TAIL

INGREDIENTS—

1 ox tail.
1 carrot.
1 onion.
1 teaspoon salt.
1 tablespoon dripping.

A bouquet garni (page 28),
  or 4 cloves.
1 tablespoon flour.
1 teaspoon lemon juice.

Stewed Ox Tail—Continued

METHOD—

1. Cut tail into neat joints removing fat. Roll in seasoned flour.
2. Heat dripping and brown sliced onions, meat and flour.
3. Put meat, bouquet garni, lemon juice and onion in saucepan, barely cover with cold water. Simmer till tender (3 to 4 hours).
4. Remove bouquet garni. Allow meat etc. to cool. Remove fat.
5. Add sliced carrot, simmer for ½ hour.
6. If necessary, thicken gravy with extra blended flour.
7. Serve on hot dish garnished with carrot.

SEA PIE

INGREDIENTS—

500 grams steak (1 lb 2 oz).	1 tablespoon flour.
1 sheep's kidney.	1 teaspoon salt.
1 carrot.	120 grams suet pastry
1 onion.	(page 91) (4 oz).
Pepper to taste.	Turnip (if liked).

METHOD—

1. Cut steak and kidney into small pieces. Cut vegetables into dice.
2. Place meat and vegetables in saucepan, barely cover with stock or water.
3. Simmer 2 hours. Stir in blended flour.
4. Make suet pastry. Roll to a round the size of the pan.
5. Place on top of meat, making a small hole in centre.
6. Cover closely and simmer ½ hour.
7. Serve very hot with pastry arranged in triangular pieces around edge of dish.

BRAISED STEAK

INGREDIENTS—

1 kilogram topside steak (2 lbs 3 oz).	1 teaspoon salt.
1 onion.	Pepper.
1 carrot.	1 cup water.
1 turnip.	Fat.
	1 dessertspoon flour.

Braised Steak—Continued

METHOD—

1. Cut onions into rings, and other vegetables into dice-shaped pieces.
2. Dip meat in seasoned flour.
3. Heat fat in saucepan, brown meat then vegetables. Put lid on pan.
4. Cook slowly for ½ hour. Add water, cook gently for 1½ hours.
5. Serve on hot dish with vegetables and gravy poured around.

Note—Any small joint may be treated in this way.

RAGOUT OF RABBIT

INGREDIENTS—

1 rabbit.	6 cloves.
2 rashers of bacon.	1 level teaspoon salt.
1½ tablespoons flour.	Pepper.
1 carrot.	Forcemeat balls (see
1 onion.	page 77).
1 bay leaf.	

METHOD—

1. Joint rabbit, soak in salted water, wash and dry.
2. Remove rind from bacon, cut each rasher in 3 or 4 pieces.
3. Fry bacon in stew pan, lift out.
4. Toss rabbit in seasoned flour, fry in bacon fat.
5. Add sufficient water to barely cover meat.
6. Scrape and slice carrot, peel and slice onion. Add to meat with bay leaf and cloves. Simmer for 1½ hours.
7. Thicken gravy with remainder of flour.
8. Ten minutes before serving add bacon and forcemeat balls.
9. Serve in a hot dish arranging bacon and forcemeat balls around edge.

BEEF OLIVES

INGREDIENTS—

500 grams steak (1 lb 2 oz).	1 tablespoon flour.
4 tablespoons veal stuffing.	1½ cups water.
1 teaspoon salt.	1 tablespoon fat.

Beef Olives—Continued

METHOD—

1. Make stuffing (see page 77).
2. Cut steak into thin slices, 10 cm (4 inch) squares; place stuffing on each. Roll up and tie firmly with string.
3. Roll in flour, brown in hot fat.
4. Remove olives, drain off fat, make brown gravy.
5. Simmer olives in gravy for 2 hours.
6. Remove string from olives, serve with gravy on a hot dish.

STUFFED STEAK

METHOD—

1. Choose a piece of thick, tender steak.
2. Cut a pocket in the steak and fill with veal stuffing (see page 77).
3. Bake until tender, 1 to 1½ hours, according to size.
4. Serve with rich brown gravy.

STEAK AND KIDNEY PIE

INGREDIENTS—

Flaky pastry, half recipe (page 139).
500 grams steak (top side) (1 lb 2 oz).
Cold water.

1 tablespoon flour.
1 or 2 kidneys (sheep's) or small piece ox kidney.
Salt and pepper.

METHOD—

1. Make pastry, roll to required size and stand in a cool place.
2. Cut steak into thin strips. Put into seasoned flour.
3. Wash, dry and cut kidney into dice. Roll a piece of kidney in each piece of steak and place rolls in a pie dish; half fill pie dish with cold water. Put pie funnel in centre.
4. Place strips of pastry around wet edges of pie dish. Damp.
5. Cover with pastry, trim and decorate edges.
6. Make a hole in centre of pie.
7. Roll out trimmings and cut out leaves and roses for decorating. Glaze with egg.
8. Cook in hot oven about 20 minutes then in a cooler oven about 1½ hours longer, protecting pastry with brown paper.
9. Serve on a dish using plain doyley.

Note—If preferred meat may be cooked first, allowed to cool before covering with pastry.

MUTTON PIE

INGREDIENTS—

750 grams leg or chump chops
(1lb 11oz.).
1 white onion.
1 cup water.
1½ teaspoons salt.
Grated rind of ½ lemon.

Rough puff or flaky pastry
(page 139).
4 peppercorns.
2 hard boiled eggs.
2 teaspoons chopped parsley.

METHOD—

1. Cut meat in suitable pieces. Peel and slice onion.
2. Put meat, onion, water, salt and peppercorns in stewpan.
   Cook gently till tender—1½-2 hours.
3. Put meat in a piedish with pie funnel.
4. Cover with sliced egg, parsley and lemon rind.
5. Thicken gravy with a little blended flour, pour over meat.
   Allow to cool.
6. Make pastry, cover pie as for Steak and Kidney Pie.

VEAL PIE

Make as for Mutton Pie using veal instead of mutton. Omit onion,
add sliced ham.

STEAK AND KIDNEY PUDDING

INGREDIENTS—

Foundation recipe suet pastry
(page 91).
500 grams beef steak
(1 lb 2 oz).
1 or 2 sheep's kidneys or
¼ ox kidney.

1 tablespoon flour.
Water.
1 teaspoon salt.
1 onion (if liked).
Pepper.

Steak and Kidney Pudding — continued

METHOD—

1. Put water on to boil. Prepare cloth and grease basin.
2. Cut meat into small pieces.
3. Sprinkle flour, salt and pepper over meat and chopped onions; mix well.
4. Make suet pastry. Cut off 1-3rd for covering basin.
5. Line basin evenly, fill centre with meat, etc.; add sufficient water to cover the meat.
6. Roll pastry for covering into a round, and cover pudding, pressing edges well together.
7. Cover with greased paper, or alfoil, tie securely.
8. Place in boiling water, water reaching ½ way up basin.
9. Steam constantly 3 to 4 hours.
10. Lift out of pan; remove cloth; make hole in centre and fill with hot stock or water.
11. Fold table napkin neatly around basin, and stand basin on dish to serve.

SAVOURY STEAK

INGREDIENTS—

500 grams blade bone or topside steak (1 lb 2 oz).
1 tablespoon of flour.
1 tablespoon of sugar.
½ teaspoon of mustard.
1 tablespoon of tomato sauce.
1 tablespoon of Worcester sauce.
1 teaspoon of salt.
1½ cups of cold water.

METHOD—

1. Cut meat into cubes.
2. Put other ingredients into casserole adding water last. Mix smooth.
3. Stir in meat.
4. Bake slowly for 2 to 3 hours.

Note—Mutton may be used.

MARINADED STEAK

INGREDIENTS—

Grilling steak cut in thick slice.
2 tablespoons vinegar, lemon juice or red wine.
2 tablespoons sugar.
2 tablespoons Worcester sauce.
2 tablespoons tomato sauce.
Pepper, salt.
Grated rind of one lemon.

Marinaded Steak — continued

METHOD—

1. Put steak into a dish. Pour marinade mixture over steak.
2. Leave for 5 or 6 hours, turning occasionally.
3. Grill steak slowly for a short time.
4. Boil up the mixture. Thicken with a little flour and pour over steak.
5. Serve hot.

ABERDEEN SAUSAGE

INGREDIENTS—

500 grams steak (topside) (1 lb 2 oz).

240 grams fat bacon (8 oz).

1 large cup of fresh breadcrumbs

1 tablespoon Worcester sauce.

1 egg.

1 tablespoon tomato sauce.

Grated lemon rind.

Salt and pepper to taste.

METHOD—

1. Mince steak and bacon. Add breadcrumbs, sauce, seasoning and beaten egg.
2. Mix well. Mould into a long roll.
3. Wrap well in greased paper or alfoil.
4. Steam 3 hours.
5. Remove paper allow to cool. Roll in brown bread crumbs.
6. Serve cold. Garnish with parsley.

TO COOK A HAM

No. 1

METHOD—

1. Soak ham 12 hours. Scrape well. Dry.
2. Prepare a dough (like scone dough) of 1 kilogram (2 lbs 3 oz) flour and water.
3. Roll out paste. Wrap ham in paste.
4. Place in baking tin with cup full of dripping.
5. Bake in a moderately hot oven 3 or 4 hours. Baste frequently.
6. Remove paste and skin, trim neatly. Sprinkle thickly with brown bread crumbs and grated nutmeg.

No. 2

1. Wash and trim ham. A large ham which may be dry or over salty should be soaked for 12 hours.
2. Put ham in a boiler or saucepan, and sufficient cold water to cover ham.
3. Bring slowly to boil. Allow to boil for one minute to each 500 grams (1 lb 2 oz) and 10 minutes over. (Example—a 7 kilogram (15½ lbs) ham . . . boil for 25 minutes).
4. Prepare a thick wrapping of old rug, blankets or bags and several sheets of paper.
5. Leave lid on pan and wrap completely to keep in heat. Leave overnight.
6. When cool, lift out ham and remove skin. Dress surface as in No. 1 recipe.

Note—This method may be used for corned beef or mutton.

OX TONGUE

INGREDIENTS—

Ox tongue.   Bunch of herbs.

METHOD—

1. Choose tongue with smooth skin.
2. Soak in cold water about 1 hour.
3. Scrape and trim.
4. Put on to boil with cold water and bunch of herbs.
5. Simmer from about 3 to 4 hours, according to size of tongue. Skim well.
6. When cooked remove skin. Cut tongue down centre lengthways.
7. Place first piece cut side down in mould. Place 2nd piece cut side up, root in space. Press.
8. When cold and set, turn on to dish. Garnish with parsley.

Note—No. 2 method for cooking ham may be used. A pressure cooker saves cooking time.

SHEEP'S TONGUES IN JELLY

INGREDIENTS—

6 sheep's tongues (corned).   1 level dessertspoon gelatine.
2 hard boiled eggs.   Bunch herbs.
Gherkins.

Sheep's Tongues in Jelly — continued

METHOD—

1. Put into saucepan; cover well with cold water; add herbs. Simmer gently till tender—about 3 hours. Skin.
2. Decorate mould with sliced hard boiled eggs and gherkins. Arrange tongues in mould.
3. Add gelatine to 1½ cups of liquor and, when thoroughly dissolved, pour over tongues.
4. When set and cold turn into a dish and garnish with sprigs of parsley.

CORNED SHEEP'S TONGUES (HOT)

1. Put sheep's tongues in saucepan with cold water and a bouquet garni.
2. Simmer for 3 hours or until tender. Remove skins.
3. Serve hot with parsley sauce.

Note—Sheep's tongues cook quickly in Pressure Cooker.

FRENCH CUTLETS

INGREDIENTS—

Cutlets.   Green butter balls.
Potato chips.   Bacon.
Salt and pepper.

METHOD—

1. Trim cutlets, leaving 2½ cms (1 inch) of bare bone.
2. Grill for 8 to 10 minutes.
3. Grill bacon in rolls.
4. Place cutlets on hot dish with potato chips.
5. Garnish with bacon rolls and green butter balls.

CRUMBED CUTLETS

INGREDIENTS—

Cutlets.   Salt.
1 egg.   Pepper.
Bread crumbs (dried).   Good dripping.

Crumbed Cutlets — continued

METHOD—

1. Trim cutlets, removing skin and gristle and leaving about 5 cms (2 inches) bare bone.
2. Beat egg on plate. Season with salt and pepper.
3. Place bread crumbs on kitchen paper.
4. Dip cutlets into egg, then bread crumbs. Press each cutlet firmly with knife and then shake off loose crumbs.
5. Melt fat in pan and when fuming hot, put in cutlets. Fry about 10 minutes.
6. Drain cutlets on kitchen paper.
7. Serve on mound or wall of mashed potatoes on a hot dish.
8. Garnish with grilled tomatoes and green peas.

AMERICAN CUTLETS

INGREDIENTS—

Leg or chump chops.	Onion.
Flour.	Thyme.
Fat.	Bacon.
Soft breadcrumbs.	Gravy.

METHOD—

1. Trim chops, dip in flour seasoned with salt and pepper.
2. Heat 2 tablespoons of fat in a baking dish.
3. For each chop prepare 2 teaspoons of breadcrumbs, 2 teaspoons finely chopped onion, ¼ teaspoon of thyme or mixed herbs, salt and pepper. Mix together then pile some of mixture on each chop. Sprinkle with paprika.
4. Place chops in baking dish, baste with fat and bake for ½ hour or until tender then cover each chop with a piece of bacon and continue baking for another 10 minutes.
5. Serve with gravy.

BRAWN

INGREDIENTS—

1 beef shin bone.	1 level tablespoon salt.
1 knuckle of veal.	Bouquet garni (page 28).
750 grams gravy beef (1lb 11oz.).	Pepper.

Brawn — continued

METHOD—

1. Place well sawn bones and knuckle in saucepan with seasonings. Cover well with cold water.
2. Simmer gently until gristle softens.
3. Remove bare bones and allow liquid to stand till cold. Remove fat.
4. Cut gravy beef into pieces, add to liquid, simmer till meat is tender.
5. Strain liquid off meat and gristle.
6. Cut up meat and gristle taking care to remove small pieces of bone.
7. Add meat to liquid, stir well, pour into wet moulds. Keep in cool place.

Note—Pig's trotters, pig's cheek, sheep tongues or bacon may be added for additional flavours.

POTTED MEAT

INGREDIENTS—

500 grams juicy beef (1 lb 2 oz).
240 grams butter (8 oz).
½ teaspoon salt.
Pepper.

½ teaspoon mustard.
¼ teaspoon mixed spice.
2 or 3 anchovies.
Pinch cayenne.
1 bay leaf.

METHOD—

1. Cut meat into small pieces, remove skin leaving any hard fat.
2. Put in stewing jar with pepper, salt, cayenne, bay leaf and rather more than half the butter. Cover jar closely.
3. Place in saucepan with water reaching half way up jar, steam until beef is tender.
4. Turn into a mortar, remove bay leaf, add anchovies; pound to a paste.
5. Add mustard and spice.
6. Rub through a fine sieve, pack in little pots.
7. Melt remainder of butter and pour over top to keep out the air.
8. This will keep indefinitely in cold place.

WINE IN COOKING

1. Wine improves the texture of inexpensive cuts of meat by softening connective tissue.

2. Wine gives zest to soups, sauces, simple stews and casseroles.

3. The alcohol content in wine evaporates with heat.

4. Suitable meats for including wine are veal, steak, lamb and mutton, chicken, rabbit.

5. Use red wines for red meats and white wines for white meats.

CASSEROLE OF CHOPS

INGREDIENTS—

4 shoulder or chump chops.
1 clove garlic.
Salt and pepper.
Flour and fat.

1 onion.
4 shallots.
1 tablespoon chopped parsley.
1 cup wine.

METHOD—

1. Rub each chop with cut clove of garlic.
2. Sprinkle each chop with flour, pepper and salt.
3. Fry chops gently till lightly browned.
4. Fry sliced onion and shallots.
5. Put meat, vegetables and parsley in casserole. Add wine.
6. Bake in a moderate oven for ½ to 1 hour or until chops are tender.

SAUTE OF CHICKEN

INGREDIENTS—

1 chicken for 4 people.	240 grams mushrooms (8 oz).
2 cloves garlic.	2 tomatoes.
Salt and pepper.	1 tablespoon chopped parsley.
Sprig of parsley.	1½ cups white wine.
Sprig of thyme.	1 tablespoon flour.
1 bay leaf.	Frying fat.

METHOD—

1. Cut chicken into suitable pieces, coat with flour.
2. Chop garlic. Slice tomatoes, peel and slice mushrooms (already washed).
3. Fry garlic till lightly browned, then brown chicken pieces.
4. Put chicken, garlic, tomatoes, mushrooms, sprigs of parsley and thyme, bay leaf, salt and pepper in a stew pan. Add wine.
5. Simmer gently until chicken is tender, approx. ¾ hour.
6. Remove herbs. Liquid may be thickened with 1 tablespoon of flour (blended).
7. Serve hot, sprinkled with chopped parsley and boiled rice.

ESCALOPES OF VEAL

INGREDIENTS—

4 thin fillets of veal (trimmed).	½ cup tomato puree or 1 tablespoon tomato paste.
1 onion.	1 cup red wine.
3 slices ham or bacon.	1 tablespoon lemon juice.
Salt and pepper.	1 clove garlic.
Flour.	Frying fat.

METHOD—

1. Chop onion and garlic, cut up bacon. Fry together till lightly browned. Remove from pan. Drain off fat.
2. Coat veal in flour, salt and pepper, fry till brown. Drain off fat.
3. Put veal, bacon, onion and garlic in a stew pan, add tomato puree, lemon juice and wine. Simmer gently until meat is tender—about 45 minutes.
4. Serve with cooked macaroni or spaghetti.

PRESSURE COOKING

Pressure cooking has three advantages—

1. Cooking time is reduced to less than one third of the usual time required by other methods such as stewing, boiling, steaming.

2. More flavours and nutritive value of food is conserved.

3. The reduced cooking time economises in fuel.

PROCEDURE—

1. Follow carefully directions provided with the pressure cooker.

2. Great care should be taken to keep the pressure cooker in sound condition and unnecessary risks should be avoided.

3. Perfect cleanliness of the pressure cooker is necessary.

RE-HEATING

1. Cold cooked food may be made into appetising dishes and re-heated.

2. The food must not be re-cooked.

3. Other ingredients added to the cooked food must be cooked first.

4. Cooked meat may be made into the following: Rissoles, Curry, Potato Pie, Mince Pies, Fritters.

5. Cooked fish may be made into Fish Cakes, Kedgeree, Fish Pie, Fritters, Fish Custard.

6. Cooked potato may be used for Fish Cakes, Potato Croquettes, Potato Scones.

7. Fish Cakes, Potato Croquettes, Rissoles. The addition of beaten egg helps to bind mixture.

8. Cooked vegetables may be re-heated in a frying pan.

RISSOLES

INGREDIENTS—

240 grams cold meat (8 oz).
1 cup fresh bread crumbs.
Nutmeg.
¼ to ½ cup stock or gravy.
1 small onion.
1 teaspoon salt.

Pepper.
1 dessertspoon parsley.
¼ teaspoon marjoram and
thyme.
1 egg and some dry bread
crumbs.

METHOD—

1. Mince meat and onion, add to it 1 tablespoon beaten egg,
chopped parsley, herbs, seasoning, fresh bread crumbs and
stock or gravy. Mix well.
2. Divide into required number of pieces. Mould into cakes
using a little flour.
3. Dip rissoles into beaten egg, then bread crumbs.
4. Deep fry a golden brown. Drain on kitchen paper.
5. Serve on paper d'oyley on hot plate. Garnish with parsley.

POTATO PIE

INGREDIENTS—

500 grams minced meat
(cooked) (1 lb 2 oz).
500 grams mashed potatoes
(1 lb 2 oz).
Little nutmeg.
½ cup gravy.

1 teaspoon salt.
Pepper.
½ teaspoon herbs or
¼ teaspoon all spice.
Grated rind ½ lemon.
1 onion (cooked).

METHOD—

1. Mix meat with gravy. Add seasoning, nutmeg, finely chopped
onion, herbs and lemon rind.
2. Turn into pie dish. Pile mashed potatoes on top. Brush over
with butter or dripping.
3. Brown evenly. Serve hot with tomato sauce.

Note—Minced bacon may be added to the mixture, or dish may
be lined with slices of tomato.

STUFFED TOMATOES

INGREDIENTS—

10 tomatoes.
1 cup minced meat (cooked).
Small onion.
2 tablespoons bread crumbs.
½ teaspoon lemon juice.
1 teaspoon sugar.

Salt and pepper.
½ teaspoon herbs.
1 teaspoon flour.
1 teaspoon chopped parsley.
¼ cup water.
Toast.

METHOD—

1. Mince meat and onion.
2. Put meat into saucepan with flour, breadcrumbs, lemon juice, seasoning, parsley and water. Cook gently 10 minutes.
3. Wash tomatoes, make hole in top and scoop out centre.
4. Add half tomato pulp to mince.
5. Fill tomatoes with mince mixture. Sprinkle few breadcrumbs over top and small piece of butter.
6. Stand in baking dish and cook in moderate oven 15 to 20 minutes.
7. Place each tomato on a round of toasted bread and serve hot, garnished with parsley.

FORCEMEAT OR STUFFING

Forcemeat is the term applied to a stuffing mixture with the addition of minced or chopped meat, bacon, kidney, liver, veal or fish. Less breadcrumbs are required.

Stuffing is the term used for a mixture of breadcrumbs, seasoning, herbs, fat and moisture.

Flavourings which may be added according to kind of poultry, meat or fish, etc. are—grated lemon rind, chopped parsley, nutmeg, onion, tomato, mushrooms, apple, prunes, nuts, oysters.

STUFFING—Basic Recipe

1 cup breadcrumbs.
1 level tablespoon butter,
   dripping or chopped suet.
Flavourings and herbs.

1 level teaspoon salt,
   pepper.
Moisture (a little milk or
   beaten egg).

For CHICKEN, TURKEY, LAMB, MUTTON, RABBIT, BEEF, VEAL, FISH

To the basic recipe add the following:—

1 level tablespoon chopped
   parsley.
¼ teaspoon nutmeg.

1 teaspoon thyme, marjoram
   or mixed herbs.
1 teaspoon grated lemon rind.

For DUCK, GOOSE, PORK

To the basic recipe add the following:—

¼ teaspoon nutmeg.
1 teaspoon grated lemon rind.

1 teaspoon powdered sage.
1 small onion, chopped finely.

METHOD—

1. Mix dry ingredients. Add fat and rub into breadcrumbs, etc.
2. Add flavourings, mix well.
3. Add sufficient moisture to make mixture hold together.

POULTRY

Poultry for roasting should be young and tender, but for boiling and stewing it may be more mature. When young the legs and feet will be pliable and the breast bone can be easily bent. The legs will also be smooth and free from heavy scale. A fowl is usually called a chicken until it is about nine months old.

When ducks and geese are young they have yellow and pliable feet and legs and the under bill is easily broken.

Turkeys when young have white, smooth legs.

TO PLUCK A FOWL—

Dip into bucket of boiling water. Wrap up quickly in a cloth. Leave a few minutes, then pluck immediately, beginning with the stiff feathers of the wings. Next work from the breast downwards, plucking the legs, turn over and pluck the back. Singe off down. Scald feet, removing scales by rubbing them with a coarse cloth. If desired the feet may be cut off.

TO DRAW A FOWL—

1. Take scaly parts of legs off old fowls, by cutting skin and snapping them at the knee joint. Pull the shank and draw away the sinews at the same time.
2. Cut off head, leaving on about 4 inches of neck.
3. Turn on to its breast and cut a slit an inch long in the skin at the back of the neck.
4. Loosen skin with the fingers and with a sharp knife under skin cut neck off close to the body.
5. Still further slit the skin, leaving a flap for folding over the back.
6. Remove crop with fingers, pulling it out whole.
7. Turn fowl on its back, neck towards you. Insert first fingers and loosen the skin, surrounding the organs at breast.
8. Turn opposite way. Make a slit crossways just beneath the tail, being careful not to interfere with the intestines.
9. Insert first finger and loosen the membrane still further, separating the organs from the bony structure.
10. Insert the fingers, grasp the gizzard and draw everything out, being careful not to break the gall bladder.
11. Flush the inside well with clean water, then dry with a clean cloth.

TO TRUSS FOR ROASTING—

1. Lay breast downward. Bend tail toward and push it through the slit into the lower opening.

2. The flap which was cut when removing the neck should be folded over the opening.

3. Cross ends of wings over back of neck.

4. Turn fowl over. Press sides well together with the legs, raising the breast. Push lower joint of legs well upwards.

5. Pass trussing needle and twine through lower point of right wing and upper joint of right leg through body, near back bone to left leg and through left wing.

6. Turn fowl on its breast again, take a stitch through the ends of the wings and flap.

7. Remove needle. Take the two loose ends of twine and draw on either side round the tail of the fowl. Bring the two legs into position so that the shanks stand up. Tie neatly down.

8. Short skewers through wings and legs tied with string may be used.

TO TRUSS FOR BOILING—

1. Draw and prepare fowl as for roasting.

2. Loosen skin round the sides of the legs.

3. Cut away skin at knee joint end.

4. Press leg joints up into the body.

5. Pull the skin well over the knee joint, pushing it upward out of sight.

6. Truss wings as before. Pass needle and twine through the narrow end of the fowl securing the legs. Bring it round body and tie.

Note—The liver, heart, neck and gizzard can be used for making gravy or stock for soup. Wash each thoroughly, removing fat. The gizzard should be cut open, the bag of stones removed from inside and then skinned.

BAKED CHICKEN

Time—1 to 1½ hours (less for small birds).

1. Draw, stuff and truss, Veal stuffing.
2. Wrap in greased paper or alfoil.
3. Place in baking tin breast side down with a little good dripping.
4. Put into moderate over for 10 minutes, then cook gently.
5. Baste frequently. Turn bird breast side up.
6. Remove greased paper about ¼ hour before serving. Sprinkle chicken with salt and pepper. Brown.
7. Serve with brown gravy and bread sauce.

Note 1—Boiled ham should be served with fowl.

Note 2—A fowl is improved by steaming 1½ to 2 hours and then baking until brown (about ¾ hour).

ROAST TURKEY

INGREDIENTS—

1 turkey.	Salt.
Stuffing (page 77).	Dripping.
1 onion.	500 grams sausages (fried)
3 cups of stock or water.	(1 lb 2 oz)
10 peppercorns.	Ham or bacon (boiled).
2 bay leaves.	Bread sauce (page 131).

METHOD—

1. Pluck, draw and singe turkey.
2. Stuff breast with stuffing and chopped onion. Truss for roasting (see page 79).
3. Wrap in greased paper and put into a hot oven, allowing 20 minutes to 500 grams (1 lb 2 oz) and 20 minutes over.
4. Cook bird gently basting frequently. Turn occasionally.
5. Put giblets into saucepan with stock, peppercorns, bay leaves and salt, simmer gently 1 hour for gravy.
6. Thirty minutes before serving, remove paper, baste, dredge with flour, baste again, put into oven and keep well basted until a rich brown.
7. Untruss; place on a hot dish. Make gravy.
8. Garnish with fried or baked sausages, slices of pineapple or orange, and serve with ham, bread sauce, gravy and vegetables.

Note—Pork sausages, oysters and walnuts may be added to forcemeat.

ROAST DUCK

METHOD—

1. Draw, stuff and truss. Sage and Onion Stuffing (page 77).
2. Allow 20 minutes cooking for each 500 grams (1 lb 2 oz) and 20 minutes extra.
3. Wrap in greased paper or alfoil.
4. Place on trivet in baking tin with a little good dripping.
5. Put into hot oven. Reduce heat after 10 minutes. Cook gently for rest of time.
6. Baste frequently. Turn occasionally.
7. Remove paper ½ hour before serving. Sprinkle with salt and pepper. Brown.
8. Remove string and skewers. Serve breast side up on hot dish garnished with sliced orange and water cress.
9. Brown gravy may be served with roast duck.

Note—Wild duck or teal may be stuffed with prunes.

BOILED FOWL

METHOD—

1. Have a saucepan half full of boiling stock or water.
2. Truss fowl. Rub with lemon and wrap in thin cloth.
3. Put into pan breast down.
4. Prepare and cut small onion, carrot and couple of sticks of celery. Add to stock.
5. Add salt and bag of herbs.
6. Bring to boil, then simmer gently till tender, 1½ to 2 hours.
7. Serve with parsley or egg sauce.
8. Rolls of bacon grilled make a nice garnish.

BAKED FOWL

METHOD—

1. Dress and stuff bird with veal stuffing. Rub over with lemon.
2. Roll tightly in thick well greased paper or alfoil. Put into saucepan of boiling water. Simmer gently one hour.
3. Leaving bird wrapped, lift into baking tin. Add fat.
4. Bake gently until tender about 1 hour. Baste well.
5. When ready, remove paper and brown evenly.
6. Serve on hot dish. Make brown gravy.
7. Serve with gravy, baked potatoes and rolls of cooked bacon or cold ham.

CHICKEN PIECES

FRIED—

1. Trim into tidy shapes for serving. Dry well.
2. Dust lightly with flour.
3. Dip in beaten egg and fine dried breadcrumbs or crushed cornflakes. Press well.
      or
4. Coat with a thin batter.
5. Deep fry for 15 minutes.
6. Drain on crumpled paper.
7. Serve hot with chipped potatoes and a tossed salad or peas, pineapple, sweet corn.

GRILLED—

1. Trim into tidy shapes for serving. Dry well.
2. Rub over with oil, butter or substitute.
3. Grill gently until cooked and golden brown about 15 to 20 minutes. Turn during cooking.
4. Serve with grilled bacon rolls or melted butter and chopped parsley.
5. A tossed salad or hot vegetables may be served with chicken.

CHICKEN DISHES

1. Steam chicken and retain stock.
2. Remove flesh from bones, cut into small pieces.
3. Make a good white sauce (page 125), mix with chicken. Chicken stock with powdered milk may be used.
4. Add flavourings such as:—
      Mushrooms, asparagus pieces, hard boiled egg (cut up), pieces of cooked ham or bacon, sweetcorn, pineapple pieces, almonds, chopped white onion (lightly fried). Mix well.
5. Additional flavourings such as curry powder, nutmeg, ginger, grated cheese, chopped parsley, chopped capsicum may be added to sauce.
6. Pour mixture into oven proof dish, sprinkle fine dried crumbs or cornflakes on surface.
7. Accompaniments—boiled rice or spaghetti, green peas.

VEGETABLES

FOOD VALUE OF VEGETABLES—

1. Vegetables and fruit are amongst the richest sources of vitamins and mineral salts. They are important "protective foods."
2. Vegetables and fruit supply water to the body, also roughage or fibre, necessary for normal bowel action.
3. A variety of vegetables is essential so that all vitamins may be included in the diet.

To obtain the greatest food value from vegetables—

   (a) Grow your own vegetables and fruit. When fully ripened and freshly picked they have greater vitamin content.
   (b) Store vegetables away from light and air.
   (c) Cook root vegetables in their skins.
   (d) Avoid cutting vegetables in small pieces.
   (e) Wash but do not soak in water.
   (f) Avoid use of soda—it lessens the vitamin content.
   (g) Cook vegetables quickly in a small quantity of fat or water and serve immediately. Long slow cooking or keeping hot destroys vitamin content.
   (h) Use water in which vegetables are cooked for gravy, soup or sauce.

Vegetables are of three classes—

1. Roots, such as parsnips and carrots.
2. Greens, such as cabbage and peas.
3. Squashes, such as marrow, cucumber, pumpkin etc.

ROOTS

PREPARATION—

Carrots and Parsnips—Wash and scrub or scrape. Cut into suitable sizes.

Turnips and Swedes—Wash and peel.

Potatoes—Wash and scrub. They may be cooked in their jackets or peeled thinly.

New Potatoes—Wash and scrub or scrape.

Artichokes—Scrape carefully. Wash.

RULES FOR COOKING ROOTS

1. Have ready boiling salted water 2 level teaspoons salt to 500 grams (1 lb 2 oz) vegetable.
2. Boil quickly with lid on pan, until tender.
3. Test with skewer. If tender at the centre they are cooked.
4. Drain through a colander or against the lid of pan.
5. Serve with white sauce or sauce made from vegetable water. Root vegetables may be mashed with butter and pepper.

POTATOES (Boiled)

New—Cook in the same way as root vegetables, 20 to 30 minutes, adding a sprig of mint to the water. When cooked, drain well. Steam until dry. Keep hot with lid on pan till ready to use. Serve with butter, pepper and salt.

Old—Cook as for new potatoes omitting mint. When old potatoes are inclined to break up, boil until half-cooked, drain off water, then steam until tender. Drain thoroughly and shake over fire to make them floury. Mash well, add 1 teaspoon butter and 1 tablespoon milk. Beat until smooth. Season.

SWEDES

Peel thickly and cleanly. Cut into neat pieces. Cook as for root vegetables, allowing about ½ hour. Strain. Mash. Serve with butter and pepper.

BEETROOT

Wash well. Cut away only half the stalks. Put into boiling water. Bring to boil, then simmer about 1½ hours, or until tender.
Plunge into cold water and skin.
Beetroot may be served hot with white sauce or cold (see page 125).
Beetroot will cook in ½ an hour in Pressure Cooker.

ONIONS

Remove skins. Cut away mat and top. Place in hot, salted water. Bring to boil. Cook 20 to 30 minutes. Strain and serve with white sauce.

Note—White onions require less cooking than brown.

RULES FOR COOKING GREENS—

(Preparation see individual directions)

1. Have ready a small amount of hot but not fuming fat or boiling water.
2. Add salt, approximately 1 level teaspoon to 500 grams (1 lb 2 oz) vegetables.
3. The addition of ½ teaspoon sugar improves the vegetable. A pinch of bi-carbonate of soda whould be added to tough vegetables or if water is hard.
4. Boil quickly until tender with lid on pan 10 to 20 minutes.
5. Drain through colander. Shake well.
6. Serve hot with butter and pepper.

BRUSSELS SPROUTS

1. Remove withered leaves and wash thoroughly.
2. Cook as for greens.
3. Drain well, leave whole, serve with butter.

CABBAGE

1. Cut in four. Remove thick stalks and rough leaves.
2. Wash in salted water to remove grubs.
3. Boil as for greens 15 to 20 minutes.
4. Strain through colander. Cut well. Press.
5. Serve hot with butter and pepper.

STEAMED CABBAGE

1. Remove outside leaves and stalk.
2. Slice cabbage thinly, wash thoroughly and drain.
3. Have ready small quantity of boiling water. Add to it ½ teaspoon sugar, ¾ teaspoon salt, 1 tablespoon butter or dripping, and if liked 1 tablespoon vinegar.
4. Add cabbage, cover saucepan and cook till tender.
5. Strain and serve.

Note—If steamer is used allow longer time for cooking.

CAULIFLOWER

1. Remove thick stalk and coarse leaves. Slit stalk.
2. Wash in salted water to remove grubs.
3. Boil 20 to 30 minutes (as for greens).
4. When tender lift out carefully. Drain off water, place in dish with flower up.
5. Serve with white sauce, to which grated cheese may be added.

Note—A cauliflower may be tied in a cloth to keep it whole while cooking.

Leaves may be cooked as green vegetables.

SILVER BEET

1. Separate leaves. Wash thoroughly. Cut across into strips.
2. Steam for 20 minutes, with a little butter. Add salt.
3. Strain through colander. Press out water.
4. Serve hot with butter and pepper.

   Turnip tops may be cooked in the same way.

Note—A sprig of mint cooked with silver beet improves flavour.

BROAD BEANS

1. Pod. Put into boiling water. Add sugar and salt.
2. Boil gently in salted water 15 to 20 minutes.
3. Strain and serve hot with butter and pepper.

Note—Fresh young pods may be cooked in the same way as French beans.

FRENCH or RUNNER BEANS

1. Wash in cold water.
2. String by cutting off ends, and then strip from both sides.
3. Shred finely or cook whole.
4. Boil as for greens (15 to 20 minutes).
5. Strain through colander. Shake.
6. Serve hot with butter and pepper.
7. French beans may be steamed.

PEAS

1. Pod.
2. Put into hot water (not boiling) with a little salt, sugar, a sprig of mint. Add a pinch of soda, if peas are old.
3. Boil gently, until tender (10 to 20 minutes).
4. Strain through colander.
5. Serve hot with butter and pepper.

CELERY

1. Remove leaves. Scrape if soiled. Scrub and cut into even lengths.
2. Cook as for greens (¾ to 1 hour).
3. Strain. Serve hot with white sauce.

RULES FOR COOKING SQUASHES—

MARROW

1. Cut into even pieces. Peel if necessary and scrape out seeds.
2. Place about 1 tablespoon of butter or dripping in saucepan with marrow. Sprinkle with salt and pepper.
3. Put on lid and allow to cook without water 20 to 30 minutes. Serve hot with thickened liquid.

Note—Marrow may be boiled and served with white sauce, or baked.

PUMPKIN

1. Cut, peel and remove seeds.
2. Cook as for roots (20 to 30 minutes).
3. Strain, mash and serve with butter and pepper.

Note—Pumpkin may be steamed or baked.

CUCUMBER

1. Peel and cut into two lengthwise without removing the seeds.
2. Cook as for roots (about 20 minutes).
3. Strain and serve hot with white sauce.

ZUCCHINI

1. Wash and dry. Cut off ends.
2. Cut lengthwise, sprinkle with herbs, olive oil or melted butter and grated cheese.
3. Bake in covered dish till tender (about 30 minutes). Remove cover to brown.

CHOKOES

1. Wash chokoes thoroughly, cut off ends and peel.
2. Cook in salted water until tender.
3. Serve with white sauce or melted butter.

EGG FRUIT

1. Wash thoroughly, cut in slices.
2. Dip in beaten egg and fine breadcrumbs.
3. Fry gently until tender.

Note—Egg Fruit may be stuffed as for Capsicum.

CAPSICUMS

1. Wash thoroughly, cut off tops. Remove centre.
2. Fill with a savoury stuffing including minced, cooked meat.
3. Put tops on, bake gently till tender (about 20 minutes).

BAKING VEGETABLES

1. Potatoes, pumpkin, parsnips, sweet potatoes, etc. may be baked with meat.
2. Allow about one hour.
3. Vegetables are nicer if partly boiled before baking.

POTATOES IN JACKETS

1. Choose sound potatoes of even size.
2. Scrub well. Prick. Rub over with oil or dripping.
3. Place in hot oven. No fat required.
4. Cook gently for 1 to 1½ hours. Turn once.
5. When tender, cut in halves lengthways.
6. Serve hot with melted butter and chopped mint.

CHIP POTATOES

1. Scrub and peel potatoes. Dry.
2. Cut in slices, then in strips, or in wafers.
3. Dry well in a towel.
4. Lower gently into fuming fat. Cook until tender. Lift out and allow fat to heat again, and plunge once more in fuming fat. Cook till brown and crisp.
5. Drain on kitchen paper. Salt and toss well.
6. Serve very hot.

Note—Use a saucepan large enough to allow fat only ½ way up saucepan.

ASPARAGUS

1. Cut stalks all one length; scrape white part lightly from tip down.
2. Wash and tie in bundles. Soak ½ hour in cold water.
3. Place in saucepan, flat. Cover with boiling water and add salt.
4. Boil gently 30 minutes. Drain well.
5. Serve hot on asparagus dish, with melted butter.

ASPARAGUS (Iced)

1. Cook as above. Drain.
2. Arrange neatly on an asparagus dish.
3. Sprinkle with few drops of tarragon vinegar.
4. Stand in refrigerator until ready.
5. Serve with iced Mousseline or Hollandaise sauce. (see page 130).

POTATO CROQUETTES

INGREDIENTS—

2 or 3 cooked potatoes.
1 teaspoon chopped parsley.
1 teaspoon butter.
Pepper and salt.
1 egg.
Fine breadcrumbs.

METHOD—

1. Mash potatoes. Add parsley, butter and a little beaten egg. Beat until smooth and firm.
2. Roll into balls, using a little flour on the hands.
3. Dip in egg and breadcrumbs; leave for 15 minutes; coat again.
4. Fry until a golden brown in deep fat. Drain.
5. Serve on paper d'oyley, garnished with parsley.

BOSTON BAKED BEANS (Lima or Haricot)

METHOD—

1. Wash, soak overnight in cold water.
2. Put in cold, salted water, boil 2 hours, adding extra water if necessary. Strain when tender.
3. Place in pie dish in layers—sliced onion, beans, bacon and a layer of breadcrumbs on top.
4. Place knobs of butter on top, bake gently for about 2 hours.

PUDDINGS

It is often hard to decide what the pudding for a meal should be. These points should help the decision:—

1. A full meal of meat and vegetables should be followed by a light and easily digested pudding.
2. Suet puddings are unsuitable for a hot summer day.
3. After a cold meal in winter, a hot pudding should be served.
4. Cold puddings are more appetising in summer than in winter.
5. Avoid similarity in meat and pudding dishes served at a meal.
6. Cold puddings should be served quite cold. Hot puddings should be served very hot.

BOILED PUDDINGS

1. The foundation for these puddings is flour and fat.
2. Breadcrumbs may be used partly or wholly in place of flour.
3. The fat may be suet, dripping, butter or lard.
4. Water, milk, or eggs may be used for mixing puddings. Eggs bind the mixture better than milk and milk better than water.
5. Suet puddings are made richer by the addition of sugar, fruit, spices and eggs.
6. Baking powder or cream of tartar and soda are used for "rising" in these puddings. Rich puddings require less "rising" than plain ones. Omit cream of tartar and use soda only in mixtures containing jam or treacle.
7. A boiled pudding should be mixed stiffer than one to be steamed.
8. Beef suet makes a richer pudding than mutton suet. Suet should be shredded, the skin removed and so finely chopped that it resembles breadcrumbs.
9. A boiled pudding should be placed in a scalded and thickly floured cloth or in a greased basin covered with a cloth. The basin may be covered first with a greased paper, then with pudding cloth.
10. Put into fast boiling water sufficient to cover the pudding. The water must be kept boiling all the time. More boiling water should be added as required to make up for loss in evaporation.
11. The pudding cloth should be made of calico. It should be washed after use, in hot water and soda, dried and put away until required.

Note—See Homely Measurements — Page 18.

SUET PASTRY

(Foundation Recipe)

INGREDIENTS—

180 grams flour (½ plain and   1 level teaspoon of salt.
  ½ S.R. flour) (6 oz).   Cold milk or water to mix.
90 grams suet (3oz).

Note—This pastry may be used for steak and kidney pudding,
fruit or roly poly puddings, dumplings.

METHOD—

1. Remove skin, shred suet, chop finely, using some of the
   measured flour to prevent sticking to knife.
2. Add sifted flour, salt.
3. Stir with a knife, mixing in sufficient water to make a light
   dough.
4. Turn on to floured board, knead lightly. Roll as required.

ROLY POLY PUDDING

INGREDIENTS—

Foundation recipe for Suet Pastry.

METHOD—

1. Use the plain suet mixture, but mix more stiffly.
2. Roll out on a lightly floured board to an oblong shape, about
   1 cm thick (¼ inch).
3. Spread with jam, allowing a 2 cms margin (¾ inch).
4. Roll up lightly. Press edges together.
5. Wrap in greased paper. Steam 1½ hours or put into greased
   fruit or jam tin and steam.
6. Other fillings may be used instead of jam—
     (a) Chopped apples with sugar and spice.
     (b) Dates, stoned and sliced with sugar.
     (c) Currants or raisins with sugar and chopped peel.
     (d) Treacle and bread crumbs.

AUSTRALIAN PLUM PUDDING

INGREDIENTS—

2 cups flour.
1 cup breadcrumbs.
1 cup sugar.
1 cup raisins.
1 cup currants.
Lemon peel to taste.

1 teaspoon bi-carbonate of
    soda.
½ packet spice.
1 tablespoon beef dripping.
1 tablespoon butter.
1½ cups boiling water.

METHOD—

1. Sift flour, add breadcrumbs, sugar, spices and fruits.
2. Mix dripping, butter, soda and boiling water in separate basin
       and add to the first basin immediately.
3. Boil in scalded floured cloth 4 hours.
4. Serve hot with sauce.

PLUM PUDDING

INGREDIENTS—

240 grams beef suet (8 oz).
240 grams sultanas (8 oz).
240 grams currants (8 oz).
240 grams raisins (8 oz).
120 grams mixed peel
    (4 oz).
120 grams breadcrumbs
    (4 oz).
120 grams flour (4 oz).
¼ teaspoon salt.
1 teaspoon bi-carbonate of
    soda.

1 teaspoon cinnamon.
1 teaspoon mixed spice.
½ teaspoon ginger.
4 eggs.
Milk as required.
2 tablespoons lemon juice,
    grated rind of one lemon.
60 grams almonds (2 oz).
½ grated nutmeg.
Brandy may be used in place
    of milk if desired.
240 grams sugar (8 oz).

METHOD—

1. Chop suet finely.
2. Prepare and mix dry ingredients.
3. Add almonds, blanched and chopped.
4. Add well beaten eggs, lemon juice. Mix thoroughly.
5. Add soda dissolved in milk.
6. Turn into greased mould or scalded and floured pudding
       cloth. Boil 5 hours or divide mixture into two moulds.
       Cover with greased paper. Steam 4½ hours.

BOILED APPLE PUDDING

INGREDIENTS—

Foundation Recipe
500 grams apples (1 lb 2 oz).
½ cup sugar.

6 cloves.
Strip of lemon rind.
3 tablespoons cold water.

METHOD—

1. Peel, quarter and core apples.
2. Make suet crust, cut off 1-3rd for covering.
3. Roll remaining 2-3rds large enough to line basin.
4. Line greased basin with paste.
5. Fill with apples and other ingredients.
6. Roll 1-3rd of paste large enough to cover pudding. Damp edges, place on top of fruit, seal tightly.
7. Cover with prepared pudding cloth.
8. Boil for 2 hours.
9. Serve with sweet sauce, or butter and nutmeg.

Note—Other fruits may be used.

DROUGHT PLUM PUDDING

INGREDIENTS—

3 cups flour.
1 cup sugar.
2 cups raisins.
2½ cups currants
1 tablespoon butter.

1 cup milk.
1 cup hot water.
2 level teaspoons bi-carbonate of soda.
1 level teaspoon salt.

METHOD —

1. Melt butter in hot water. Dissolve soda in milk.
2. Mix dry ingredients together. Stir in water and butter then milk and bi-carbonate of soda.
3. Put into a scalded and floured pudding cloth. Tie securely.
4. Boil for 4 hours.
5. Serve with a suitable sauce or custard.

STEAMED PUDDINGS

1. Boiling water is required to produce steam.
2. Steaming can be done in a steamer made to fit a saucepan, or by standing a basin or mould containing the pudding in boiling water sufficient to come half-way up the sides of the mould.
3. The pudding mould or basin should be greased and covered with greased paper or alfoil.
4. The mould or basin should be two thirds full of the mixture.
5. Those containing eggs should be steamed slowly.
6. Steaming takes half as long again as boiling.
7. Steamed puddings are lighter than boiled.
8. Water must be kept boiling.
9. Replenish with boiling water.
10. The steamer must have a tight-fitting lid.
11. Allow pudding to stand for a few minutes before turning out.

Note—See Homely Measurements — Page 18.

DATE PUDDING

INGREDIENTS—

60 grams butter or substitute (2 oz).
60 grams sugar (2 oz).
1 egg.
120 grams dates (4 oz).
180 grams S.R. flour (6 oz).
Milk.
Pinch of salt.

METHOD—

1. Put the saucepan of water on to boil.
2. Grease the mould.
3. Cut a piece of white paper, the same shape as the mould and large enough to fasten down.
4. Stone the dates and cut them into four.
5. Beat the butter and sugar to a cream in a basin.
6. Beat the egg and mix it well into the butter and sugar. Add dates.
7. Stir in half flour and mix. Stir in a little milk.
8. Add remainder of flour.
9. Add sufficient milk to make a fairly soft mixture.
10. Turn into a greased mould, cover with lid or greased paper.
11. Put into the steamer and steam 1½ hours.
12. Turn out and serve on a hot dish with white sauce or boiled custard.

RAISIN PUDDING

INGREDIENTS—

360 grams flour — ½ plain
and ½ self raising (12 oz).
180 grams suet (6 oz).
240 grams raisins (8 oz).

¼ teaspoonful grated nutmeg.
1¼ cups milk.
120 grams sugar (4 oz).
Pinch of salt.

METHOD—

1. Chop suet finely. Stone raisins. Sift flour and salt.
2. Mix all dry ingredients. Add milk. Stir well.
3. Turn into a greased pudding basin or scalded and floured pudding cloth. Steam 3½ hours or boil 2½ hours.

CUP OF TEA (Plum) PUDDING

INGREDIENTS—

1 cup flour.
1 cup finely chopped suet.
1 cup breadcrumbs.
1 cup clean dry currants.
¼ cup candied peel.
1 cup raisins.
1 cup sultanas.

1 cup sugar.
1 cup tea, black.
1 teaspoon bi-carbonate of
soda.
1 teaspoon mixed spice.
An egg may be added.

METHOD—

1. Mix all dry ingredients. Add beaten egg.
2. Dissolve soda in the tea and add immediately.
3. Two thirds fill greased pudding basin.
4. Cover with lid or greased paper.
5. Steam 2½ hours.
6. Serve hot with white sauce or custard.

BROWN PUDDING — No. 1

INGREDIENTS—

2½ cups flour.
½ cup of fresh dripping or butter.
¾ cup sugar.
1½ teaspoons ginger.
½ cup treacle.

½ cup milk.
1 teaspoon bi-carbonate of
soda.
2 eggs.

Brown Pudding — No. 1 — continued

METHOD—

1. Sift flour and bi-carbonate of soda, rub in dripping with tips of fingers.
2. Add sugar and ginger and beaten egg.
3. Heat milk, add to it the treacle. Stir well.
4. Add milk and treacle to dry ingredients.
5. Two thirds fill a greased pudding basin. Cover with lid or greased paper. Steam 3 hours.

BROWN PUDDING — No. 2

INGREDIENTS—

1½ cups flour.
½ cup of fresh dripping or butter.
½ cup sugar.
½ cup milk.

2 tablespoons raspberry jam.
1 teaspoon bi-carbonate of soda.

METHOD—

1. Sift flour. Rub in dripping. Add sugar.
2. Stir in the jam. Add the milk in which the soda has been dissolved.
3. Two thirds fill a greased pudding basin. Cover with lid or greased paper.
4. Steam 1½ to 2 hours. Serve with sweet sauce.

Note—Chopped dates may be added.

MARGUERITE PUDDING

INGREDIENTS—

120 grams self-raising flour (4 oz).
60 grams sugar (2 oz).
60 grams butter or substitute (2 oz).

2 tablespoons jam.
1 egg.
A little milk.
Grated lemon rind.

METHOD—

1. Cream butter and sugar, add well beaten egg.
2. Add sifted flour, milk and grated lemon rind.
3. Place jam in bottom of greased basin.
4. Pour in mixture, cover with lid or greased paper.
5. Steam 1½ hours.
6. Serve with white sauce or jam sauce.

Note—Other flavourings, sultanas, coconut or cocoa may be used.

GINGER PUDDING

INGREDIENTS—

240 grams plain flour (8 oz).
90 grams suet, finely chopped
(3 oz).
1 tablespoon preserved ginger
or candied peel (chopped).
90 grams sugar (3 oz).

1 level teaspoon ground
ginger.
1 level teaspoon
bi-carbonate of soda.
¼ cup treacle.
¼ cup milk.

METHOD—

1. Sift flour, salt and ground ginger.
2. Add finely chopped suet and preserved ginger.
3. Make a well in centre. Add treacle, slightly warmed.
4. Heat milk, add to soda. Add to mixture and mix well.
5. Pour into well greased pudding basin. Cover with lid or
   greased paper.
6. Steam of 2½ hours.
7. Serve hot with sweet sauce.

SAGO RAISIN PUDDING

INGREDIENTS—

4 tablespoons sago.
¾ cup milk.
1 cup breadcrumbs.
1 tablespoon butter.
4 tablespoons sugar.

1 cup raisins.
½ teaspoon essence.
½ teaspoon bi-carbonate of
soda.

METHOD—

1. Wash sago and soak in milk ½ hour.
2. Mix breadcrumbs, sugar, raisins, soda together.
3. Melt butter, add to mixture, then pour in sago and milk.
4. Turn into greased basin. Cover with lid or greased paper.
5. Steam 3 hours. Serve with a sauce.

FIG PUDDING

INGREDIENTS—

240 grams figs (preserved)
(8 oz).
240 grams suet (8 oz).

240 grams breadcrumbs (8 oz).
240 grams sugar (8 oz).
3 eggs.

Fig Pudding — continued

METHOD—

1. Shred and chop suet finely.
2. Chop figs.
3. Mix suet, figs, breadcrumbs.
4. Beat eggs well, add sugar and beat.
5. Mix eggs and sugar into other ingredients.
6. Pour mixture into greased basin, cover with lid or greased paper.
7. Steam 3 hours.
8. Serve with a sweet sauce.

MARMALADE PUDDING

INGREDIENTS—

360 grams breadcrumbs (12 oz).
240 grams suet (8 oz).
3 tablespoons marmalade.
3 tablespoons sugar.
Grated rind and juice 1 lemon.
1 teaspoon bi-carbonate of soda.
3 eggs.

METHOD—

1. Chop suet finely.
2. Beat eggs well.
3. Mix all ingredients together, adding well beaten eggs last.
4. Put into greased basin, cover with lid or greased paper. Steam 3 hours.
5. Serve with lemon sauce.

Milk Puddings, Custards, Etc.

Plain Milk Puddings contain milk and starchy food, such as rice, wheaten flour, sago, tapioca, arrowroot, cornflour, rice flour, or semolina. Starch is found in the cells of these grains. The walls of the cells are softened by cold liquid and broken down by boiling liquid, cooking the starch. Milk puddings are nourishing and easily digested. They are heat and energy-producing as well as flesh forming and are particularly suitable for children. Milk puddings may be baked or boiled. Eggs and butter may be added to make them richer. If skim milk is used 1 dessertspoon butter or finely chopped suet should be added to 2½ cups of milk to make up for loss of cream. Milk puddings should not be allowed to boil after eggs are added. Boiling hardens the albumen, rendering it indigestible. Flavourings for milk puddings may be vanilla, almond, lemon essence, a piece of cinnamon stick or thin strip of lemon rind, removed after boiling.

GENERAL RULES

1. Wash grain. Soak tapioca overnight before cooking. Mix cornflour, arrowroot, wheaten flour and semolina with a little cold liquid before cooking to prevent lumps.

2. When baking puddings containing eggs, stand the pie dish in a baking tin containing water.

3. Allow 2 tablespoons of grain and 1 tablespoon of sugar to 2½ cups of milk for grain pudding.

4. A plain milk pudding may be converted into a custard, cream or snow, according to method of adding eggs.

Extra milk is required in proportion of 1 cup to 1 egg for a grain custard.

Custards—2 eggs and 1 tablespoon sugar to 2 cups of milk, or 3 eggs to 2½ cups for richer mixture.

BAKED RICE PUDDING (Plain)

INGREDIENTS—

1 tablespoon rice.
2½ cups milk.
1 tablespoon sugar.

1 tablespoon butter or
finely chopped suet.
Pince salt.

METHOD—

1. Put washed rice, sugar, salt and butter into a pie dish. Add milk, stir well.
2. Bake in a slow oven until thick and creamy, stirring occasionally. Add more milk if necessary.

Note—For STEAMED RICE use the same list of ingredients.

BOILED RICE

METHOD—

1. Wash rice. Sprinkle into fast boiling water, to which salt has been added.
2. Boil 15 to 20 minutes with the lid off. Do not stir.
3. When tender strain through colander.
4. If necessary pour over some hot or cold water to separate grains.

Note—One cup of rice, eight cups of water, one level dessertspoon of salt will make three cups of cooked rice.

RICE CUSTARD

INGREDIENTS—

1½ tablespoons rice.
2½ cups milk.
1½ cups water.
1½ tablespoons sugar.

2 eggs.
½ teaspoon butter.
Flavouring (vanilla or lemon).

METHOD—

1. Wash; boil rice in water for 10 minutes. Drain. Turn into pie dish.
2. Beat eggs well and mix with sugar and milk.
3. Pour eggs and milk over rice. Mix lightly.
4. Add butter and flavouring.
5. Grate nutmeg on top.
6. Stand pie dish in baking tin containing water. Bake gently till set, about 30 minutes.

SAGO CUSTARD

INGREDIENTS—

2 tablespoons sago.
1½ tablespoons sugar.
3¾ cups milk.
2 eggs.

1 teaspoon butter.
¼ teaspoon vanilla.
Pinch of salt

METHOD—

1. Wash sago, put in saucepan with 2½ cups of milk, pinch of salt, 1 tablespoon sugar. Cook until sago is clear, stirring frequently.
2. Pour mixture into a pie dish.
3. Beat eggs and ½ tablespoon of sugar. Add 1¼ cups of milk and vanilla. Pour over sago, stir slightly.
4. Sprinkle with grated nugmeg or cinnamon. Put small pieces of butter on top.
5. Stand pie dish in baking dish containing water. Bake in moderate oven until custard is set and lightly browned.
6. Serve hot or cold.

SAGO PUDDING (Plain)

INGREDIENTS—

2 tablespoons sago.
1 tablespoon sugar.
2½ cups milk.
1 teaspoon butter.

Flavouring.
Nutmeg.
Pinch of salt.

METHOD—

1. Wash sago, add sugar and salt.
2. Stir into the boiling milk.
3. Stir until thickened.
4. Remove spoon. Place lid on tightly and allow sago to finish cooking in its own steam.
5. When sago is clear, add butter.
6. Pour into dish.
7. Grate nutmeg on top.

Note—A double saucepan saves a lot of stirring.

SAGO CREAM

INGREDIENTS—

2 tablespoons sago.
2½ cups milk.
Whites and yolks of 2 eggs.
2 tablespoons sugar.

Vanilla essence.
Pinch of salt.
Teaspoon butter.

METHOD—

1. Wash sago, add to hot milk. Add salt.
2. Stir over heat until sago is clear. Cool slightly.
3. Add beaten egg yolks, butter and essence. Beat well.
4. Beat egg whites stiffly, add sugar gradually beating well.
5. Stir half of egg white mixture into cooled sago mixture. Pour into pie dish.
6. Pile remaining egg white mixture on top.
7. Stand pie dish in baking dish containing a little water.
8. Bake slowly till set and lightly browned. Serve hot or cold.

MACARONI CUSTARD

INGREDIENTS—

2 tablespoons macaroni or vermicelli.
2½ cups milk.
1½ tablespoons sugar.
2 eggs.

1 teaspoon butter.
Nutmeg, grated rind of lemon.
Pinch of salt.

METHOD—

1. Boil macaroni in water until cooked.
2. Drain away water.
3. Add to macaroni the milk, sugar, butter and well-beaten eggs.
4. Pour into a greased pie dish. Grate nutmeg on top. Stand in a baking dish containing water, bake in a moderate oven till set and lightly browned.
5. Serve hot or cold.

SEMOLINA PUDDING

INGREDIENTS—

2 tablespoons semolina.
2½ cups milk.
2 tablespoons sugar.
2 eggs.

Jam.
Thin rind of lemon.
1 teaspoon butter.
Pinch of salt.

Semolina Pudding — continued

METHOD—

1. Heat milk. Mix semolina to a smooth paste with a little cold water. Stir into milk.
2. Add thin strips of lemon rind.
3. Stir mixture over heat until it thickens, boil 3 minutes. Remove lemon rind and cool mixture.
4. Beat yolks of eggs, butter and ½ tablespoon of sugar. Stir into semolina mixture.
5. Turn mixture into pie dish. Stand in a baking dish containing water. Bake in slow oven till set. Cool off a little.
6. Spread a thin layer of jam over surface.
7. Whip whites of eggs to a stiff froth. Add 1½ tablespoons sugar gradually. Beat well.
8. Pile meringue mixture on top of pudding. Lightly brown in oven.
9. Serve hot or cold.

Note—Digestive meal, wheaten meal, ground rice may be used in same way.

BREAD AND BUTTER CUSTARD

INGREDIENTS—

2 small slices bread.	Butter.
2½ cups milk.	1 tablespoon currants or
1 tablespoon sugar.	sultanas.
2 eggs.	Grated nutmeg.

METHOD—

1. Cut bread in thin slices.
2. Remove dark crusts, butter bread, cut into oblongs.
3. Place in pie dish with fruit.
4. Beat egg and sugar. Add milk,
5. Pour mixture over the bread and fruit. Grate nutmeg on top.
6. Allow to stand about ½ an hour.
7. Place in baking tin containing a little water.
8. Bake in a moderate oven until set and lightly browned.
9. Serve hot or cold.

CUSTARD SAUCE

INGREDIENTS—

2½ cups milk.   1 tablespoon sugar.
3 eggs.   Flavouring essence.

METHOD—

1. Beat eggs with sugar. Add milk. Mix well.
2. Pour into a jug. Stand jug in a pan of water. Place on stove.
3. Let water boil gently. Stir mixture until it begins to coat the spoon.
4. Remove jug from water. Add flavouring.
5. Allow to cool. Serve in jug.

CORNFLOUR CUSTARD

INGREDIENTS—

2½ cups milk.   1 egg.
1 tablespoon sugar.   Essence.
2 teaspoons cornflour.

METHOD—

1. Blend cornflour with a little of milk.
2. Heat remainder of milk, pour into cornflour gradually.
3. Return mixture to saucepan, stir over heat until boiling. Boil for 3 minutes.
4. Beat eggs and sugar well. Gradually add hot milk and cornflour, beat well.
5. If custard does not thicken, return mixture to saucepan, stir over low heat until custard thickens. Do not boil.
6. Add essence and allow to cool.
7. Serve in a jug or dish with a little sprinkling of nutmeg.

CUSTARD WITH YOLKS

INGREDIENTS—

2 yolks of eggs.   1 teaspoon cornflour.
1¼ cups milk.   1 dessertspoon sugar.

METHOD—

1. Heat milk.
2. Beat yolks and sugar. Add to blended cornflour.
3. Pour hot milk very gradually on to eggs etc. Stir well.
4. Return to saucepan. Stir over low heat until custard thickens. Add essence.
5. When cold, serve in a glass dish.

BAKED CUSTARD

INGREDIENTS—

2 eggs.
2 cups milk.
1 tablespoon sugar.
1 teaspoon butter.
Flavouring.
Nutmeg.

METHOD—

1. Beat eggs and sugar together. Add milk and flavouring.
2. Pour mixture into greased pie dish. Sprinkle with nutmeg.
3. Stand dish in baking dish containing a little water.
4. Place in a slow oven until custard is set and lightly browned—about 30 minutes.

Note—This custard may be steamed

CRUMB CUSTARD

INGREDIENTS—

2 tablespoons breadcrumbs or cake crumbs.
1 teaspoon of butter.
2½ cups milk.
2 eggs.
1 tablespoon sugar.
Flavouring.

METHOD—

1. Beat eggs and sugar together. Add milk, flavouring and butter.
2. Pour mixture over breadcrumbs in greased pie dish.
3. Stand pie dish in baking tin containing water.
4. Bake until set and browned in slow oven, about 30 minutes.
5. Serve hot or cold.

BANANA CUSTARD

INGREDIENTS—

Cornflour Custard (page 104).
3 bananas.

METHOD—

1. When custard is cool, pour it over sliced bananas.
2. Serve cold with whipped cream.

CARAMEL CUSTARD

INGREDIENTS—

For Custard—
3 eggs.
2½ cups milk.
1 tablespoon sugar.
4 drops flavouring essence.

For Caramel—
4 tablespoons sugar.
2 tablespoons cold water.
Pinch of cream of tartar,
   or ½ teaspoon lemon juice.

METHOD—

1. Make custard mixture.
2. Make caramel by placing sugar, lemon juice and water in saucepan. Boil until sugar turns golden brown.
3. Pour into mould or basin, turning basin to bring caramel up the side.
4. Pour in custard mixture, cover with lid or butter paper.
5. Steam slowly until set, about 30 minutes.
6. Allow to stand in basin until ready to serve.

Note—May be baked in oven—stand in dish with water.

QUEEN PUDDING

INGREDIENTS—

1 cup bread or cake crumbs.
2½ cups milk.
2 eggs.

2 tablespoons sugar
   (less for cake crumbs).
1 tablespoon rasberry jam.

METHOD—

1. Place crumbs in pie dish. Beat yolks and one white of egg with 1 tablespoon sugar.
2. Add milk and pour over the crumbs. Stand piedish in water.
3. Bake till set and a light brown. Cool off. Spread with jam.
4. Beat remaining white of egg very stiffly. Add remaining sugar, beat well.
5. Heap high on top of pudding. Brown very lightly.
6. Serve hot or cold with whipped cream.

CORNFLOUR SNOW

INGREDIENTS—

2 tablespoons cornflour.
2½ cups milk.
White of 2 eggs.

1½ tablespoons sugar.
Juice of 1 lemon
   and ½ the rind.

Cornflour Snow — continued

METHOD—

1. Boil 2-3rds of milk with strips of lemon rind.
2. Blend cornflour with remainder of milk.
3. Stir into hot milk.
4. Stir over heat till boiling. Boil 3 minutes. Cool.
5. Add lemon juice and sugar. Remove rind.
6. Whip white of eggs stiffly. Stir lightly into cornflour. Turn into wet mould to set.
7. Serve on glass dish with boiled custard made from yolks of eggs or stewed fruit.

JUNKET

INGREDIENTS—

3 cups unscalded milk
½ junket tablet.
3 drops vanilla.

1 tablespoon sugar.
1 tablespoon cold water.

METHOD—

1. Soak tablet in cold water. Crush.
2. Warm milk slightly (blood heat).
3. Put dissolved tablet and sugar in a glass dish, pour on warm milk.
4. Stir slightly, leave to set in a warm place.
5. Cover with grated nutmeg, serve with stewed fruit.

BANANA PUDDING

INGREDIENTS—

3 ripe bananas.
2 tablespoons sugar.

2 eggs.
2½ cups milk (hot)

METHOD—

1. Peel bananas and rub through a strainer.
2. Beat eggs well.
3. Mix banana pulp, sugar and eggs.
4. Stir in hot milk.
5. Pour into greased pie dish. Stand in dish containing water.
6. Bake slowly until set, about 30 minutes.
7. Serve hot or cold with cream.

BLANC MANGE

INGREDIENTS—

6 level teaspoons
   gelatine.
2½ cups milk (unscalded).

Lemon rind or
   other flavouring.
1 tablespoon sugar.

METHOD—

1. Soften gelatine in a little cold water.
2. Place milk with sugar and lemon rind in white lined saucepan. Make hot.
3. Add gelatine. Dissolve but do not boil. Remove from heat. Remove lemon rind.
4. Pour into a wet mould. Put in a cool place till set and firm.
5. Serve in a glass dish with stewed fruit.

CORNFLOUR MOULD

INGREDIENTS—

2½ cups milk.
2 tablespoons cornflour
1 tablespoon sugar.

1 teaspoon butter.
4 drops vanilla.

METHOD—

1. Mix cornflour with some of the milk.
2. Heat remainder of milk. Stir in blended cornflour. Stir until boiling. Cook 3 minutes.
3. Add sugar, butter, vanilla.
4. Pour into wet mould. Leave to set. Turn out when cold.
5. Serve with stewed fruit or jam.

CHOCOLATE MOULD

INGREDIENTS—

2½ cups milk.
4 drops vanilla.
1½ tablespoons sugar

2 tablespoons dark cocoa or
   1½ tablespoons shredded
   chocolate.
2 tablespoons cornflour.

METHOD—

1. Mix cornflour and cocoa with a little of the milk.
2. Heat remainder of milk, stir in blended cornflour and cocoa; boil for 3 minutes.
3. Add sugar and vanilla.
4. Pour into a wet mould. Turn out when cold.
5. Serve with boiled custard or cream.

Variation—Add 2 tablespoons of mixed fruit (cherries etc.) and chopped nuts.

SAGO SNOW

INGREDIENTS—

½ cup sago.
2 cups cold water.
3 tablespoons sugar.

2 lemons, rind of one,
   juice of 2.
Whites of 2 eggs.

METHOD—

1. Wash sago and boil in water, adding sugar and grated rind of lemon. Stir occasionally.
2. When boiled, add juice of lemons. Stir well.
3. When nearly cold add stiffly beaten white of eggs.
4. Serve quite cold, with a custard made of the yolks of the eggs.

CHOCOLATE PUDDING (Baked)

INGREDIENTS—

1 cup cake or breadcrumbs.
2 tablespoons sugar.
2 eggs.
2½ cups milk.

2 dessertspoons cocoa.
2 to 3 drops of vanilla
   or almond essence.
Pinch of salt.

METHOD—

1. Put cake crumbs into an oven dish. Add salt and ¼ of milk.
2. Separate yolks from whites of eggs.
3. Beat egg yolks, stir into cake crumbs and milk.
4. Mix cocoa with another ¼ of milk. Heat remainder of milk, stir in cocoa, bring to boil.
5. Stir milk and cocoa into cake crumbs etc.
6. Whip whites of eggs stiffly, add sugar gradually, beating well. Stir into cake crumb mixture.
7. Stand dish in baking tin containing cold water. Bake in moderate oven until set, about 30 minutes.
8. Serve hot or cold with cream or custard.

VELVET PUDDING

INGREDIENTS—

2 eggs.
1½ tablespoons cornflour.
Vanilla essence.
Jam or jelly.
Lemon juice.

1 tablespoon sugar.
2½ cups milk.
Butter.
Pinch of salt.

Velvet Pudding — continued

METHOD—
1. Separate yolks from egg whites.
2. Beat yolks and sugar, add cornflour then a little milk.
3. Heat remainder of milk, stir into mixture, boil for 3 minutes stirring all the time.
4. Add essence, pour mixture into a buttered pie dish. When cool and set, spread a thin layer of jam or jelly on top.
5. Beat egg whites and salt till stiff, add 2 tablespoons of sugar gradually, add 1 teaspoon of lemon juice.
6. Pile meringue on top of pudding, sprinkle lightly with sugar, brown slightly.
7. Serve hot.

LEMON SAGO

INGREDIENTS—

½ cup sago.
2 cups cold water.
Juice of 2 lemons,
Rind of lemon.

2 tablespoons
  golden syrup.
1 tablespoon sugar.

METHOD—
1. Soak the sago in water.
2. Add the juice and grated lemon rind.
3. Add golden syrup and sugar.
4. Boil until sago is cooked, stirring all the time.
5. Pour into a wet mould or glass dish.
6. Serve quite cold with cream or boiled custard.

LEMON PUDDING

INGREDIENTS—

90 grams Castor sugar
  (3 ozs.).
Lemons.
3 eggs.

½ cup of cream or milk.
1 cup cake or breadcrumbs.
Rough puff pastry —
  Half quantity (page 139).

Lemon Pudding — continued

METHOD—

1. Make rough puff pastry, line a deep cooking plate, 22cm. diam. (9 inches). Leave in cool place.
2. Grate yellow of lemon rind of one lemon — **Squeeze** half a cup of lemon juice.
3. Beat yolks of eggs, lemon rind and juice.
4. Add cake crumbs, stir well. Add cream or milk.
5. Beat egg whites stiffly, add sugar gradually, beating well.
6. Stir half of egg white mixture into cake crumbs etc. Pour this into pastry.
7. Bake in a hot oven, reducing heat after ten minutes, until pastry is cooked and filling set. (10 to 15 minutes).
8. Pile remaining egg white mixture on top. Brown lightly.
9. Serve hot.

LEMON PUDDING (Two Basin)

INGREDIENTS—

No. 1 Basin.

2 tablespoons arrowroot.	3 tablespoons cold water.
Grated rind and juice of 2 lemons.	2½ cups boiling water.

No. 2 Basin.

½ cup sugar.	1 tablespoon butter.
2 yolks of eggs.	

METHOD—

1. Blend arrowroot, cold water, juice and rind of lemons.
2. Add boiling water, stirring until it looks semi-transparent.
3. Mix well contents of No. 2 basin.
4. Combine the two mixtures, beating well.
5. Pour into a glass dish. Decorate with stiffly beaten whites of eggs to which 3 dessertspoons of sugar have been added.
6. Serve quite cold.

Note—If cornflour is used instead of arrowroot the mixture should be boiled.

Variation—Line an oven dish with half apricot pieces (cooked). Add mixture, pile meringue mixture on top. Lightly brown. Serve hot.

PASSION FRUIT FLUMMERY

INGREDIENTS—

1 tablespoon gelatine.
3 cups cold water.
½ cup sugar.
1 tablespoon plain flour.

Juice and rind of
2 oranges, 1 lemon.
6 passion fruit.
2 eggs.

METHOD—

1. Soak gelatine in 2 cups of cold water.
2. Blend flour and sugar with 1 cup cold water.
3. Add fruit juices and rind.
4. Put all into saucepan. Stir continuously until boiling.
5. Remove from stove. Take out fruit rind. Cool, then add passion fruit pulp.
6. Add stiffly beaten whites of eggs and beat mixture until thick and white.
7. Turn into glass dish to set.
8. Serve cold with custard made of yolks of eggs.

Note—Fruits other than passion fruit may be used.

APPLE CAKE (Pudding)

INGREDIENTS—

60 grams butter (2 ozs.)
6 tablespoons
  self-raising flour.
2 tablespoons sugar.
2 teaspoons cinnamon.

1 egg. Milk if required.
500 grams apples cooked
  (1lb. 2oz.)
Sugar to taste
  (about 3 or 4 tablespoons).

METHOD—

1. Prepare a moderately hot oven.
2. Grease a sandwich tin.
3. Stew or bake apples and mash pulp. Drain off syrup.
4. Cream butter and sugar, add beaten egg.
5. Sift in flour and mix lightly.
6. Spread ½ of mixture in a greased sandwich tin.
7. Cover with a layer of mashed apple.
8. Spread remainder of mixture over apple.
9. Cook in a moderately hot oven about 40 minutes.
10. Turn on to a hot plate.
11. While still hot spread lightly with butter sprinkle with cinnamon and sugar.
12. Serve hot or cold with custard or cream.

Variation—Add 1 level teaspoon cinnamon and ½ cup chopped raisins to the mixture.

APPLE SNOW

INGREDIENTS—

3 or 4 large
  cooking apples.
2 or 3 tablespoons sugar.

Whites of two
  or three eggs.
Strips of lemon rind.

METHOD—

1. Bake apples or stew them with a tablespoon of sugar, a little water and lemon rind.
2. Pass pulp through a strainer.
3. Beat the whites of eggs stiffly. By degrees add remainder of sugar.
4. Beat the apple pulp gradually into the whites until the mixture is light and soft like snow.
5. Pile it roughly on to a glass dish.
6. Decorate with pieces of apple jelly or crystallised cherries.

Note—This may be served with whipped cream or with custard made with yolks of eggs.

CAKE PUDDING

INGREDIENTS—

1 cup self-raising
  flour.
1 tablespoon butter.
½ cup sugar.

1 egg.
½ cup milk.
Pinch salt.
Few drops vanilla.

METHOD—

1. Cream butter and sugar. Add beaten egg.
2. Add sifted flour and salt and sufficient milk to make a soft dough. Turn into a greased pie dish. Bake in a moderate oven about 30 minutes.
3. Serve with jam sauce.

LEMON FLUFF

INGREDIENTS—

1 tablespoon butter.
3 tablespoons sugar.
2 tablespoons flour.

1 lemon.
1 cup milk.
2 eggs.

Lemon Fluff — continued

METHOD—
1. Cream butter, sugar and egg yolks.
2. Add grated rind and juice of lemon, then flour.
3. Add milk.
4. Add stiffly beaten whites of eggs.
5. Pour into pie dish. Stand in a dish of water.
6. Bake gently for 1 hour.
7. Pudding should be lightly set on top and soft underneath.

PRUNE PUFF

INGREDIENTS—

240 grams prunes (8 ozs).   2 teaspoons lemon juice.
1/3 cup sugar.   2 egg whites.

METHOD—
1. Soak prunes then cook till soft. Drain.
2. Remove stones and chop fruit finely.
3. Add lemon juice and sugar.
4. Add stiffly beaten whites of eggs.
5. Pour into greased oven dish, stand in dish containing water.
   Bake in moderate oven for 20 minutes.
6. Serve with lemon sauce (page 127), custard or cream.

COLD CHOCOLATE SOUFFLE

INGREDIENTS—

4 eggs.   3 tablespoons cocoa.
4 cups milk.   Sugar to taste
4 level dessertspoons gelatine   (about 3 or 4 tablespoons).

METHOD—
1. Beat egg yolks and sugar.
2. Boil cocoa in milk then add gradually to egg and sugar.
3. Heat mixture until it thickens like custard.
   Allow to cool.
4. When cool add gelatine which has been dissolved in a little
   boiling water.
5. Add stiffly beaten egg whites.
6. Set in a mould till firm.
7. Turn out and put whipped cream on top.
8. Sprinkle with chopped almonds.

APRICOT AND ORANGE MOUSSE (Cold)

INGREDIENTS—

240 grams dried
  apricots (8 ozs.)
2½ cups boiling water.
4 tablespoons sugar.
3 egg whites.

2 level dessertspoons
  gelatine.
4 tablespoons cold water.
Juice and rind
  of 1 orange.

METHOD—

1. Soak and cook apricots in the boiling water until soft.
2. Add sugar, stir till dissolved.
3. Soak gelatine in the cold water.
4. Rub apricots through strainer. Reheat.
5. Add gelatine, stir until dissolved. Cool off.
6. Add orange juice and rind (grated).
7. When cold fold in stiffly beaten whites of eggs.
8. Put in serving dish or mould. Chill.
9. Serve with custard, cream or icecream.

Note—Use egg yolks for custard recipe, (page 104).

PINEAPPLE SPONGE (Cold)

INGREDIENTS—

1 tin crushed pineapple
  (450 grams) (15ozs).
2 level teaspoons
  gelatine

2 egg whites.
1¼ cups juice and water
Juice ½ lemon.

METHOD—

1. Drain syrup from pineapple.
2. Dissolve gelatine in juice and water. Cool well.
3. Whisk egg whites till stiff, and sugar gradually. Add lemon
   juice.
4. Add gelatine and juice gradually, beating well after each
   addition.
5. Fold in fruit. Pile in serving dish. Chill.
6. Serve with custard, cream or icecream.

Note—Use egg yolks for custard — recipe page 104.

COFFEE VELVET (Cold)

INGREDIENTS—

1 egg
2 tablespoons sugar.
1 cup hot, strong milky
  coffee.

½ cup evaporated milk
1 dessertspoon gelatine.
1 tablespoon brandy.
¼ teaspoon vanilla.

METHOD—

1. Beat egg and sugar.
2. Add milky coffee, stir over low heat till mixture thickens as for custard. Do not boil.
3. When cold, add evaporated milk which has been stiffly beaten. Add gelatine dissolved in a little hot water. Stir in brandy and vanilla.
4. Pour mixture into a wet mould. Chill.
5. Serve with cream or icecream.

ORANGE DELIGHT (Cold)

INGREDIENTS—

Stale sponge cake.
Orange juice (extra).
3 eggs.
1 dessertspoon butter.

Juice of 3 oranges.
Juice of ½ lemon.
½ cup sugar.

METHOD—

1. Cut sponge cake in thin slices. Place in serving dish and soak with extra orange juice.
2. Separate yolks from whites of eggs.
3. Beat egg yolks and sugar, add butter, lemon and orange juice. Stir over heat until thick.
4. When cold, fold in stiffly beaten whites of eggs, pour over cake.

COCONUT PIE

INGREDIENTS—

1 kilogram apples
  (2lb. 3 ozs)
½ cup water.
1 cup sugar.
Juice half lemon.

1 cup of breadcrumbs.
½ cup of
  dessicated coconut.
Butter.

METHOD—

1. Cook apples with water and half of sugar. Put in a pie dish.
2. Mix in crumbs, remainder of sugar and coconut.
3. Place mixture over the apples.
4. Place knobs of butter on top.
5. Bake in moderate oven until browned.
6. Serve with custard or cream.

BROWN BETTY

INGREDIENTS—

1 kilogram apples.
(2 lb 3 oz).
½ cup water.
1 cup sugar.

3 cloves.
Dried breadcrumbs
or cornflakes.
Butter.

METHOD—

1. Stew apples with sugar, water and cloves until soft and pulpy.
2. Well butter a pie dish. Cover thickly with dried crumbs.
3. Fill up pie dish with stewed apples.
4. Cover apples with dried crumbs.
5. Place knobs of butter on top.
6. Bake in moderate oven until nicely browned..
7. Serve with custard or cream.

APPLE CHARLOTTE

INGREDIENTS—

500 grams apples
(1 lb 2 oz).
½ cup sugar.
¾ cup water.

Strips of lemon rind.
6 cloves.
Bread.
Butter.

METHOD—

1. Stew apples with water, sugar, lemon rind, cloves.
2. Butter well inside of piedish.
3. Cut bread in thin slices, cut into neat pieces, butter well.
4. Line piedish neatly with buttered bread.
5. Remove lemon rind from apples. Put apples in piedish, keeping back syrup.
6. Cover with slices of buttered bread.
7. Bake in a hot oven until brown.
8. Turn out on a hot dish. Serve hot with syrup, custard or cream.

NEW APPLE PUDDING

INGREDIENTS—

1 large tablespoon butter.
2 tablespoons flour.
1½ cups milk.
2 eggs.

½ teaspoon vanilla.
750 grams apples (1 lb 11 oz).
5 tablespoons sugar.
6 cloves.

New Apple Pudding — continued

METHOD—

1. Peel apples, cut in slices.
2. Put apples in pie dish, sprinkle with 4 tablespoons sugar.
3. Melt butter in saucepan, add flour, stir till smooth.
4. Add milk, boil 3 minutes, stirring all the time.
5. Beat eggs well, add gradually to mixture.
6. Add 1 tablespoon sugar and few drops vanilla.
7. Pour mixture over apples. Bake in a moderate oven for 20 or 30 minutes or until apple is soft. Serve hot.
8. Other fruit may be used instead of apples.

PASSION FRUIT SAGO

INGREDIENTS—

½ cup sago.　　　　　　　2 tablespoons sugar.
1 cup water.　　　　　　　6 passion fruit.
Pinch salt.

METHOD—

1. Wash sago and sprinkle into boiling water, stirring until cooked. Add sugar and salt and 4 of the passion fruit. Stir well.
2. Scoop two passion fruit into wet mould and pour in the passion fruit sago.
3. When cold and set turn into glass dish and serve with boiled custard or cream.

FRUIT — STEWED

1. Fruit is best cooked in syrup.
2. The syrup is made in proportion of half as much sugar as water and brought to boiling point.
3. To each 500 grams (1 lb 2 ozs) of fruit allow ½ cup of sugar and one cup of water. Very sour fruit requires more sugar.
4. Peel and cut apples in quarters, remove core.
5. Peel pears, cut in half, core need not be removed.
6. Peel quinces, cut in neat sections, remove core. Cores of quinces should be put in a muslin bag and cooked with quinces.
7. Large pieces cook more quickly than slices.
8. Wipe nectarines, apricots, plums. If large cut in two, remove stone.

Fruit — Stewed — continued

9. To remove skin from peaches, drop into boiling water, then in cold.
10. Berry fruits should be washed.
11. Put fruit into boiling syrup and simmer gently till tender.
12. Berries are stewed with sugar and very little water.
13. Fruit may be cooked in a casserole in oven.
14. If pears and quinces are cooked slowly for a long time, they assume a deep rich colour.
15. Cloves, lemon rind, cinnamon stick may be used to flavour.

Note—The syrup may be thickened with sago after fruit is cooked.

TRIFLE

INGREDIENTS—

6 stale sponge cakes or substitute.
Blanched almonds.
Custard sauce (page 104).
Jelly.

½ cup of sherry.
½ cup of cream.
Raspberry jam.
Cherries and angelica.

METHOD—

1. Spread the sliced cake with jam and arrange in a glass bowl.
2. Pour over the sherry gradually and allow to stand 15 minutes.
3. Add the cooled custard.
4. Just before serving add the whipped cream and decorate with sliced almonds, cherries, angelica, and chopped jelly.
5. Lemon juice, milk or fruit juice may be substituted for the sherry.

ORANGE CUSTARD

INGREDIENTS—

Cornflour custard (page 104), using twice the amount of cornflour.

3 or 4 oranges.
Sugar.

METHOD—

1. Remove peel and pith from oranges. Slice thinly and sprinkle with sugar. Stand half an hour.
2. Make custard. Allow to get cold. Pour it over the fruit.

Note—This may be served with whipped cream.

SPONGE FOR FRUIT

INGREDIENTS—

750 grams apples or other
   fruit (stewed)
   (1 lb. 11 ozs).
1 cup self raising
   flour

1 tablespoon butter.
½ cup milk.
1 egg.
½ cup sugar.
Essence.

METHOD—

1. Warm butter, add sugar and beat.
2. Add egg. Beat well.
3. Stir in sifted flour.
4. Add flavouring and sufficient milk to make a soft mixture.
5. Pour over boiling hot fruit in pie dish (dish must only be half
   full of fruit).
6. Bake in moderate oven about 20 to 30 minutes.
7. Serve hot with custard or cream.

LEMON OR ORANGE CREAM JELLY

INGREDIENTS—

30 grams gelatine (1 oz)
½ cup boiling water.
240 grams castor sugar
   (8 ozs) for lemons
2½ cups milk.

120 grams castor sugar
   (4 ozs) for oranges.
Rinds and juice of 3 lemons
   or oranges.
3 eggs.

METHOD—

1. Soak gelatine in cold water to cover. Add boiling water.
2. Add sugar and grated rinds. Dissolve.
3. Add milk, egg yolks and juice of fruit.
4. When setting, stir in whipped whites of eggs.
5. Pour into wet moulds or serving dish.
6. Serve with cream or custard.

BATTERS

PANCAKES

INGREDIENTS—

1 cup flour.	1¼ cups milk.
¼ teaspoon salt.	1 lemon.
1 egg.	Sugar.

METHOD—

1. Sift flour and salt. Make well in centre.
2. Drop in egg. Stir lightly, adding half the milk gradually, gathering in flour slowly.
3. Beat with wooden spoon for 10 minutes.
4. Add remainder of milk.
5. Stand in cool place for at least ½ an hour.
6. Heat a little dripping in pan. Drain off and pour in sufficient mixture (about 3 tablespoons) to thinly cover the bottom of pan.
7. Cook till lightly brown and set. Loosen edges.
8. Toss cake. Cook other side.
9. Turn on to kitchen paper. Sprinkle with sugar and lemon juice. Roll.
10. Serve on paper d'oyley on hot dish.
11. Garnish with slices of lemon.

YORKSHIRE PUDDING

1. Use pancake recipe with 2 eggs and half the milk. If only one egg is used add ½ teaspoon of baking powder just before putting pudding into baking tin.
2. Batter should be poured into hot fat and baked about 30 minutes.

Note—Long standing improves this batter.

BATTER FOR FRIED FISH

1. Make pancake batter adding two extra level tablespoons of flour.
2. Economical batter — coat fish in dry plain flour.
   Mix a small cup of self raising flour and ¼ teaspoon salt to a batter consistency with cold water.

BATTER FOR MEAT OR FRUIT FRITTERS

1. Use Apple Fritter recipe (page 122).
2. Make pancake batter using half of milk. (page 121).
   Self-raising flour may be used.

APPLE FRITTERS

INGREDIENTS—

¾ cup flour.
1 level tablespoon butter.
½ cup lukewarm water.
¼ teaspoon salt.

1 egg.
2 large apples, peeled,
   cored and sliced
   in rings.

METHOD—

1. Sift flour and salt. Make well in centre.
2. Melt butter, pour into well with lukewarm water and yolk of
   egg.
3. Gradually stir in flour. Beat until smooth.
4. Stir the stiffly beaten white of egg lightly into mixture.
5. Dip apple slices in batter.
6. Deep fry a golden brown. Drain on kitchen paper.
7. Serve on paper d'oyley on dish. Sprinkle with castor or icing
   sugar.

Note—Other fruits may be used.

PIKELETS

INGREDIENTS—

1½ cups flour.
4 level teaspoons
   cream of tartar.
Pinch salt.
Grated nutmeg to taste.

2 tablespoons sugar.
2 eggs.
2 level teaspoons
   bi-carbonate of soda.
1 cup milk.

METHOD—

1. Sift flour, salt, cream of tartar, nutmeg.
2. Beat eggs and sugar well.
3. Dissolve soda in milk.
4. Add flour etc. and milk alternately in two lots. Mix well.
5. Cook immediately in dessertspoonful on hot greased iron
   gridle or heavy fry pan.
6. When bubbles rise turn with a broad knife or spatula to
   brown.
7. Lift onto cake cooler, cover with a cloth. Makes
   approximately 40.

GEM SCONES

INGREDIENTS—

1½ cups self-raising
flour.
1 egg.
¾ cup milk.

¼ teaspoon salt.
1½ tablespoons sugar,
or grated cheese.
1 tablespoon butter.

METHOD—

1. Heat gem iron.
2. Sift flour and salt and add sugar, or cheese.
3. Add melted butter, beaten egg and milk. Mix to a stiff batter.
4. Half fill iron with batter. Cook in a hot oven about five minutes.
5. May be served buttered, hot or cold.

Note—Gem iron and not ordinary cake tins must be used.

POTATO SCONES

INGREDIENTS—

1 cup self-raising flour,
or 1 cup wheat meal with
1 teaspoon baking powder.
Salt.

1½ cups well mashed
potatoes.
1 tablespoon butter.
Milk.

METHOD—

1. Sift flour and salt, then rub in well the potatoes and butter.
Add milk to consistency of scone dough.
2. Knead and roll out. Cut into scone shapes.
3. Lay on greased baking tin and bake in a hot oven about 20 minutes.

Note— These scones may be cooked on a griddle or fried in deep fat. A little grated cheese may be added to the mixture.

DOUGH NUTS

INGREDIENTS—

1½ cups S.R. flour.
1 rounded tablespoon butter.
1 tablespoon sugar.

1 egg.
Little milk.
Jam.

Dough Nuts — continued

METHOD
1. Sift flour. Rub in butter, add sugar.
2. Beat egg, add milk and add to flour. Mix with knife to a stiff paste.
3. Roll out 1 cm. (¼ in.) thick; cut into rounds.
4. Put a little jam on each alternate round and damp edges of the others. Place two together. Press edges well.
5. Deep fry until brown. Drain on kitchen paper.
6. Roll in castor sugar and serve very hot.

Note—The fat must not be quite as hot as for ordinary frying. If preferred, the dough may be rolled into balls with a little jam in centre of each ball or cut in rings.

SAUSAGES IN BATTER

INGREDIENTS—
500 grams sausages (1 lb 2 ozs).
Yorkshire Pudding Batter (page 121).

METHOD—
1. Make batter, allow to stand.
2. Prick sausages, spread in oven dish. Partly cook to release fat.
3. Drain off surplus fat.
4. Pour batter over sausages.
5. Bake in moderately hot oven until batter is well risen and brown (about 30 minutes).
6. Serve with Tomato Sauce (see recipe page 131).

SAUCES

The following rules should be observed when making sauces:—

1. Careful measurements and good proportions. (One table-spoon thickening, flour or cornflour, to 2½ cups liquid).
2. The thickening must be mixed till quite smooth before adding remainder of liquid.
3. After thickening has been added, the sauce must be stirred continually while it is over the heat.
4. Sauces should be boiled for 3 minutes in order to cook the starch in flour and cornflour.
5. Flavouring essence should be added after sauce is cooked.
6. Sauces should be made just before they are required. If made earlier cover sauce with thin layer of water or milk. Put on lid.
7. Lemon juice may be used instead of vinegar in most cases.

WHITE SAUCE (Melted Butter)

INGREDIENTS—

2½ cups milk.
1½ tablespoons flour.

1 tablespoon butter.
Pinch salt.

METHOD—

1. Melt butter in saucepan, and remove from heat.
2. Add flour, stir till smooth. Cook 2 minutes.
3. Add milk gradually.
4. Stir over heat until sauce has boiled for 3 minutes.
5. Add salt.

WHITE SAUCE

INGREDIENTS—

2½ cups milk.
Pinch salt.

1 tablespoon flour.
1 teaspoon butter.

METHOD—

1. Mix flour to a smooth paste with some of the milk.
2. Put remainder of milk on to heat.
3. When nearly boiling, stir in blended flour.
4. Boil for 3 minutes, stirring all the time.
5. Add salt and butter.

SWEET CORN SAUCE

INGREDIENTS—

Melted butter sauce
(page 125).
Cayenne to taste.

1 teaspoon
lemon juice.
Small tin sweet corn.

METHOD—

1. Make sauce. Add sweet corn. Heat together.
2. Remove from stove, add lemon juice and cayenne.
3. Serve with fried fish or as a vegetable.

MUSHROOM SAUCE

INGREDIENTS—

240 grams mushrooms
(8 ozs.)
1 tablespoon butter.
Juice half lemon.

Pepper, salt.
1 tablespoon flour.
1 cup milk.
Nutmeg.

METHOD—

1. Peel and remove stalks of mushrooms, wash and drain.
2. Melt butter in stewpan, add juice of half a lemon and
   mushrooms.
3. Cover pan and simmer till tender.
4. Add blended flour and milk, stirring all the time. Bring to
   boil. Add nutmeg, pepper and salt.
5. Serve hot.

OYSTER SAUCE

INGREDIENTS—

White sauce (Melted
Butter) (page 125).

1 tin oysters.
Cayenne and lemon juice.

METHOD—

1. Make sauce, using oyster liquor and milk. Remove from
   stove.
2. Add cut up oysters, lemon juice and cayenne (to taste).

CORNFLOUR SAUCE (Sweet)

INGREDIENTS—

2½ cups milk.
1 dessertspoon sugar.
¼ teaspoon vanilla.

1 tablespoon cornflour.
1 teaspoon butter.

METHOD—

1. Mix cornflour to smooth paste with some of the milk.
2. Put remainder of milk on to heat.
3. Stir cornflour into milk.
4. Boil for three minutes, stirring all the time.
5. Add sugar, butter, vanilla.

Note— 1 tablespoon of dissolved cocoa or 1½ tablespoons of golden syrup make nice flavourings.

JAM SAUCE

INGREDIENTS—

2½ cups water.
1 tablespoon of
   cornflour.

3 tablespoons of jam.
Sugar and colouring
   as necessary.

METHOD—

1. Mix cornflour with a little of the water.
2. Put jam and remainder of water on to boil.
3. Strain liquid.
4. Stir in cornflour. Boil 3 minutes stirring all the time.
5. Add sugar and colouring if necessary.

LEMON SAUCE

INGREDIENTS—

2½ cups water.
1 lemon.

1 tablespoon of sugar.
1 tablespoon of cornflour.

METHOD—

1. Mix cornflour to smooth paste with some of the water.
2. Put 2 or 3 strips of thin lemon rind with remainder of water. Bring to boil.
3. Remove lemon rind from water, then stir in cornflour and boil 3 minutes stirring all the time.
4. Add sugar and lemon juice.

PLUM PUDDING SAUCE

INGREDIENTS—

1 cup water.
2 tablespoons treacle
    or golden syrup.
1 teaspoon of butter.

2 teaspoons of
    lemon juice.
1 dessertspoon of
    cornflour.

METHOD—

1. Blend cornflour with a little of the water.
2. Put remainder of water and treacle on to boil.
3. When boiling, stir in blended cornflour and allow to boil 3
      minutes stirring all the time.
4. Add lemon juice and butter.

PARSLEY SAUCE

INGREDIENTS—

White sauce (page 125).
1 tablespoon finely chopped parsley.
Add parsley to white sauce when cooked.

CAPER SAUCE

INGREDIENTS—

White sauce (page 125).
2 tablespoons of capers.
Make white sauce.
Drain vinegar off capers. Add them to sauce.

ONION SAUCE

INGREDIENTS—

White sauce (page 125).
1 large onion (white).
Boil onion till tender, then chop it up finely.
Make white sauce, add onion.

EGG SAUCE

INGREDIENTS—

White sauce (page 125).
2 hard boiled eggs.
Chop hard boiled egg finely, add to white sauce.

CHEESE SAUCE

INGREDIENTS—

White sauce (page 125).
2 heaped tablespoons grated cheese.
Small pinch cayenne pepper.
Make white sauce, add cheese and cayenne pepper.

HORSE-RADISH SAUCE

INGREDIENTS—

White sauce (page 125).   1 teaspoon lemon juice.
3 tablespoons   ¼ teaspoon mustard.
  grated horse-radish.   Pinch cayenne pepper.

METHOD—

1. Mix horse-radish, lemon juice, mustard and cayenne.
2. Make white sauce.
3. Add horse-radish mixture.
4. May be served hot or cold.

Note—Horse-radish may be grated and covered with vinegar, to serve with roast beef.

APPLE SAUCE

INGREDIENTS—

2 apples.   1 dessertspoon
½ cup water.   lemon juice.
2 teaspoons sugar.   Pinch salt.
1 teaspoon butter.

METHOD—

1. Peel and quarter apples.
2. Put apples in saucepan with water, sugar and lemon juice. Boil until soft.
3. Add butter.
4. Beat well.
5. Cayenne and nutmeg may be added if liked.

MINT SAUCE

INGREDIENTS—

2 tablespoons
chopped mint.
½ cup vinegar.

3 tablespoons sugar.
3 tablespoons
boiling water.

METHOD—

1. Pour boiling water on sugar and mint. Cover and stand for few minutes.
2. Add vinegar. Stir well.

MOUSELLINE SAUCE

INGREDIENTS—

1½ tablespoons butter.
1 tablespoon vinegar.
2 tablespoons water.
2 yolks of eggs.
Salt, pepper.

Squeeze of
lemon juice.
Cayenne to taste.
2 tablespoons
whipped cream.

METHOD—

1. Put water, vinegar and yolks of eggs into a basin.
2. Stand basin over pot of hot water. Stir until sauce thickens.
3. Add butter in small pieces gradually.
4. Add seasoning and lemon juice.
5. Add cream just before serving.

Note—This sauce must not be allowed to boil.

HOLLANDAISE SAUCE

Follow recipe for Mouselline Sauce, omitting cream.

CORNED BEEF SAUCE

INGREDIENTS—

2 tablespoons of sugar.
3 tablespoons of
vinegar.
1 dessertspoon of butter.

5 tablespoons of
corned beef water.
1 teaspoon of
mustard.

METHOD—

Place ingredients in saucepan. Add one well beaten egg. Stir over heat. Do not boil.

TOMATO SAUCE

INGREDIENTS—

3 large tomatoes.
1 small onion.
1 level tablespoon butter.
½ tablespoon flour.
½ teaspoon salt.
¼ teaspoon pepper.

1 teaspoon sugar.
1 cup stock or water.
Cayenne and nutmeg
   to taste.
2 cloves.

METHOD—

1. Skin tomatoes, then cut into slices. Prepare onion.
2. Place tomatoes, onion, stock, salt, pepper and sugar in saucepan with cayenne, nutmeg and cloves.
3. Cook till tender.
4. Melt butter in saucepan, then add flour, stirring constantly.
5. Add liquid and pulp gradually.
6. Return to stove and stir until boiling. Boil 3 minutes.
7. Serve in a sauce tureen.

BREAD SAUCE

INGREDIENTS—

2 tablespoons
   breadcrumbs.
½ blade mace, 1 clove.
Salt, cayenne.

1 cup milk.
1 teaspoon butter.
½ small white onion
   (sliced).

METHOD—

1. Put onion, milk, mace and clove into saucepan. Simmer gently for 10 minutes.
2. Strain milk and return to saucepan.
3. Sprinkle in breadcrumbs. Add butter and salt and cayenne.
4. Beat well and stand at side of stove for 10 minutes. Do not boil.
5. Serve in sauce tureen.

PASTRY

NOTES ON PASTRY

1. Pastry is flour made crisp and light by shortening.

2. Shortening may be butter, lard, or clarified fat.

3. Kinds—Short, flaky, rough puff, puff. These are named according to the method of making and quantity of shortening used.

4. Have utensils cool and clean, fat firm.

5. Short Pastry—Use ½ fat to flour.
   Flaky Pastry—Use ¾ fat to flour.
   Rough Puff Pastry—Use ¾ fat to flour.
   Puff Pastry—Use equal quantities of fat and flour.
   Note—Directions for making Puff Pastry not included.

6. Never use self-raising flour or baking powder if correct proportions of flour and fat are used.

7. Handle pastry lightly and quickly.

8. Use as little water as possible for mixing.

9. Roll pastry evenly with short, quick strokes, using very little flour.

10. Cut edges rise best.

11. If tarts are cooked without fillings, prick well to prevent rising in centre.

12. Custard tarts, brush pastry with white of egg before putting in custard, to prevent custard soaking through paste, or make custard with hot milk.

13. Glaze before cooking:— using beaten egg, yolk of egg, or milk for meat dishes; sugar and water for sweet dishes; fruit pies (short pastry), sprinkle with sugar before serving.

14. Pastry must be baked in a hot oven so that starch cells will burst quickly and absorb fat before it escapes.

15. Covering contents of pies while hot makes pastry sodden.

SHORT PASTRY

INGREDIENTS—

240 grams flour
(8 ozs).
Cold water.

120 grams butter,
or substitute (4 ozs).
Salt, 1 level teaspoon.

METHOD—

1. Sift flour and salt.
2. Add shortening and rub in with finger tips until it looks like bread crumbs.
3. Add a little cold water and mix to a stiff dough, using a knife.
4. Turn dough on to a lightly-floured board or slab. Knead.
5. Roll once without folding. Cut to shape.
6. Cook in a hot oven.
7. Short pastry is used for Cornish pasties, mince patties, fruit pies, tarts.

Note—See Homely Measurements — Page 18.

RICH SHORT PASTRY

INGREDIENTS—

240 grams flour (8 ozs)
180 grams fat (6 ozs)
1 yolk of egg.

½ teaspoon lemon juice.
Cold water.
Salt, 1 level teaspoon.

METHOD—

Use same method as for short pastry, adding beaten yolk and lemon juice before the water. 1 tablespoon of sugar may be added. This pastry keeps well.

SWEET SHORT PASTRY (No. 1)

INGREDIENTS—

120 grams
plain flour (4 ozs).
120 grams self-raising
flour (4 ozs).
1 level teaspoon salt.

120 grams shortening
(4 ozs).
90 grams castor
sugar (3 ozs).
1 egg.

METHOD—

1. Sift flours and salt. Rub in shortening.
2. Add sugar then beaten egg gradually making a firm dough.
3. Roll out thinly.
4. Bake in a moderately hot oven.

SWEET SHORT PASTRY (No. 2)

INGREDIENTS—

150 grams self-raising
   flour (5 ozs).
60 grams cornflour (2 ozs).
1 level teaspoon salt.
1 egg.

90 grams shortening
   (3 ozs).
45 grams icing
   sugar (1½ ozs).
1 tablespoon milk.

METHOD—

Follow same method as for Sweet Pastry No. 1. Both pastries
   may be used for tartlets with sweet filling, small pies, e.g.
   fruit mince, plate tart or pie.

MINCE PATTIES (Meat)

INGREDIENTS—

Short pastry as per
   recipe (page 133).
1 cup of cooked,
   minced meat.
¼ cup breadcrumbs.
1 dessertspoon flour.

Small onion.
1 dessertspoon parsley
   (chopped).
Salt and pepper.
Cold water or stock.
¼ teaspoon herbs.

METHOD—

1. Chop onion, put into a saucepan with seasoning, herbs, flour
   and water or stock.
2. Simmer gently 10 minutes, stir occasionally. Add meat,
   breadcrumbs and parsley.
3. Turn on to a plate to cool.
4. Make pastry, roll out rather thinly and cut into rounds to fit
   tins.
5. Line patty tins with pastry and fill with mince.
6. Damp edges, cover with pastry. Press and decorate edges.
7. Glaze and cook in a hot oven about 15 minutes.
8. Serve hot, garnished with parsley.

JAM TART

INGREDIENTS—

Short pastry,
   ¾ of recipe (page 133).

Jam.

Jam Tart — continued

METHOD—

1. Make pastry, turn on to floured board, knead lightly.
2. Roll to ½ cm. (¼ inch) thickness and a little larger than plate.
3. Cut strip of pastry and put round edge of plate. Damp strip.
4. Place pastry on plate. Trim and ornament edges.
5. Prick pastry all over to prevent rising in centre.
6. Bake in quick oven about 10 minutes.
7. Spread with jam.

Note— Jam may be added before cooking.

LEMON TART

INGREDIENTS—

Rich short pastry
  ¾ recipe (page 133).
1 egg.
2 level tablespoons sugar.

¾ tablespoon butter.
1 lemon.
½ cup water.
1 teaspoon arrowroot.

METHOD—

1. Make pastry and roll to ½ cm. (¼ in.) thickness, and roll a little larger than plate.
2. Cut strip of pastry and put it around edge of plate. Damp strip.
3. Place pastry on plate, trim and ornament edges.
4. Prick pastry all over to prevent rising in centre.
5. Bake in a quick oven about 10 minutes.

LEMON FILLING

METHOD—

1. Mix grated rind and juice of lemon in saucepan, with butter, sugar, yolk of egg, arrowroot and water.
2. Stir over heat until thick.
3. When cold put in tart.
4. Whisk white of egg until stiff, add 3 dessertspoons of sugar. Beat well.
5. Pile on top of tart.
6. Bake in a cool oven until lightly browned.

CORNISH PASTIES

INGREDIENTS—

Short pastry
¾ recipe (page 133).
120 grams meat (4 ozs).
1 onion (small).

1 potato
(medium size).
½ a small turnip.
Salt and pepper.

METHOD—

1. Wash and peel potatoes and onions.
2. Cut meat finely and vegetables into small dice or very thin slices.
3. Put into a basin, add salt, pepper and two tablespoons water and mix thoroughly.
4. Make pastry and roll out about ½ cm. (¼ inch) thick.
5. Cut into 4 or 5 rounds the size of a saucer and place mixture in centre of each.
6. Damp edges and join together on top.
7. Pinch neat frill round edges.
8. Glaze. Bake in a quick oven 15 minutes, then more gently 15 minutes later.
9. Serve garnished with sprigs of parsley.

EGG and BACON PIE (No. 1)

INGREDIENTS—

300 grams plain
flour (10 ozs).
150 grams dripping
or lard (5 ozs).
Cold water.

4 or 5 small rashers
of bacon.
4 or 5 eggs.
Oven plate 22 cm.
diam. (9 inch).

METHOD—

1. Make short pastry with flour, dripping, salt and cold water.
2. Divide pastry in two, roll into rounds.
3. Cover plate with pastry, lay pieces of bacon on pastry and break an egg on each piece. Prick yolks.
4. Sprinkle with pepper and a little salt.
5. Damp edges and cover with 2nd piece of pastry. Press edges together. Decorate. Glaze with egg.
6. Bake in hot oven 15 to 20 minutes.

Note—Slices of cold, cooked mutton may be substituted for bacon, use more salt.

EGG and BACON PIE (No. 2)

INGREDIENTS—

CHEESE PASTRY

¾ cup plain flour.
¾ cup S.R. flour.
90 grams butter
  or substitute (3 ozs).
90 grams tasty cheese
  (grated) (3 ozs)

1 level teaspoon salt.
Cold water.
Baking tin
  28 cms x 18 cms
  (11 ins x 7 ins).

Make as for Short Pastry.

FILLING

1 large white onion.
2 rashers of bacon.
1 level teaspoon salt.
Pinch of cayenne pepper.
3 eggs.

1 level teaspoon
  dry mustard.
2½ cups warm milk.
1 dessertspoon
  chopped parsley.

METHOD—

1. Peel and chop onion finely. Cut bacon into small pieces.
2. Fry onion and bacon together for 5 minutes. Do not brown.
3. Add salt, pepper, mustard, parsley, beaten eggs and milk.
4. Roll out pastry and line baking tin.
5. Pour in mixture. Bake in a hot oven for 10 minutes. Reduce heat then cook until custard sets. (about 20 minutes.)
6. Serve hot with lettuce salad.

BAKED CURRANT ROLL

INGREDIENTS—

Short pastry as per
  recipe (page 133).
2 apples.
½ cup currants.
4 tablespoons sugar.
Grated nutmeg.

½ teaspoon mixed spice
  or cinnamon.
1 tablespoon of candied
  peel (chopped).
1 teaspoon lemon
  juice.

METHOD—

1. Make pastry and roll into an oblong ½ cm. (¼ inch) thick.
2. Spread with currants, grated apple, spice, peel, lemon juice, and ½ sugar, well mixed.
3. Roll up, put in a pie dish.
4. Dissolve 2 tablespoons of sugar in 1 cup of boiling water and pour over pastry.
5. Bake in a hot oven ½ an hour.

APPLE DUMPLINGS (Baked)

INGREDIENTS—

Short pastry as per
  recipe (page 133).
4 or 5 apples.

Sugar.
Cloves.

METHOD—

1. Peel and core apples.
2. Make short pastry.
3. Divide pastry in same number of pieces as apples.
4. Roll each piece into a round large enough to cover apple.
5. Place apple in centre of pastry, fill centre with sugar and a clove.
6. Damp edges of pastry, fold around apple, mould into a good shape.
7. Place a clove in top, glaze with water and sugar.
8. Bake in hot oven to cook pastry, then decrease heat and cook till apple is soft.
9. Serve hot with custard or cream.

Note—Apple dumplings may be baked in pie dish with syrup. See Baked Currant Roll.

AMBER PIE

INGREDIENTS—

Short pastry as
  per recipe (page 133).
1 kilogram apples
  (2 lbs. 3 ozs).
1 lemon.

Sugar.
2 eggs.
1 rounded tablespoon
  butter.
Cherries and angelica.

METHOD—

1. Peel and cut up apples. Put in saucepan with 4 tablespoons sugar, grated lemon rind, one tablespoon lemon juice and butter.
2. Stew gently until pulped, stirring frequently.
3. Rub through strainer, add beaten egg yolks.
4. Make pastry and line a large oven plate or pie dish. Pour in apple mixture.
5. Bake in hot oven until pastry browns — 20 to 30 minutes.
6. Beat egg whites stiffly. Add 2 tablespoons sugar gradually, beat well.
7. Pile meringue on pie, decorate with cherries and angelica. Brown lightly.
8. Serve with custard or cream.

Variation—Two tablespoons of coconut may be added to pastry mixture.

FLAKY PASTRY

INGREDIENTS—

240 grams flour (8 ozs).   Salt, 1 level teaspoon.
90 grams lard (3 ozs).   Very cold water.
90 grams butter (3 ozs).   ½ teaspoon lemon juice.

Note—See Homely Measurements — Page 18.

METHOD—

1. Sift flour and salt.
2. Add a quarter of the shortening and rub in with finger tips.
3. Add lemon juice and sufficient cold water to mix to a stiff dough.
4. Turn on to a floured board. Toss into a ball.
5. Roll thinly to an oblong shape. Mark into 3 sections — A, B, C.
6. Spread ¼ of fat in small lumps on sections A and B. Sprinkle lightly with flour.
7. Fold section C over section B then fold section A over section B. Press open edges firmly with rolling pin.
8. Turn folded edge to right, roll into oblong shape.
9. Repeat nos. 6, 7, 8 twice.
10. Roll to required shape.
    Bake in hot oven.

Note—Pastry is improved by standing in a cool place before cooking.

ROUGH PUFF PASTRY

INGREDIENTS—

240 grams flour (8 ozs).   ½ teaspoon lemon juice.
90 grams butter (3 ozs).   Cold water.
90 grams lard (3 ozs).   Salt, 1 level teaspoon.

Note—See Homely Measurements — Page 18.

Rough Puff Pastry — continued

METHOD—
1. Sift flour and salt.
2. Cut lard and butter into pieces size of marbles, add to flour.
3. Add lemon juice and sufficient very cold water to mix to a stiff dough.
4. Turn on to a lightly floured board.
5. Roll out very thinly lengthways.
6. Fold in three, press edges to imprison air. Turn top edge to right. Roll with short quick rolls.
7. Repeat Nos. 5 and 6 four or five times.
8. Roll to required shape.
9. Bake in a hot oven.

Note—Oyster patties, cream horns, etc., are usually made with puff pastry, but rough puff forms a good substitute.

SAUSAGE ROLLS.

INGREDIENTS—

Flaky or rough puff pastry
    ½ recipe (page 139).
240 grams sausage meat
    (8 ozs).

Salt, pepper,
    cold water.

METHOD—
1. Make pastry, roll out thinly and cut in long strips wide enough to roll.
2. Add salt, pepper and a little water to meat; mix well.
3. Place meat along strips of pastry. Damp edges, fold over and press edges with back of knife. Cut into even sections.
4. Glaze with egg and bake in hot oven 15 to 20 minutes, reducing heat after pastry is brown.

CHEESE CAKES

INGREDIENTS—

Flaky pastry or short
  pastry as per recipes
  (page 139 or 133).

Lemon cheese filling
  or jam.

Cake Mixture—

90 grams butter (3 ozs).
90 grams sugar (3 ozs).
1 egg.
Little milk.

60 grams plain flour
  (2 ozs).
60 grams self-raising
  flour (2 ozs).

METHOD—

1. Make pastry and line patty tins.
2. Make cake mixture — 2nd cake method.
3. Place ½ level teaspoon of jam or lemon cheese filling in each
     pastry.
4. Put a teaspoon of cake mixture over lemon cheese and strips
     of pastry crossways on top.
5. Cook in a hot oven about 15 minutes.

Note—The mixture used for date shells (see page 182) may be
  used instead of pastry if desired.

NAPOLEONS

INGREDIENTS—

Rough puff pastry
  (as per recipe (page 139).
Lemon juice.
Jam.

4 tablespoons
  icing sugar.
Chopped almonds.

Cake Mixture—

75 grams butter (2½ ozs).
75 grams sugar (2½ ozs).
2 eggs.

180 grams self-raising
  flour (6 ozs).
Milk if necessary.

METHOD—

1. Make pastry, roll out thinly and cut in two pieces the size of
     cake tin. Prick well. Bake in hot oven about 10 minutes.
2. Make cake by 2nd Cake Method. Bake.
3. When cold, jam one layer of pastry, place cake on top, jam
     cake and place second layer of pastry over sponge.
4. Make thin icing with lemon juice and icing sugar and pour
     over top. Sprinkle well with chopped almonds.
5. Allow to set, trim edges and cut into small oblongs.

DATE ROLLS

INGREDIENTS—

Rough puff or good
  short pastry, ½ quantity
  recipe (page 139 or 133).

120 grams dates (4 ozs).
30 grams almonds
  (1 oz).

METHOD—

1. Stone and chop dates. Put into saucepan with 2 tablespoons of boiling water. Stir until softened. Add chopped almonds.
2. Make pastry roll into oblong, cut into strips wide enough to roll.
3. Place filling on each strip, damp edges and fold over, cut into sections.
4. Glaze with sugar and water.
5. Cook in hot oven about 7 minutes.

CURRANT SLICE

INGREDIENTS—

Rough puff pastry
  ¾ recipe (page 139)
¾ cup sultanas
  and currants mixed.
1 finely chopped apple.

Rind and juice
  of ½ a lemon.
1 teaspoon mixed spice.
1 tablespoon sugar.
1 dessertspoon peel.

METHOD—

1. Make pastry and roll thinly in a long slice. Cut in half.
2. Put one piece of pastry on baking tin, spread with mixture.
3. Cover with other piece of pastry. Prick over top with fork. Damp and seal edges.
4. Mark into squares with back edge of knife.
5. Cook in a hot oven about 15 minutes. Glaze with sugar glazing.

CREAM HORNS

INGREDIENTS—

Flaky or rough puff
  pastry, ¾ recipe
  (page 139).

Cream.
Sugar.
Flavouring.

Cream Horns — continued

METHOD—
1. Make pastry, roll thinly, cut in strips 2½ cm. (1 inch) wide.
2. Twist strips of pastry round the outside of greased cornet-shaped moulds.
3. Wet joints with a little cold water or egg.
4. Glaze and cook in a hot oven for 10 to 15 minutes.
5. Cool slightly before removing moulds.
6. When cold, fill with whipped cream sweetened and flavoured.
7. A little jam may be put in before the cream.

APPLE PIE

INGREDIENTS—

Flaky or rough puff pastry
 ¾ recipe (page 139)
Lemon.
½ cup water.

1 kilogram apples
 (2 lbs 3 ozs).
1 cup sugar.
3 cloves.

METHOD—
1. Make pastry.
2. Peel apples and cut into large pieces.
3. Place in pie dish with sugar, cloves, water, thin slice of rind and 1 teaspoon of juice.
4. Cut strips of pastry for rim of pie dish. Damp edges.
5. Cover with pastry. Trim and cut edges. Glaze.
6. Bake in a hot oven 10 minutes and in cooler part until apples are tender.
7. Serve hot or cold.

FRUIT MINCE PIES

INGREDIENTS—

120 grams suet (4 ozs).
120 grams sugar (4 ozs).
120 grams seeded
 raisins (4 ozs).
120 grams sultanas (4 ozs).
120 grams currants (4 ozs).
½ cup of brandy.

60 grams blanched and
 chopped almonds (2 ozs).
2 large apples.
1 teaspoon mixed spice.
½ teaspoon ground ginger.
Grated rind of lemon,
 yellow part only.

Fruit Mince Pies — continued

METHOD—

1. Skin and chop suet finely.
2. Peel, core and grate apples. Chop raisins.
3. Mix all ingredients thoroughly together.
4. Bottle and cover.
5. Make Rich Short Pastry (page 133). Use for small or large pies.

FISH PIE

INGREDIENTS—

360 grams lightly cooked
 fish (12 ozs).
1 teaspoon chopped
 parsley.
1 hard boiled egg.
Salt and pepper.

1 or 2 tablespoons white
 sauce.
A little grated lemon.
 rind and juice.
Pinch cayenne.
Rough Puff Pastry (page 139).

METHOD—

1. Flake fish. Chop up egg.
2. Mix fish, egg, salt, pepper, sauce, lemon rind and juice, cayenne.
3. Make pastry. Roll to a square ½ cm (¼ inch) thick. Trim edges.
4. Place fish mixture in centre of pastry.
5. Damp corners of pastry, fold over fish to join in centre. Decorate with pastry leaves. Brush over with beaten egg.
6. Bake in a hot oven till pastry is cooked (about 15 minutes).

Note—Other fillings such as chicken may be used instead of fish.

ICE CREAM
ICE CREAM No. 1

INGREDIENTS—

2½ cups cream.
3 dessertspoons castor sugar.
Whites of 3 eggs.
Vanilla.

METHOD—

1. Whip cream until stiff.
2. Beat whites of eggs until firm adding sugar gradually.
3. Add flavouring.
4. Fold cream into egg mixture.
5. Half freeze then beat well and return to freezer.

ICE CREAM No. 2.

INGREDIENTS—

1 small level cup of ice cream mixture.
1 small cup boiling water.
1/3rd cup of evaporated milk.
Vanilla (½ teaspoon).

METHOD—

1. Blend mixture with boiling water.
2. Add evaporated milk.
3. Half freeze, then beat until thick.
4. Add vanilla.
5. Freeze.

ICE CREAM No. 3.

INGREDIENTS—

2½ cups fresh milk.
2 tablespoons full cream powdered milk.
3 tablespoons condensed milk.
½ tin evaporated milk.
1 large teaspoon gelatine.
2 tablespoons sugar.
Vanilla.

METHOD—

1. Soak gelatine in ½ cup cold water to dissolve.
2. Mix all milks together and whip.
3. Add sugar and dissolved gelatine.
4. Put into freezer until nearly set.
5. Whip well and add vanilla.
6. Freeze.

CAKES

1. There are three methods of cake making. First, Second and Third methods.

2. The First Method is used for scones and the plainer kinds of cake in which the proportion of fat to flour is half or less than half.

3. The Second Method is for richer cakes, and is generally used where half or more fat to flour is allowed such as Queen Cakes, Madeira and fruit cakes.

4. The Third Method is used for sponges or cakes in which little or no fat is used, the lightness of the cake depending on number and beating of eggs and sugar.

GENERAL NOTES

1. Attend to the oven. Collect necessary utensils.
2. Measure and prepare ingredients.
    (a) Fruit should be picked over and, if necessary, cleaned by washing and drying well or rubbing with a little flour and sifting.
    (b) Cut candied peel finely.
    (c) Blanch almonds—pour boiling water over them and stand for a few minutes. Skin and drop into cold water. Dry.
3. The plainer the cake mixture the more "rising" necessary.
4. Rising may be (a) baking powder, (b) cream of tartar, combined with bi-carbonate of soda, (c) sour milk and soda, (d) treacle and soda. Allow 8 level teaspoons of baking powder or 5 level teaspoons of cream of tartar and 2 level teaspoons of bi-carbonate of soda to 480 grams (1 lb.) of flour.
5. Omit baking powder or cream of tartar and use soda only when mixture contains treacle, jam or sour milk.
6. If bi-carbonate of soda is used, crush well or dissolve in milk or water before adding.
7. Self raising flour is flour with the rising already added to it.
8. Rich cakes require little or no rising.
9. Test freshness of eggs by breaking each into a cup. 2 tablespoons milk or water may be substituted for one egg in a cake mixture.
10. Flour should be added last in both the Second and the Third methods. Stir mixture as little as possible after flour is added or cake will be "leathery".

General Notes on Cakes — continued

11. Good, clean beef dripping or marrow may be used instead of butter for economical cakes.
12. Brandy is often used to extract flavour from fruit. It prevents drying and preserves the cake.
13. Cake containing baking powder should be put into the oven at once, as its action is quicker than that of cream of tartar and soda.

PREPARATION OF TINS

1. Flour tins for scones. Grease for small cakes, biscuits, buns, sponges, swiss rolls and bread.
2. For rich cakes line tins with three layers of paper.
3. Tins for sponge cakes are often greased and sprinkled with equal parts of castor sugar and cornflour.
4. Patty tins should be half filled with mixture. Large cakes fill two-thirds of tin.

THE OVEN

1. Scones and milk loaves require a very hot oven.
2. Small cakes a moderate oven.
3. Rich cakes a moderately hot oven, with a gradually decreasing heat and a low, even temperature maintained after cake is well risen and browned. The heat bursts the starch cells which then absorb the fat, thus setting cake and preventing fruit from sinking.
4. Biscuits and ginger cakes should be cooked in a cooler oven.
5. Avoid slamming oven door.
6. If cake is browning too quickly cover with brown or white paper.
7. Test cakes by passing skewer or straw through thickest part, when, if a cake is cooked it comes out dry.
8. Cool cakes on cake cooler.
9. Use baking tins of correct size.

OVEN TEMPERATURES

	Degrees Farenheit	Degrees Celsius
Very slow	200–250	93–121
Slow	250–300	121–149
Very Moderate	300–350	149–177
Moderate	350–375	177–190
Moderately hot	375–425	190–218
Hot	425–450	218–232
Very Hot	450–500	232–260

OVEN TESTS (To be used when no regulator available)—
  Sprinkle tablespoon flour on a baking dish. Put in the oven for
    five minutes:—
  (a) Hot—the flour becomes dark brown.
  (b) Moderate—the flour becomes golden brown.
  (c) Cool—the flour becomes pale brown.

RULES FOR FIRST CAKE METHOD
1. Sift flour, salt and rising.
2. Rub fat into flour with tips of fingers till mixture resembles
     breadcrumbs.
3. Add dry ingredients (fruit, sugar, spices, etc.). Mix well.
4. Add sufficient moisture (beaten egg, milk or water) to make
     a stiff mixture.
5. Bake in a hot oven on greased oven slide.
Note—See Homely Measurements— Page 18.

ROCK CAKES

INGREDIENTS—
240 grams self-raising
  flour (8 ozs).
60 grams butter
  (2 ozs).
90 grams sugar (3 ozs).
1 egg.

60 grams currants and
  chopped lemon peel
  (2 ozs).
Milk.
Sugar to sprinkle
  over top.

METHOD—
Mix by First Cake Method (to stiff mixture). Put in dessertspoon
  heaps on greased slide and bake in hot oven 10 minutes.

APRICOT BUNS

INGREDIENTS—

240 grams flour
(S.R.) (8 ozs).
Pinch salt.
60 grams butter (2 ozs).

90 grams sugar (3 ozs).
2 tablespoons
apricot jam.
1 egg.

METHOD—

1. Make by First Cake Method (page 148), leaving out the fruit. The mixture must be firm.
2. Turn on to lightly floured board, knead slightly.
3. Divide mixture into 12 or 16 pieces.
4. Roll each piece into a ball, place on greased slide.
5. Press a hole in centre and fill with jam.
6. Bake in a hot oven for 10 to 15 minutes.

LONDON BUNS

INGREDIENTS—

240 grams flour,
(S.R.) (8 ozs.)
Pinch of salt.
90 grams butter (3 ozs).

Thin slices of
candied peel.
90 grams sugar (3 ozs).
1 egg, milk.

METHOD—

1. Mix by First Cake Method (page 148), Place in spoonsful on tin. Put slice of lemon peel across. Sprinkle lightly with sugar.
2. Bake for 10 minutes in hot oven.

SUNBEAMS

INGREDIENTS—

240 grams self-raising
flour (8 ozs).
90 grams butter (3 ozs).

90 grams sugar (3 ozs).
1 egg.
Pinch salt, jam.

METHOD—

1. Mix by First Cake Method (page 148), omitting the jam. The mixture must be firm enough to roll.
2. Turn on to a lightly floured board. Roll out evenly about ½ cm (¼ in.) thick. Spread thinly with jam.
3. Roll up and cut in slices ½ cm (¼ in.) thick.
4. Place on greased slide. Bake 10 minutes in a moderate oven.

SURPRISES

1. Use sunbeam recipe, substituting dates for jam.
2. Take 1 teaspoon of mixture, and roll lightly between hands. Make hole in middle and enclose half a date. Bake on greased slide 10 minutes in moderate oven.

BACHELOR BUTTONS

INGREDIENTS—

120 grams self-raising
   flour, (4 ozs)
   pinch salt.
45 grams butter (1½ ozs).

45 grams sugar (1½ ozs).
1 egg.
Essence vanilla.
Extra sugar for dipping.

METHOD—

1. Prepare by First Cake Method (148), making a fairly stiff mixture.
2. Take teaspoon of mixture and roll into a ball. Dip in sugar. Place on greased tin.
3. Bake 10 minutes in a hot oven.

Note—One tablespoon coconut may be added if liked.

GINGER BREAD (Plain)

INGREDIENTS—

3 cups self-raising flour.
120 grams butter
   or dripping (4 ozs).
3 tablespoons of sugar.
2 tablespoons treacle
1 tablespoon chopped peel.

4 tablespoons currants
   or sultanas.
1 teaspoon of ginger.
2 eggs.
Milk.
Pinch salt.

METHOD—

1. Clean currants. Chop peel.
2. Sift flour and salt.
3. Rub in fat.
4. Stir in fruit, sugar and ginger.
5. Mix with melted treacle, beaten eggs and sufficient milk to make a thick batter.
6. Place in tin lined with greased paper.
7. Bake 1 to 1½ hours in a fairly hot oven.

Note—Is best kept a week before cutting.

SCONES

INGREDIENTS—

2 cups self-raising flour
Pinch salt.

2 teaspoons butter.
Nearly 1 cup milk.

METHOD—

1. Sift flour and salt. Add butter and rub into flour.
2. Add sufficient milk to make a soft dough.
3. Turn on to a floured board. Knead very slightly.
4. Roll out 2 cms (¾ in.) thick. Cut into shapes.
5. Put on hot, floured tin. Bake for 7 to 10 minutes in very hot oven.
6. Scones may be glazed by brushing over with milk before putting into oven.

SWEET SCONES

Make as Scones (page 151), and add 1 tablespoon sugar, ½ cup sultanas, and, if liked, 1 egg (beaten).

SCONE LOAF

INGREDIENTS—

3 cups self-raising flour.
1½ tablespoons sugar.
1 tablespoon butter.
Milk.

4 tablespoons sultanas,
currants or dates.
1 egg.

METHOD—

1. Make as for scones.
2. Knead into loaf, put on floured slide or in a loaf tin.
3. Bake in hot oven for 15 to 20 minutes.
4. Cover with a thin icing, sprinkle with chopped nuts or cinnamon.

CHEESE LOAF

INGREDIENTS—

2 cups S.R. flour.
1 cup of grated
cheese.

Level teaspoon of salt.
1 egg beaten in cup and
then filled with milk.

Cheese Loaf — continued

METHOD—

1. Mix all ingredients together. Add egg and milk.
2. Put mixture into long narrow greased tin.
3. Bake in moderately hot oven for ½ hour.
4. Slice and butter.

CHEESE SCONES

Plain scone mixture. Add to flour 3 tablespoons grated cheese, ¼ teaspoon of mustard and pinch cayenne and 1 beaten egg. Glaze with milk. Sprinkle with grated cheese.

BRAN SCONES

INGREDIENTS—

1 cup flour.
2 cups bran.
1 cup milk.
1 egg.
2 tablespoons butter.

1 teaspoon bi-carbonate of soda, dissolved in ¼ of milk,
¼ cup treacle.
2 tablespoons brown sugar.

METHOD—

1. Beat egg and sugar together.
2. Add treacle, melted butter, milk and soda.
3. Add flour and bran. Mix well. Roll out, cut as for scones.
4. Bake in moderate oven about ¼ hour.

WHEATEN LOAF

INGREDIENTS—

1 cup fine wheaten meal.
1 small teaspoon cream of tartar.
1 cup self-raising flour.

½ teaspoon bi-carbonate of soda.
3 teaspoons treacle.
Milk.

METHOD—

1. Mix dry ingredients.
2. Dissolve treacle in a little milk and add to mixture with sufficient milk to make a soft dough.
3. Pour into 2 greased tins (tall tins with lids). Bake in hot oven ½ hour.

PUMPKIN SCONES

INGREDIENTS—

1½ tablespoons butter.
½ cup sugar.
1 egg.

1 cup cold
  mashed pumpkin.
2 cups self-raising flour.

METHOD—

1. Cream butter and sugar, add egg.
2. Add pumpkin.
3. Add sifted flour and mix well.
4. Put in tablespoon heaps on a greased tin.
5. Bake in hot oven about 15 minutes.

WHEATEN MEAL SCONES

INGREDIENTS—

1 cup plain flour.
1½ cups wheaten
  meal.
1 teaspoon bi-carbonate
  of soda.

2 teaspoons cream tartar.
2 tablespoons butter.
1 teaspoon sugar.
1 cup milk.
1 level teaspoon salt.

METHOD—

1. Sift plain flour, rising and salt.
2. Add wheaten flour.
3. Rub in butter.
4. Add sugar and mix to a soft dough with milk.
5. Roll out 2½ cms (1 in.) thick, cut in rounds.
6. Bake in a very hot oven 8 to 10 minutes.

NUT BREAD

INGREDIENTS—

1 tablespoon butter.
½ cup sugar.
1 egg.
½ cup chopped nuts.

1½ cups self-raising
  flour.
½ cup milk.
½ cup of fruit if liked.

METHOD—

1. Cream butter and sugar, add egg. Beat well.
2. Stir in nuts and flour.
3. Add milk.
4. Put into 2 greased tins, (tall tins with lids). Put on lids. Bake in moderate oven for about 1 hour.

DATE LOAF

INGREDIENTS—

1 cup boiling water.
240 grams chopped
   dates. (8 ozs).
2 tablespoons butter
   or margarine.

¾ cup sugar.
1 teaspoon bi-carbonate
   of soda.
1¾ cup S.R. flour.
1 well beaten egg.

METHOD—

1. Cook dates, butter, sugar and soda in boiling water for 2 to 3
      minutes. Cool.
2. Add egg and S.R. flour.
3. Bake in long narrow greased tin for ¾ hour in moderate oven.
4. Slice and butter.

RULES FOR SECOND CAKE METHOD

1. Cream butter and sugar.
2. Add eggs one at a time. Beat well.
3. Stir in fruit and flavouring.
4. Sift in flour and rising. Mix well. Add milk if necessary.
5. Rich fruit cakes should be stiff enough to hold a wooden
      spoon upright.
6. Bake in moderate oven.
7. Leave block cakes in tins, standing on cooler until cold.

Note—See Homely Measurements — **Page 18.**

PLAIN CAKES

INGREDIENTS—

60 grams butter (2 ozs).
60 grams sugar (2 ozs).
120 grams self-raising
   flour (4 ozs).

1 egg.
Milk.
Flavouring.

METHOD—

1. Second Cake Method, (see above).
2. Put into greased patty tins.
3. Bake in moderate oven for 10 to 15 minutes.

QUEEN CAKES

INGREDIENTS—

120 grams self-raising
flour (4 ozs).
60 grams plain
flour (2 ozs).
120 grams butter (4 ozs).
120 grams sugar (4 ozs).

2 eggs.
2 tablespoons currants.
Little candied peel.
Few drops essence.
1 or 2 tablespoons
of milk.

METHOD—

1. Second Cake Method (page 154).
2. Turn into greased patty tins. Bake in moderate oven 10 to 15 minutes.

CORNFLOUR CAKES

INGREDIENTS—

60 grams self-raising
flour (2 ozs).
60 grams cornflour
(2 ozs).
60 grams butter. (2 ozs)

60 grams sugar (2 ozs).
1 egg, pinch salt.
4 drops essence lemon
or vanilla.
Little milk.

METHOD—

1. Second Cake Method (page 154).
2. Half fill greased patty tins.
3. Bake in a moderate oven 10 to 15 minutes.

COFFEE ROLLS

INGREDIENTS—

3 cups self raising
flour.
2 tablespoons sugar.

2 tablespoons butter.
1 egg.
¾ cup milk.

METHOD—

1. Cream butter and sugar, add egg. Beat well.
2. Add sifted flour and milk alternately.
3. Knead lightly, roll out 1½ cms. thick. Cut into rounds or squares, fold in halves or cornerwise.
4. Bake in a hot oven for 10 to 15 minutes.

TEA CAKE

INGREDIENTS—

1 tablespoon butter.
½ cup sugar.
1 egg.
Vanilla.

1½ cups self-raising
  flour.
½ to ¾ cup milk.

METHOD—

1. Second Cake Method (page 154).
2. Put in greased sandwich tin, bake 15 to 20 minutes in moderate oven.
3. While hot spread butter on top of cake, sprinkle with cinnamon and sugar.
4. When cold, cut through centre, spread with butter, rejoin.

KISSES

INGREDIENTS—

90 grams butter (3 ozs).
90 grams sugar (3 ozs).
1 egg (large).
90 grams self-raising
  flour (3 ozs)

90 grams cornflour (3 ozs).
1 tablespoon milk.
Essence.
Raspberry jam.
Icing sugar.

METHOD—

1. Second Cake Method (page 154).
2. Drop teaspoons of mixture on greased oven slide.
3. Bake in moderate oven 10 minutes.
4. When cakes are cool, place two together with jam and sprinkle with icing sugar.

CREAM CAKES

INGREDIENTS—

120 grams self-raising
  flour (4 ozs).
pinch salt
75 grams sugar (2½ ozs).

75 grams butter
  (2½ ozs).
2 eggs
Flavourings.

Cream Cakes — continued

METHOD—
1. Second Cake Method (page 154)
2. Put mixture into greased patty tins.
3. Bake in a moderate oven 10 to 15 minutes.
4. When cakes are cold, cut a small round out of each, fill space with cream and replace top.
5. If preferred cake may be filled with jam or lemon cheese.

Note Bramble Cakes: Make as above, fill with raspberry jam or black currant jam, replace top and cover with pink icing.

SEED CAKE

INGREDIENTS—

1 cup self-raising flour.
½ cup plain flour.
¾ cup sugar.
3 eggs.

120 grams butter (4 ozs).
1 tablespoon carraway seeds.
¼ teaspoon lemon essence.

METHOD—
1. Second Cake Method (page 154)
2. Put in cake tin lined with greased paper.
3. Bake about 1 hour in moderate oven.

APPLE BLOSSOM CAKES

INGREDIENTS—

½ cup self-raising flour.
½ cup plain flour.
½ cup sugar.

90 grams butter (3 ozs).
Apple pulp (cooked).
1 egg.
Essence of lemon.

METHOD—
1. Make cake mixture by the Second Cake Method (page 154). omitting the apple pulp.
2. Grease patty tins. Put 1 teaspoon of mixture into each, hollowing the centre slightly.
3. Put in a little apple pulp on each cake and cover with a little of cake mixture.
4. Bake in a moderate oven about 15 minutes.
5. When cold, decorate with pink icing.

*Note—*Pulped bananas or chopped nuts with apricot jam, could be used instead of apple filling.

GINGER CAKE (No. 1)

INGREDIENTS

180 grams butter (6 ozs).
240 grams sugar (8 ozs).
240 grams plain
  flour (8 ozs).
¾ cup treacle.
120 grams whole meal. (4 ozs)
1 tea cup milk.

4 eggs.
½ grated nutmeg.
1½ level teaspoons
  bi-carbonate of soda.
2 teaspoons ginger.
1 teaspoon cinnamon.
½ teaspoon spice.

METHOD—

1. Soak whole meal in milk half an hour.
2. Cream butter and sugar.
3. Add beaten eggs.
4. Add treacle, beat well.
5. Add the whole meal, flour and all spices.
6. Add soda dissolved in a little hot water.
7. Put into greased tin and cook in moderate oven for about 1 hour.
8. When cold, ice with chocolate icing and sprinkle with chopped walnuts.
9. Do not cut until next day.

GINGER CAKE (No. 2)

INGREDIENTS—

3 cups plain
  flour
180 grams butter (6 ozs).
240 grams sugar (8 ozs).
½ cup treacle.
¼ cup milk.
2 level teaspoons
  bi-carbonate of soda.

1 level teaspoon
  cream of tartar
6 level teaspoons
  ground ginger
2 level teaspoons
  mixed spice.
3 eggs.

METHOD—

1. Cream butter and sugar. Add eggs one at a time, beat well.
2. Add treacle, mix well.
3. Sift flour, bicarbonate of soda, cream of tartar, ground ginger and spice. Add gradually to mixture. Add milk as necessary.
4. Put into a greased paper lined tin.
5. Bake in moderate oven for 1 to 1½ hours.
6. This cake improves with keeping.

SNOW BALLS

INGREDIENTS—

120 grams butter (4 ozs).

120 grams sugar (4 ozs).

3 eggs.

180 grams S.R. Flour
  (6 ozs).

Milk as necessary.

METHOD—

1. Make by Second Cake Method (page 154.)
2. Bake in hot greased gem irons for 10 minutes.

FILLING

INGREDIENTS—

1 cup of milk.

2 tablespoons icing
  sugar.

2 tablespoons butter.

1 tablespoon cornflour.

Essence of vanilla
  (¼ teaspoon).

METHOD—

1. Cream butter and sugar.
2. Cook cornflour and milk.
3. Combine both mixtures. Beat well.
4. Put filling between two cakes.
5. Completely cover cake with filling. Roll in coconut.

COFFEE CAKE

INGREDIENTS—

120 grams butter (4 ozs.)

120 grams sugar (4ozs.)

2 eggs.

240 grams S. R. Flour (8 ozs.).

Milk (about ½ cup).

Topping.

Topping— 2 tablespoons castor sugar mixed with 2 teaspoons
  cinnamon.

METHOD—

1. Grease deep cake tin (19 cms. or 7½ inches across), placing
   greased paper in bottom.
2. Cream butter and sugar.
3. Add eggs one at a time, beat well.
4. Add flour alternately with milk.
5. Put mixture in cake tin, smooth surface.
6. Sprinkle topping evenly on mixture.
7. Bake in moderate oven for 30 to 40 minutes.

COCONUT CAKE

INGREDIENTS—

240 grams self-raising
  flour (8 ozs).
120 grams butter. (4 ozs)
120 grams sugar (4 ozs).
2 eggs.

60 grams coconut (2 ozs).
¼ cup milk.
Grated rind of lemon,
  or vanilla essence.
Salt.

METHOD—

1. Soak coconut in milk.
2. Make by Second Cake Method (page 154).
3. Bake in well-greased tin in moderate oven for 30—40 minutes.

CANBERRA CAKE

INGREDIENTS—

1½ cups flour.
120 grams butter (4 ozs).
¾ cup sugar.
¼ cup milk.
½ cup raisins.
3 eggs.

1 level tablespoon
  cinnamon.
1 teaspoon cream
  of tartar.
½ teaspoon bi-carbonate
  of soda.

METHOD—

1. Make by Second Cake Method (page 154), adding the soda dissolved in milk last.
2. Bake in moderate oven 30 to 40 minutes.

Icing—Follow recipe for icing Pumpkin Fruit Cake (page 163) spread over cake and sprinkle with coconut.

FEATHER CAKE

INGREDIENTS—

120 grams butter (4 ozs).
1 cup sugar.
3 cups flour.
Flavouring
1 cup milk.
2 eggs.

1 teaspoon bi-carbonate
  soda.
2 teaspoons cream
  of tartar.
Pinch salt.
Fruit flavoured icing.

Feather Cake — Continued.

METHOD—

1. Second Cake Method (page 154).
2. Put into prepared tin and bake in moderate oven about 1 hour.
3. When cold, ice with fruit flavoured icing.

JEWISH CAKE

INGREDIENTS—

120 grams butter (4 ozs).
1 cup sugar.
1½ cups flour.
2 teaspoons cinnamon
3 eggs.

6 tablespoons milk.
1 teaspoon cream
   of tartar.
½ teaspoon bi-carbonate
   of soda.

METHOD—

1. Second Cake Method (page 154).
2. Bake in greased sandwich tins about 15 to 20 minutes in moderate oven.
3. Fill with lemon filling or cream.
4. Sift icing sugar on top.

MADEIRA CAKE

INGREDIENTS—

150 grams self-raising
   flour (5 ozs).
90 grams plain
   flour (3 ozs).
150 grams butter (5 ozs).
150 grams sugar (5 ozs).

3 eggs or
   2 eggs and milk.
Finely chopped
   candied peel.
Essence or 1 teaspoon
   grated lemon rind.

METHOD—

1. Second Cake Method (page 154). Decorate with thin strips of candied peel or split almonds.
2. Bake in greased papered tin in moderate oven 1 hour.

SULTANA CAKE

INGREDIENTS—

1 cup self-raising flour.
½ cup plain flour.
120 grams butter (4 ozs).
¾ cup sugar.
¾ cup sultanas.

3 eggs.
½ cup of milk.
Lemon peel.
Essence lemon.
Pinch salt.

METHOD—

1. Second Cake Method (page 154).
2. Turn into a prepared tin. Bake 45 minutes in moderate oven.
3. This mixture will also make very nice small cakes.

BOIL and BAKE FRUIT CAKE

INGREDIENTS—

1 cup sugar.
2 cups raisins, sultanas,
    currants, mixed.
60 grams butter (2 ozs).
1 cup cold water.
½ teaspoon salt.

1 cup plain flour.
1 cup self-raising
    flour.
1 teaspoon bi-carbonate
    of soda.
½ cup boiling water.

METHOD—

1. Put sugar, fruit, butter, cold water, 1 teaspoon spice, salt in a
    saucepan, boil for 3 minutes.
2. Allow to cool.
3. When mixture is cold, sift in flour.
4. Dissolve soda in boiling water, stir into cake mixture.
5. Put into prepared tin, bake in moderate oven for 1 hour.

Note—Some chopped lemon peel may be added to fruit and one
    beaten egg may be added with flour. Use less boiling water
    with soda when an egg is added.

RAISIN CAKE

INGREDIENTS—

360 grams butter (12 ozs).
360 grams sugar. (12 ozs).
240 grams self-raising
    flour (8 ozs).
240 grams plain flour
    (8 ozs)
360 grams raisins
    (12 ozs)

4 eggs.
1 tablespoon chopped peel.
½ tablespoon mixed
    spice.
About ½ a cup of
    milk or water.

Raisin Cake — Continued.

METHOD—

1. Cut up raisins.
2. Chop peel finely.
3. Beat butter and sugar to a cream.
4. Add eggs one at a time. Beat well.
5. Stir in fruit and spice.
6. Sift in flour.
7. Add sufficient milk to make moist mixture.
8. Turn into tin lined with greased paper.
9. Bake in moderate oven about 2 hours.

SCOTCH CAKE

INGREDIENTS—

420 grams flour (14 ozs)
  pinch salt.
240 grams butter. (8 ozs)
240 grams sugar (8 ozs).
2 eggs.
360 grams mixed fruits
  (dates, sultanas, raisins
  and currants). (12 ozs)

60 grams lemon peel
  (2 ozs).
60 grams almonds, (2 ozs).
¼ cup milk.
½ cup strong coffee.
1 teaspoon bi-carbonate
  soda.

METHOD—

1. Second Cake Method (page 154).
2. Dissolve soda in milk and add last.
3. Turn into a greased papered tin. Bake 1½ to 2 hours in moderate oven.

PUMPKIN FRUIT CAKE

INGREDIENTS—

240 grams butter
  or margarine (8 ozs).
1 cup sugar (brown
  sugar in preference).
2 cups S.R. flour
  Pinch of salt.

1 cup cold mashed pumpkin.
3 eggs.
480 grams mixed
  fruit (1 lb).
½ teaspoon each of nutmeg,
  ginger, cinnamon.

Pumpkin Fruit Cake — Continued.

METHOD—

1. Cream butter and sugar.
2. Add eggs one at a time. Beat well.
3. Add fruit, spices, then pumpkin.
4. Add sifted flour.
5. Add milk if necessary.
6. Put mixture into square tin lined with greased paper.
7. Bake in moderate oven 1¼ hours.

ICING

1 tablespoon butter.
2 tablespoons sugar.
3 tablespoons water.
Boil 3 minutes.
Cool mixture. Add sufficient powdered milk (about 3 tablespoons) to thicken mixture.
Spread on cake.

LAMINGTONS

INGREDIENTS—

1 cup butter.
1½ cups sugar.
4 eggs.
1 cup milk.

3 cups self-raising flour.
1 teaspoon essence vanilla.

METHOD—

1. Second Cake Method (page 154).
2. Bake in a flat, greased tin. Keep for 2 days before icing (see page 185).
3. Cut into 4 cms (1½ ins.) cubes.
4. Coat with chocolate icing and coconut.

ORANGE CAKE

INGREDIENTS—

2 cups flour, pinch salt.
120 grams butter (4 ozs).
1 cup sugar.
3 eggs.
Juice of one orange.

Grated rind of two oranges.
1½ teaspoons cream tartar.
¾ teaspoon bi-carbonate of soda.

Orange Cake — Continued.

METHOD—
1. Cream butter and sugar, add eggs.
2. Add grated rind and juice of orange.
3. Add sifted flour and cream tartar.
4. Add soda dissolved in a little milk or water.
5. Bake in orange cake tin (greased) about ¾ hour in moderate oven.
6. Ice top of cake with orange icing.
7. Decorate with fine shreds of orange rind.

CHERRY CAKE

INGREDIENTS-

180 grams butter (6 ozs)
180 grams castor sugar (6 ozs).
3 eggs.
Milk (about ½ cup).
Essence (as desired).

180 grams S.R. flour (6 ozs).
90 grams plain flour (3 ozs).
120 grams cherries (4 ozs).

METHOD—
1. Second Cake Method. (page 154).
2. Put in a greased papered tin.
3. Cook in a moderate oven about ¾ to one hour.
4. May be iced when cold and decorated with cherries.

FRUIT CAKE

INGREDIENTS—

480 grams flour (1 lb)
pinch salt
360 grams butter (12 ozs).
360 grams sugar (12 ozs).
1 teaspoon cream of tartar.
½ teaspoon bi-carbonate soda.

1 cup raisins.
1 cup sultanas.
1 cup currants.
60 grams candied peel (2 ozs).
1 teaspoon lemon essence.
4 eggs.
Milk as required.

METHOD—
1. Second Cake Method (page 154). adding soda dissolved in milk last.
2. Turn into greased paper lined tin and bake in a moderate oven 2 to 2½ hours.

CHRISTMAS CAKE (Twelfth Cake)

INGREDIENTS—

480 grams butter (1lb).
480 grams sugar (1 lb).
9 eggs.
480 grams plain
   flour (1 lb).
120 grams S.R.
   flour (4 ozs).
480 grams currants (1 lb).
480 grams sultanas (1 lb).
480 grams raisins (1 lb).
240 grams dates (8 ozs).
120 grams almonds (4 ozs).
60 grams cherries (2 ozs).

180 grams mixed
   peel (6 ozs).
1 teaspoon essence
   of lemon.
1 teaspoon essence
   of almond.
½ teaspoon nutmeg.
1 teaspoon ground ginger.
1 teaspoon cinnamon.
¼ teaspoon crushed
   cloves.
½ cup of brandy,
   sherry or rum.

METHOD—

1. Prepare fruit, blanch and slit almonds, chop peel. Put into bowl. Add spirits. Cover and leave for an hour or two.
2. Line cake tins with one layer of brown paper or alfoil and one layer of greased paper.
3. Cream butter and sugar well.
4. Add eggs one at a time, beating well between each.
5. Add fruit, peel and essence.
6. Sift in flour and spice. Stir and mix well.
7. Two thirds fill cake tin. Make shallow hollow in centre of cake.
8. Put cake in slow oven. If mixture is made into one cake it will take 5 to 6 hours to cook, two cakes 3 to 4 hours.
9. Test centre of cake with fine skewer. If cake is cooked skewer will come away clean.
10. Leave in tins until cake is cold.

CHOCOLATE CAKE 1 (Two Minutes)

INGREDIENTS—

1 cup S.R. flour.
¾ cup sugar.
30 grams butter (1 oz).
2 dessertspoons cocoa.

¾ cup milk.
1 egg.
Flavouring.

Chocolate Cake 1 (Two Minutes) — Continued.

METHOD—

1. Sift flour and cocoa.
2. Add sugar. Make well in centre.
3. Melt butter.
4. Pour into well, butter, unbeaten egg, milk and flavouring Stir well.
5. Beat mixture for 2 minutes.
6. Turn into greased sandwich tin. Bake in moderate oven 25 minutes.

CHOCOLATE CAKE No. 2

INGREDIENTS—

120 grams butter (4 ozs).
150 grams sugar (5 ozs).
2 eggs.
Vanilla essence.
180 grams S.R. flour (6 ozs).
Cake tin — 17 cms (7 inch).

3 level tablespoons cocoa.
1 dessertspoon coffee essence.
Milk — about 4 tablespoons.

METHOD—

1. Cream butter and sugar. Add eggs one at a time, beat well.
2. Sift flour and cocoa.
3. Mix coffee essence and vanilla essence with half the milk.
4. Mix flour and milk alternately into the butter, sugar and eggs.
5. Bake in a greased cake tin for 45 minutes in moderate oven. Ice when cold.

SHERRY ICING

4 tablespoons icing sugar mixed with 1 dessertspoon of butter and a little sherry.

CHOCOLATE GLACE ICING

½ cup brown sugar.
1 level teaspoon butter.
1 tablespoon water.

1 level tablespoon glucose.

METHOD—

1. Bring above ingredients to boil. Cool slightly.
2. Stir in 2 tablespoons of grated cooking chocolate. Mix till smooth.

RAINBOW CAKE

INGREDIENTS—

240 grams butter (8 ozs).
240 grams sugar (8 ozs).
4 eggs.
2 cups flour.
2 teaspoons cocoa.
Small cup milk.

2 teaspoons cream
  of tartar.
1 teaspoon bi-carbonate of
  soda.
Pinch salt.
Cochineal.

METHOD—

1. Second Cake Method (page 154).
2. Divide into three parts colouring one with cocoa and another with cochineal. Put in 3 greased sandwich tins.
3. Bake in a moderate oven for 15 to 20 minutes.
4. When cold, put cakes together with filling. See recipe filling for Snow Balls (page 159).

SHORT BREAD (No. 1).

INGREDIENTS—

240 grams butter (8 ozs).
150 grams castor
  sugar (5 ozs).

Yolk of egg.
480 grams flour (1 lb).

METHOD—

1. Second Cake Method (page 154).
2. Turn to a floured board, and knead till soft and even.
3. Press into shape with hand, roll perfectly smooth 1½ cms. thick (½ in.).
4. Pinch round edges with fingers and prick all over with fork.
5. Place on a greased scone tray.
6. Bake in a very moderate oven 30 to 40 minutes.

Note—May be decorated with dried fruits, candied peel or carraway seeds. The mixture may be used for biscuits.

SHORT BREAD (No. 2)

INGREDIENTS—

420 grams flour. (14 ozs)
60 grams rice flour
  or arrowroot (2 ozs).

240 grams butter (8 ozs).
150 grams castor
  sugar (5 ozs).

Short Bread (No. 2) — Continued.

METHOD—

1. Sift flours on to board.
2. Mix in sugar.
3. Place butter in centre and gradually knead in flour and sugar.
4. When well kneaded, roll out 1½ cms (½ inch) thick.
5. Mark edge and decorate. Place on greased slide.
6. Bake in very moderate oven 30 to 40 minutes.

RULES FOR THIRD CAKE METHOD

1. Beat eggs and sugar until thick and creamy.
2. Add flavouring, sifted flour and cream of tartar.
3. Fold flour in lightly using knife.
4. Dissolve bi-carbonate soda in a little warm water or milk and add to mixture.
5. Pour into well-greased tins dusted with corn flour.
6. Bake in moderate oven.

Note—See Homely Measurements (page 18).

VICTORIA SANDWICH (No. 1)

INGREDIENTS—

4 eggs.
¾ cup sugar.
1 cup flour.
½ teaspoon cream
   of tartar.

¼ teaspoon bi-carbonate
   soda.
Flavouring.
Self-raising flour may
   be used if preferred.

METHOD—

Third cake method (page 169).

Note—If only 3 eggs are used add 2 tablespoons of boiling water last.

Bake in a moderate oven about 15 minutes.

VICTORIA SANDWICH (No. 2)

INGREDIENTS—

3 eggs.

3 tablespoons self-
raising flour.

3 tablespoons sugar.

1½ tablespoons boiling
water.

METHOD—

1. Put sugar in bowl, add boiling water.
2. Add eggs, beat well 15 to 20 minutes.
3. Sift in flour. Mix lightly.
4. Pour into greased tins (small size).
5. Bake in moderate oven 10 to 15 minutes.

SWISS ROLL

INGREDIENTS—

1. Use No. 1 Sandwich Recipe, turning mixture into a
   well-greased tin. Cook in moderate oven 10 to 15
   minutes.
2. When cooked turn on to clean tea towel, slightly damp. Roll
   quickly and leave 3 minutes.
3. Unroll, spread with jam. Roll tightly.
4. When cold, trim ends, dust with icing sugar.

GOLDEN WATTLE SPONGE

INGREDIENTS—

4 eggs and weight of 3 eggs in castor sugar and weight of 2 eggs
in plain flour.

Flavouring.

METHOD—

1. Beat yolks and sugar well.
2. Beat whites until stiff. Stir yolks into whites.
3. Add flavouring and twice sifted flour. Fold in lightly.
4. Put into greased mould or deep tin which has been sprinkled
   lightly with equal parts of cornflour and castor sugar.
5. Bake about ¾ hour in a moderate oven.

Note—This recipe is suitable for sponge fingers.

GOLDEN WATTLE SANDWICH

INGREDIENTS—

4 eggs
¾ cup sugar.
1 cup flour.
3 teaspoons butter.
3 tablespoons milk.

1 level teaspoon of
  cream of tartar.
½ level teaspoon
  bi-carbonate soda.
Flavouring.

METHOD—

1. Beat whites of eggs to stiff froth.
2. Beat yolks of eggs and sugar 5 minutes.
3. Add whites to yolks and sugar. Beat 15 minutes.
4. Add sifted flour and cream of tartar, mix lightly.
5. Add melted butter, then soda dissolved in warm milk.
6. Add flavouring.
7. Pour mixture into prepared tins.
8. Bake in moderate oven 15 ot 20 minutes.

Note—This recipe may be used for chocolate sponge, by adding 1
   tablespoon of cocoa or chocolate (melted).

CINNAMON SPONGE

INGREDIENTS—

3 eggs.
1 cup sugar.
1 cup plain flour.
2 tablespoons butter.
2 teaspoons cinnamon.

1 tablespoon hot water.
1 teaspoon cream
  of tartar.
½ teaspoon bi-carbonate
  of soda.

METHOD—

1. Beat eggs and sugar till thick.
2. Sift in flour, cream of tartar, soda, cinnamon. Mix lightly.
3. Melt butter in hot water, then add.
4. Pour into greased tins (large).
5. Bake in moderate oven 15 minutes.

PERTH SPONGE

INGREDIENTS—

4 eggs.
120 grams sugar (4 ozs).
30 grams cornflour (1 oz).

90 grams self-raising
  flour (3 ozs).
1 tablespoon water.
Essence.

Perth Sponge — Continued.

METHOD—

1. Beat eggs and water.
2. Add sugar gradually beating till thick, about 7 minutes.
3. Fold in sifted flour and cornflour.
4. Add essence, put in prepared tins.
5. Bake in moderate oven for 15 to 20 minutes.

GINGER SPONGE

INGREDIENTS—

4 eggs.
½ cup sugar.
½ cup cornflour.
2 tablespoons flour.
2 teaspoons ground ginger.
2 teaspoons cinnamon.
1 teaspoon cocoa.
1 small teaspoon cream of tartar.
½ small teaspoon bi-carbonate of soda.
1 dessertspoon golden syrup.

METHOD—

1. Beat eggs well, add sugar, beat till thick.
2. Add golden syrup.
3. Sift in cornflour, flour, ginger, cinnamon, cocoa, cream of tartar and soda.
4. Stir in very lightly.
5. Put in well greased tins, bake in moderate oven for 15 to 20 minutes.
6. Fill with whipped cream.

AIRLIE SANDWICH

INGREDIENTS—

4 eggs.
Weight of 3 eggs in sugar.
Weight of 2 eggs in self-raising flour.

METHOD—

1. Beat yolks and sugar.
2. Add stiffly beaten whites of eggs, beat 5 minutes.
3. Mix in flour lightly.
4. Pour into prepared tins.
5. Bake in moderate oven for 15 to 20 minutes.

MERINGUES

INGREDIENTS—

Whites of 4 eggs.
¼ teaspoon cream of
    tartar or
1 teaspoon vinegar.

Flavouring.
8 tablespoons
    castor sugar.
Cream.

METHOD—

1. Beat whites stiffly.
2. Add sugar half tablespoon at a time. Beat well.
3. Add cream of tartar and flavouring. Beat well.
4. Place in teaspoon heaps on greased paper. Bake in a very slow oven about 2 hours.
5. When cooked store for use as required.

Note—Meringues may be cooked for 1 hour only, taken out, the soft centre removed, and shell filled with whipped cream.

PAVLOVA CAKE

INGREDIENTS—

Whites of 4 eggs.
8 tablespoons castor sugar.
¼ teaspoon cream of tartar
    or
1 teaspoon vinegar

½ teaspoon vanilla
Cream, strawberries,
    pineapple or passion
    fruit.

METHOD—

1. Whip whites of eggs till stiff.
2. Gradually add sugar, beating well.
3. Add vanilla and cream of tartar or vinegar.
4. Put mixture into tin lined with rice paper or grease tin and wet.
5. Cook in slow oven for ½ hour and stored heat for ¾ hour.
6. Allow to stand a few minutes.
7. Turn on to serving dish (bottom side up).
8. Cover with whipped cream.
9. Garnish with strawberries, chopped pineapple or passion fruit.

GOLDEN LILIES

INGREDIENTS—

4 eggs.
3 tablespoons sugar.
Flavouring.

2 heaped tablespoons
self-raising flour.

METHOD—

1. Third Cake Method (page 169). Drop in tablespoonsful on
   cold greased oven tray. Bake in moderate oven for 10
   minutes.
2. Take out and twist into cone shaped moulds immediately.
3. When cold fill with whipped cream. Decorate with angelica
   and cherries.

OTHELLOS AND DESDEMONAS

INGREDIENTS—

4 eggs.
90 grams castor
   sugar (3 ozs).

90 grams flour (3 ozs).
Flavouring.
Pinch salt.

METHOD—

1. Cream yolks of eggs and half the sugar.
2. Beat whites of eggs stiffly, add the remainder of the sugar
   and beat well. Add to the yolks.
3. Fold in the twice sifted flour, adding flavouring and salt.
4. Place in teaspoon heaps on a greased paper and bake in a
   moderate oven about 5 minutes.
5. Place two together with cream between, ice and decorate.
6. These shells should be made at least one day before they are
   to be iced.
7. Ice Desdemonas with white icing and decorate with
   chocolate.
8. Ice Othellos with chocolate icing and decorate with white
   icing.
9. Shells will keep for an indefinite period in an air tight box.

CREAM PUFFS

INGREDIENTS—

120 grams flour
  (plain) (4 ozs).
3 eggs.
60 grams butter (2 ozs).
1¼ cups water.

½ teaspoon vanilla.
1 tablespoon icing.
  sugar.
Unscalded cream.

METHOD—

1. Put water and butter in a saucepan. Bring to boil.
2. Add flour, beat till smooth. Stir over heat until mixture leaves the side of saucepan.
3. Beat eggs well.
4. When mixture is cool add eggs gradually, beating well.
5. Mix well, put in small heaps on greased slide.
6. Bake in a moderately hot oven 20 to 30 minutes. Decrease heat when brown and set.
7. When cold, make an opening in side. Remove centre.
8. Whip cream, add icing sugar and vanilla.
9. Fill puffs with cream, sprinkle with icing sugar.
10. A little rasberry jam may be put in before cream.

ECLAIRS

METHOD—

1. Use cream puff recipe and method.
2. Pipe mixture on to greased tin in lengths, 7 cms. (3 ins).
3. Cook in moderately hot oven.
4. When cold fill with whipped cream, flavoured with vanilla and a little icing sugar.
5. Ice with chocolate or coffee icing.

DUTCH CAKE

INGREDIENTS—

120 grams plain
  flour (4 ozs).
Pinch of salt.

90 grams butter
  or lard (3 ozs).
Cold water. Lemon juice.

Make into flaky pastry (see page 139).

Dutch Cake — Continued.

Cake Mixture

90 grams butter (3 Ozs)
60 grams sugar (2 ozs).
1 egg.
1 cup self-raising
  flour.

½ teaspoon cinnamon
  or mixed spice.
2 tablespoons chopped
  walnuts.
Milk (if necessary)

METHOD—

1. Make pastry and line a large sandwich tin. Keep some strips for top of cake.
2. Spread pastry thinly with jam.
3. Make cake mixture by second method cake making (page 154).
4. Spread cake mixture in tin, place strips of pastry on top, lattice fashion.
5. Bake in a moderate oven with good heat at bottom to cook pastry.
6. Bake 15 to 20 minutes. Test carefully to make sure cake is cooked underneath.
7. Ice with thin icing.

TOPPING FOR TEA CAKE

INGREDIENTS—

Grated rind and juice of half a large lemon.
2 tablespoons sugar.

METHOD—

1. Mix lemon rind, juice and sugar until dissolved.
2. Pour over cake when it is still fairly hot.

BISCUITS

Note—See Homely Measurements — Page 18.

GINGER NUTS

INGREDIENTS—

½ cup treacle.
½ cup sugar.
2 tablespoons hot water.
3 tablespoons butter or
  good beef dripping.
Sufficient flour to make
  a very stiff paste.
  (approximately 3 cups).

2 teaspoons cinnamon.
2 teaspoons ginger.
2 teaspoons mixed spice.
1 teaspoon bi-carbonate
  soda.
1 teaspoon cream
  of tartar.
½ teaspoon salt.

METHOD—

1. Sift 1 cup of flour, with the cream of tartar, soda and salt, and add spices. Mix well.
2. Stir treacle, sugar, hot water and melted butter together. Add to mixture as much extra flour as is necessary to make a firm dough.
3. Roll out thinly, cut in rounds, Bake on greased tin in slow oven for 10 to 15 minutes.

Note—This mixture makes about 100 biscuits.

GINGER SNAPS

INGREDIENTS—

180 grams S.R.
  flour (6 ozs).
120 grams sugar (4 ozs).
60 grams butter
  or substitute (2 ozs).
1 egg.

1½ level teaspoons
  ground ginger.
1½ level teasoons
  bi-carbonate of soda.
1 tablespoon
  golden syrup.

METHOD—

1. Mix all dry ingredients.
2. Melt butter with golden syrup. Cool.
3. Beat egg then add to butter and syrup.
4. Add dry ingredients.
5. Roll into small balls, put on greased oven slide, flatten with a fork. Leave room for biscuits to spread.
6. Bake in a moderate oven for 10 to 15 minutes.
7. Store in airtight container.

NUTTIES

INGREDIENTS—

½ cup butter.
¾ cup sugar.
1 egg.
1 cup chopped dates.
1 cup chopped walnuts.

1 teaspoon of cinnamon.
1½ cups plain flour.
1 teaspoon bicarbonate of soda,
   dissolved in 1 tablespoon
   boiling water.

METHOD—

1. Cream butter, sugar. Add egg, beat well.
2. Add dates, nuts and cinnamon.
3. Add sifted flour.
4. Add dissolved soda.
5. Put in small heaps well apart on a greased slide.
6. Bake in a moderate oven for 10 to 15 minutes.

VANILLA BISCUITS

INGREDIENTS—

240 grams flour (½ plain
   and ½ selfraising)
   (8 ozs).
120 grams sugar (4 ozs).

1 egg.
120 grams butter (4 ozs).
Blanched almonds.
Essence vanilla.

METHOD—

1. Make by Second Cake Method (page 154). using yolk of egg
   only.
2. Turn on to a floured board, knead lightly.
3. Roll out thinly, stamp into rounds.
4. Glaze with white of egg and put half an almond on each
   biscuit. Place on greased slide.
5. Bake in a very moderate oven about 10 minutes.

SHREWSBURY BISCUITS

INGREDIENTS—

150 grams butter (5 ozs).
120 grams sugar (4 ozs).
Grated rind of lemon.
1 egg.

240 grams flour (½ plain
   and ½ selfraising)
   (8 ozs).
Pinch salt.

Shrewsbury Biscuits - Continued.

METHOD—

1. Second Cake Method (page 154).
2. Turn on to a floured board. Roll out ½ cm. thick (¼ inch)..
3. Cut into shapes. Place on greased slide.
4. Bake in moderate oven about 15 minutes.

Note—Biscuits may be sprinkled with cinnamon and castor sugar before baking.

ALMOND FINGERS

INGREDIENTS—

120 grams butter (4 ozs).
240 grams flour (½ plain and ½ selfraising) (8 ozs).
1 egg.

120 grams sugar (4 ozs).
½ cup chopped almonds.
120 grams icing sugar (4 ozs).
Essence.

METHOD—

1. Make by Second Cake Method (page 154) keeping white of egg for top.
2. Turn on to floured board, roll out ½ cm. thick (¼ inch). Trim. Brush lightly with white of egg.
3. Beat white of egg stiffly, adding icing sugar and spread over pastry. Sprinkle thickly with chopped almonds.
4. Cut in finger shaped biscuits and place on greased oven slide.
5. Cook in a very moderate oven with good heat at bottom for about 10 to 15 minutes.

BRAN BISCUITS

INGREDIENTS—

1¼ cups self-raising flour.
2 cups bran.

120 grams butter (4 ozs).
½ cup sugar.
2 eggs and milk.

METHOD—

1. Cream butter and sugar.
2. Add eggs. Beat well.
3. Add flour, bran. Mix in a little milk.
4. Mix and knead on a board.
5. Roll out, cut in rounds.
6. Put on greased slide, bake in moderate oven till light brown, about 15 minutes.

WHEAT MEAL BISCUITS

INGREDIENTS—

240 grams flour (8 ozs).
240 grams fine
  wheatmeal (8 ozs).
180 grams butter (6 ozs).
1 egg.

120 grams sugar (4 ozs).
½ teaspoon bicarbonate of soda.
1 teaspoon cream of
  tartar.
Little milk.

METHOD—

1. First Cake Method (page 148).
2. Turn on to a floured board, roll out thinly.
3. Stamp into rounds, place on greased slide and bake a pale
    brown in moderate oven, about 15 minutes.

Note—Oatmeal may be used instead of wheatmeal.

CRISPIES

INGREDIENTS—

240 grams butter
  or substitute (8 ozs).
1 cup sugar.
2 teaspoons treacle.
2 cups rolled oats.
1 teaspoon vanilla.

2 cups self-raising
  flour.
1 teaspoon bi-carbonate
  soda.
3 tablespoons boiling
  water.

METHOD—

1. Beat butter and sugar to a cream. Add treacle.
2. Dissolve soda in hot water, then add.
3. Add oats and flour, then vanilla.
4. Mix and put into small heaps well apart on a greased slide.
5. Bake in moderate oven till brown (about 15 minutes).
6. Keep in air tight tins.

CORNFLAKE BISCUITS

INGREDIENTS—

120 grams butter (4 ozs).
1 egg.
2 tablespoons sugar.
½ cup chopped dates.

¼ cup chopped walnuts.
1 cup self-raising
  flour.
Cornflakes.

Cornflake Biscuits — Continued.

METHOD—
1. Cream butter and sugar, add egg, mix well.
2. Add dates, nuts, flour, mix.
3. Take small heaps of mixture, roll in cornflakes.
4. Place on greased slide, bake in moderate oven for 10 to 15 minutes.

DATE SLICE

INGREDIENTS—

180 grams plain flour (6 ozs).
60 grams cornflour (2 ozs).
1 teaspoon cream of tartar.
Pinch of salt.

½ teaspoon bi-carbonate of soda.
120 grams butter. (4ozs).
60 grams castor sugar (2 ozs).
1 egg.

FILLING

240 grams dates (8 ozs).
60 grams chopped walnuts (2 ozs).
1 teaspoon cinnamon.

Juice and rind of one orange.
1 tablespoon water.

METHOD—
1. Put ingredients for filling in a saucepan, cook to a smooth paste. Cool.
2. Sift flour, cornflour, rising and salt.
3. Rub butter into flour etc. Add sugar.
4. Mix to a stiff dough with beaten egg and a little water if necessary. Cut into two even pieces.
5. Roll one piece of dough to size and shape of oblong baking tin. Spread on greased tin.
6. Spread date filling on biscuit mixture.
7. Roll out second piece, cover date filling. Flatten and prick surface.
8. Bake in moderate oven for 20 to 30 minutes.
9. While still warm ice with orange icing and sprinkle with chopped nuts.
10. When cold cut into fingers.

CORNFLAKE MERINGUES

INGREDIENTS—

Whites of 2 eggs.
1 small cup sugar.
2 tablespoons butter

¾ cup chopped walnuts.
½ cup coconut.
4 cups cornflakes.

METHOD—

1. Beat egg whites till stiff. Add sugar gradually, beating well.
2. Add melted butter, nuts, coconut, pinch of salt and cornflakes. Mix well.
3. Place in heaps on greased slide, bake in slow oven till firm (about 20 minutes).
4. Keep in airtight tin.

DATE SHELLS

INGREDIENTS—

180 grams S.R. flour (6 ozs)
180 grams plain
   flour (6 ozs).
180 grams butter (6 ozs).

180 grams sugar (6 ozs).
480 grams dates (1 lb).
1 egg.

METHOD—

1. First Cake Method (page 148).
2. Turn on to floured board.
3. Roll out thinly. Cut into oblong strips.
4. Place a stoned date on each strip and roll up.
5. Place on greased slide.
6. Bake in moderate oven about 10 minutes.

VENETIAN BISCUITS

INGREDIENTS—

120 grams butter (4 ozs).
120 grams sugar (4 ozs).
3 yolks of eggs.
Vanilla essence.

240 grams plain flour (8 ozs).
120 grams chopped
   nuts (4 ozs).

METHOD—

1. Cream butter and sugar. Add egg yolks, beat well.
2. Add chopped nuts and vanilla.
3. Mix in sifted flour.
4. Roll into small balls, put on greased slide. Press with fork.
5. Bake in very moderate oven for 10 to 15 minutes.

RICH CHOCOLATE BISCUITS

INGREDIENTS—

120 grams margarine
or substitute (4 ozs).
60 grams castor
sugar (2 ozs).
180 grams S.R. flour (6 ozs).

2 level tablespoons sweetened
condensed milk.
120 grams dark cooking
chocolate (4 ozs).

METHOD—

1. Cream margarine and sugar. Add milk, mix well.
2. Add chocolate cut in small pieces or grated.
3. Add flour. Roll into small balls. coat with extra castor sugar.
4. Place on greased tray, press with fork.
5. Cook in moderate oven for 10 to 15 minutes.

RICE BUBBLES AND HONEY BISCUITS
(No Cooking)

INGREDIENTS

120 grams butter
or substitute (4 ozs).
90 grams sugar (3 ozs).
2 tablespoons honey.

Pinch bi-carbonate
of soda.
4 cups rice bubbles.

METHOD—

1. Dissolve butter, sugar and honey.
2. Add pinch of soda then rice bubbles. Mix well.
3. Press into oblong tin.
4. When cold, cut in fingers.

WALNUT AND FRUIT FINGERS

INGREDIENTS—

120 grams butter
or substitute (4 ozs).
120 grams sugar (4 ozs).
1 egg.

1 cup S.R. flour
½ cup chopped walnuts.
1 cup chopped dates or
raisins or mixed fruit.

METHOD—

1. Melt butter and sugar. Add walnuts and fruit.
2. Add flour and beaten egg. Mix well.
3. Put into greased oblong tray. Press evenly.
4. Cook in moderate oven for 15 to 20 minutes.
5. Cut with sharp knife while still warm.

MELTING MOMENTS

INGREDIENTS—

120 grams butter (4 ozs).   30 grams cornflour (1 oz).
60 grams icing sugar   1 cup S.R. flour.
   (2 ozs).

METHOD—

1. Melt butter, beat in icing sugar.
2. Add sifted flour and cornflour. Mix well.
3. Roll into balls, place on greased tray, press down with a fork.
4. Bake in very moderate oven till golden brown (about 15 to 20 minutes).
5. When cold stick two together with filling.

FILLING

4 tablespoons icing sugar   1 tablespoon milk.
1 tablespoon butter (melted). 1 teaspoon vanilla.

METHOD—

Mix all ingredients to make a creamy mixture.

BISCUIT CUTTING — USEFUL HINT

1. Knead biscuit mixture into an even roll.
2. With a sharp knife cut across roll in thin slices.
3. Place rounds on greased oven slide, bake as for various biscuit recipes which require rolling and stamping out with cutter.
4. If necessary, put rolls in refrigerator to set firmly before cutting.
5. Rolls of mixture may be kept in refrigerator and used as required.

ICINGS and FILLINGS

LEMON ICING

INGREDIENTS—

1 cup icing sugar
  (sifted).
Sufficient fruit juice
  to mix.

Other fruit juices may
  be substituted for lemon.

CHOCOLATE ICING

INGREDIENTS—

1 cup icing sugar.
1 or 2 tablespoons
  boiling water.

1 tablespoon cocoa
  (dark).
1 teaspoon butter.

METHOD—

1. Mix cocoa with boiling water.
2. Add melted butter and sifted sugar.
3. Beat well. Warm slightly.

ALMOND ICING

INGREDIENTS—

480 grams icing
  sugar (1 lb).
240 grams almond
  meal (8 ozs).

3 yolks of eggs.
Sherry, orange juice or
  rum to moisten.
½ teaspoon almond essence.

METHOD—

1. Roll and sift sugar. Add almond meal. Mix well.
2. Add beaten yolks of eggs, almond essence and sherry. Take
   care not to make mixture too moist.
3. Roll mixture out to required shape.
4. Brush cake with beaten white of egg.
5. Apply icing, pressing it to cake. Smooth.

ROYAL ICING

INGREDIENTS—

960 grams icing sugar
(2 lbs).
Whites of 4 eggs.
Few drops of blue water.

Lemon or rose water
flavouring.
1 small tablespoon
glucose.

METHOD—
1. Roll and sift sugar.
2. Beat whites of eggs slightly.
3. Stir in sugar gradually. Add flavouring and blue water and glucose.
4. Beat till perfectly smooth and glossy.
5. Cover with a damp cloth while icing.
6. Use less glucose when icing is to be used for piping.

7 MINUTE FROSTING

INGREDIENTS—

¾ cup sugar.
2 tablespoons water.

1 white of egg.
Pinch cream of tartar.

METHOD—
1. Put all ingredients in double saucepan. Stand over heat and whip till stiff (about 7 minutes).
2. Remove from stove and whip a little longer.
3. Pour over cake. Decorate as desired — chopped nuts, ginger, orange rind, angelica, etc.

MOCHA ICING or CAKE FILLING

INGREDIENTS—

180 grams butter (6 ozs).
or 120 grams butter
(4 ozs) and 1 table-
spoon boiling water.
Flavouring.

240 grams icing sugar
(8 ozs).
1 teaspoon strong black
coffee or coffee
essence.

METHOD—
1. Cream butter and sugar.
2. Add flavouring. Beat well.

VIENNA ICING or CAKE FILLING

INGREDIENTS—

As for Mocha Icing substituting other flavouring for coffee and adding colouring.

METHOD—

As for Mocha Icing.

GLACE ICING

INGREDIENTS—

360 grams icing sugar (12 ozs).
3 tablespoons boiling water or hot fruit juice.
Mix well and use immediately.

COFFEE GLACE

INGREDIENTS—

360 grams icing sugar (12 ozs).
3 tablespoons of hot, black strong coffee.
Mix well and use at once.

PLASTIC ICING

INGREDIENTS—

1 cup sugar.
½ cup water.
240 grams liquid glucose (8 ozs).

1 kilogram and 130 grams icing sugar (2½ lbs).
1 teaspoon gelatine.

In hot weather 1 tablespoon of glycerine may also be used.

METHOD—

1. Put sugar, water, glucose into saucepan. Boil to 110C (230F) degrees or soft ball stage. Remove from heat. Cool.
2. Add gelatine dissolved in warm water, colouring and essence.
3. Stir in small quantity icing sugar.
4. When stiff enough to pour, turn into well of sifted icing sugar on table.
5. Knead until firm and pliable. Roll and cut into shape.
6. Brush cake with white of egg and cover with plastic icing. Press and smooth.

BOILED ICING

INGREDIENTS—

1 cup sugar.
½ cup water.

¼ teaspoon cream of
tartar.

METHOD—

1. Boil all together for 15 minutes.
2. Cool a little, beat until creamy. Flavour.

COCONUT ICING

INGREDIENTS—

1 teaspoon butter.
¾ cup milk.

2 cups sugar.
1 cup coconut.

METHOD—

1. Boil sugar, water and butter ¼ hour.
2. Pour into basin. Stir till cold. Add coconut.

PASSION FRUIT FILLING

INGREDIENTS—

8 tablespoons icing sugar.
1 tablespoon butter.

2 passion fruit.

METHOD—

1. Mix all together till smooth and creamy.

DATE FILLING

INGREDIENTS—

240 grams stoned dates
(8 ozs).
½ teaspoon butter.

1 tablespoon boiling
water.
Juice of ½ a lemon.

METHOD—

1. Cut dates small.
2. Melt butter. Add water, lemon juice and dates.
3. Beat until smooth and soft.

MOCK CREAM (1)

INGREDIENTS—

2 tablespoons butter.
2 tablespoons icing
  sugar.
2 tablespoons milk.

1 tablespoon boiling
  water.
Flavouring.

METHOD—

1. Mix butter and sugar to a cream.
2. Add milk very gradually, mixing well all the time.
3. Add boiling water last, beat well.
4. Add flavouring.

MOCK CREAM (2)

INGREDIENTS—

2 tablespoons sugar
  (icing).

1 teaspoon fruit juice.
1 tablespoon butter.

METHOD—

1. Beat butter and sugar till creamy.
2. Add fruit juice.

MOCK CREAM (3)

INGREDIENTS—

1 small dessertspoon
  cornflour.
¼ cup icing sugar.

1 cup milk.
1 small tablespoon
  butter.

METHOD—

1. Blend cornflour with milk, stir over heat till boiling. Cool.
2. Cream butter and sugar.
3. Add cornflour a little at a time to butter and sugar. Beat until smooth.
4. Add flavouring.

LEMON CHEESE

INGREDIENTS—

120 grams sugar (4 ozs).
Juice of 2 lemons, grated
  rind of 1 lemon.

2 eggs (yolks only).
60 grams butter (2 ozs).

Lemon Cheese — Continued.

METHOD—

1. Beat egg yolks.
2. Put all ingredients into saucepan.
3. Stir over heat until thickness of honey.

BANANA FILLING

INGREDIENTS—

1 banana.   ½ cup cream.
1 teaspoon sugar.   3 or 4 drops vanilla.

METHOD—

1. Pulp banana, sprinkle with sugar.
2. Add whipped cream and vanilla. Do not beat.

TOPPING FOR TEA CAKE

INGREDIENTS—

60 grams butter (2 ozs)   60 grams blanched
60 grams sugar (2 ozs)   almonds (2 ozs)
1 tablespoon milk.   1 teaspoon flour.

METHOD—

1. Mix above ingredients and boil for 3 minutes.
2. Spread over cooked cake.
3. Return to slightly hotter oven until topping is brown and crisp.

BREAD MAKING

NOTES ON BREADMAKING

INGREDIENTS—
1. Bread is composed of flour, yeast, sugar, salt and tepid water.
2. Flour is composed mainly of starch and gluten cells.
3. Yeast is a minute plant composed of tiny cells.
4. Warmth, moisture and food (starch and sugar) cause these cells to grow and multiply.
5. Great heat or cold kills the yeast plant; salt retards its growth.
6. Yeast breaks sugar up into carbon dioxide (CO_2) and alcohol. The gas thus formed causes bread to rise.
7. Tepid water is made up of 1 part boiling water and 2 parts cold water.
8. Potato water is preferable to plain.

Note—See Homely Measurements — Page 18.

HOP YEAST

INGREDIENTS—
1 large potato.
2½ cups water.
1 teaspoon hops.
1 tablespoon flour.
1 tablespoon sugar.

METHOD—
1. Boil potato, add hops while still boiling. Boil 20 minutes.
2. Strain and cool. Add flour and sugar.
3. Bottle and cork tightly.
4. The yeast should work in a few hours in a bottle previously used for yeast, 24 hours in a new bottle.
5. A fig or a raisin added to yeast will make it work more quickly.

ACID YEAST

INGREDIENTS—
Medium potato.
1½ tablespoons sugar.
2 teaspoons flour.
½ teaspoon citric or tartaric acid.
1 cup warm water

Acid Yeast — Continued.

METHOD—

1. Boil and mash potato. Add other ingredients and sufficient water to keep mixture at cupful.
2. Bottle and cork tightly.
3. Keep in a warm place 12 hours in an old yeast bottle and 24 hours (at least) in a new bottle.

WHITE BREAD

INGREDIENTS—

720 grams flour (1½ lbs).
2 cups of tepid water.
2 teaspoons sugar.
1 teaspoon salt.

2 tablespoons home-made or 1 level tablespoon brewers' yeast, or 15 grams (½ oz) compressed yeast.

METHOD—

1. Sift and warm 480 grams (1 lb.) of the flour. Make well in centre.
2. Beat yeast and sugar.
3. Pour yeast and tepid water into flour and stir to a moist dough. Beat well.
4. Cover and stand in a warm place till the dough doubles its size (brewers' yeast takes about 1 hour and home-made several hours).
5. Turn on to a floured board and knead in the extra 240 grams (½ lb.) flour and salt until the dough is of even texture.
6. Shape into loaf. Put into greased and floured tins.
7. Allow to rise in a warm place until double its size, about ½ hour.
8. Cook in a hot oven until the loaf is well risen and brown, then in a cooler part until the bread is cooked through — 40 to 50 minutes in all.
9. When cooked, the bread should give a hollow sound when tapped on the bottom.

Vienna Bread—The above mixture, if made with milk instead of water, will make Vienna Bread and plain rolls.

WHEATEN MEAL BREAD

Follow recipe for White Bread using fine wheaten meal or half wheaten meal and half plain white flour.

More moisture and longer cooking may be required.

YEAST BUNS

INGREDIENTS—

480 grams flour (1 lb).
Level tablespoon yeast.
60 grams butter (2 ozs).
1 egg.
1½ cups milk.

½ cup sugar.
½ cup mixed fruit.
Level teaspoon salt.
Pinch of cinnamon, spice,
    ginger and nutmeg.

METHOD—

1. Sift and warm flour, cream yeast and teaspoon of sugar.
2. Melt butter, add milk and beaten egg.
3. Add warm liquids to yeast. Stir into flour. Mix until smooth. Beat well.
4. Cover and allow to rise until double the size (about 1 hour). Keep warm.
5. Stir in sugar, spices, fruit and salt.
6. Turn on to a floured board. Knead in 1 cup extra flour.
7. Divide into 16 or 18 buns, quickly knead each into a smooth ball.
8. Put on a greased baking tin about 1½ cms (½ in.) apart.
9. Cover and allow to rise until double the size. Keep warm.
10. Bake in a hot oven about 15 minutes.
11. Glaze immediately they are removed from the oven.
12. *Glaze*—2 tablespoons sugar, 2 tablespoons water and ¼ teaspoon of cream of tartar boiled for five minutes. Apply boiling with a brush.

Note—This mixture may be put in a tin for a currant loaf. If fruit and spices are omitted it may be used for milk rolls.

FRUIT LOAF

INGREDIENTS—

Bread dough as per
  recipe (page 192).
60 grams butter (2 ozs).
30 grams mixed
  peel (1 oz).

½ cup currants.
1 tablespoon sugar.
½ cup sultanas.
1 teaspoon mixed spice.

METHOD—

1. Make dough as for bread. When ready knead in melted
    butter, fruit, sugar, spice and chopped peel. Mix well.
2. Knead lightly and put into greased and floured tin.
3. Allow to rise until double the size. Keep warm.
4. Bake in a hot oven until well cooked, about 40 minutes.
5. Glaze with boiled sugar and water.

SALLY LUNNS

INGREDIENTS—

480 grams flour (1 lb).
30 grams butter (1 oz).
1 dessertspoon yeast.
1 teaspoon sugar.

1 egg.
1¾ cups milk.
Pinch salt.

METHOD—

1. Warm sifted flour and salt.
2. Cream yeast and sugar, add warm milk, beaten egg and
    melted butter.
3. Add to the warm flour and beat thoroughly.
4. Put into a greased cake tin.
5. Allow to rise in a warm place about 1 hour.
6. Bake in a hot oven about 20 minutes.
7. Glaze with boiled sugar and water as soon as removed from
    oven.

Note—May be cooked in three or four separate tins if liked.

VIENNA BREAD

INGREDIENTS—

720 grams flour (Vienna
if possible) (1½ lbs).
2 teaspoons sugar.
1 tablespoon yeast.

30 grams butter (1 oz).
1½ cups milk.
1 teaspoon salt.

METHOD—

1. Sift flour and warm. (Keep about 1/3 of flour for kneading).
2. Melt butter and add milk.
3. Cream yeast and sugar and add to it the tepid butter and milk. Add salt.
4. Add to the flour and beat to a stiff batter.
5. Cover and allow to rise double the size.
6. Turn on to a well floured board, knead and cut into small rolls, horseshoe twists or any fancy shape desired.
7. Place on a greased and floured baking tin. Allow to rise about ½ hour.
8. Bake in a hot oven about 10 minutes.
9. Brush with egg or milk, put back in oven for 5 minutes.

Note—TO MAKE THE HORSESHOE TWIST.

1. Roll out dough ½ cm (¼ inch) thick and cut into triangular shapes. Damp edges.
2. Roll base of triangle to the apex — the apex ends on the top side of the roll.
3. Curve to a horseshoe shape.

CRUMPETS

INGREDIENTS—

480 grams flour (1 lb).
30 grams butter (1 oz).
1 level dessertspoon
yeast.

1 dessertspoon sugar.
1 cup milk.
Level teaspoon salt.
1 egg.

Crumpets — Continued.

METHOD—

1. Sift flour and salt and warm.
2. Melt butter and add milk.
3. Cream yeast and sugar. Add beaten egg, warmed milk and butter.
4. Add mixture to flour. Beat well.
5. Cover and set to rise in a warm place about 1 hour or until double the size.
6. Drop in tablespoon heaps on a greased and hot girdle.
7. Brown well on both sides. One side should be porous.
8. Serve hot, toasted and buttered.

SAVOURIES

1. The Savoury is quite an important feature at a dinner, luncheon or supper party.

2. Savouries should be dainty, appetising and tasty.

3. They are more tedious than difficult to make, and require a little thought to gain variety.

4. An after dinner savoury must be simple. At luncheon where the savoury very often takes the place of the entree, something more substantial may be given, the latter would also apply to the supper.

5. Savouries may be served hot or cold, and they must be daintily garnished.

Note—See Homely Measurements — Page 18.

SAVOURY EGGS

INGREDIENTS—

6 eggs
60 grams butter (2 ozs).
1 dessertspoon finely
  chopped parsley.

1 teaspoon lemon juice.
Salt and pepper to
  taste.
Lettuce.

Other Flavourings—Curry powder, mayonnaise, anchovy sauce or other savoury sauces.

Garnishes Sliced olives or gherkins, small pieces capsicum, cocktail onions.

METHOD—

1. Hard boil eggs, see page 22. Cool and shell carefully.
2. Cut eggs in halves, removing yolk. Cut a small piece off end of each half white so that egg will stand.
3. Rub yolks through a strainer, add butter, mix well.
4. Add lemon juice, salt and pepper and another flavouring if desired.
5. Fill egg whites with mixture. Garnish.
6. Stand eggs on a dish of lettuce leaves.

BAKED TOMATOES and EGGS

INGREDIENTS—

Even sized tomatoes.   Eggs.
Seasoning.

METHOD—

1. Slice tops off tomatoes.
2. Scoop out pulp. (Keep for soups, etc.)
3. Break egg into cup, then pour into tomato. Add seasoning.
4. Bake gently until tomato is soft and egg is set.
5. Serve on rounds of buttered toast.

SCOTCH EGGS

INGREDIENTS—

4 hardboiled eggs.   1 egg.
2 large sausages.   Breadcrumbs.
Salt, pepper if necessary.   Fat for frying.

METHOD—

1. Hard boil eggs (page 22). Remove shells.
2. Remove skins from sausages, divide sausage meat into 4
   sections.
3. Flatten out sections of sausage meat, brush over with beaten
   egg. Cover each egg with meat, keeping the mould.
4. Dip in egg and breadcrumbs.
5. Fry in deep fat till brown.
6. Cut each egg in half.
7. Arrange in a bed of cress or lettuce leaves. Can be served hot
   or cold.

CELERY SAVOURY

INGREDIENTS—

Celery   Egg mixture as for
Salt.   savoury eggs.
Lettuce.

METHOD—

1. Wash celery, scrub and cut into 10 cms (4 in.) lengths.
2. Sprinkle lightly with salt.
3. Fill groove with mixture as for savoury eggs.
4. Place on a plate of young lettuce leaves.
5. Garnish with cress.

DEVILLED ALMONDS

INGREDIENTS—

120 grams almonds (4 ozs).   Salt.
Level teaspoon butter.   Cayenne.

METHOD—

1. Blanch and dry almonds and place in an enamel pan with butter.
2. Cook gently, turning frequently until a light brown.
3. Turn on to kitchen paper, sprinkle with salt and cayenne.
4. Shake off loose salt.

SAVOURY BISCUITS

INGREDIENTS—

Dry biscuits.   Parmesan cheese.
Butter.   Salt and cayenne.

METHOD—

1. Butter the biscuits.
2. Put grated cheese in heaps.
3. Sprinkle with salt and cayenne.
4. Place in a moderate oven or toast until lightly browned.
5. Serve hot.

Note—Thick biscuits may be split.

CHEESE PUFFS

INGREDIENTS—

½ quantity Flaky or   1 hard boiled egg.
   rough pastry (page 139).   Cayenne and salt.
120 grams cheese (4 ozs).   Beaten egg.
30 grams butter (1 oz).

METHOD—

1. Make pastry, roll out thinly and cut into 7 cms (3 in.) squares.
2. Melt butter in saucepan, add grated cheese, salt, cayenne and finely chopped egg. Heat slowly stir well. Allow to cool.
3. Put a little mixture on each pastry.
4. Brush edges with egg, double opposite corners together.
5. Brush with egg.
6. Cook in a hot oven until brown, 10 to 15 minutes.
7. Serve hot.

CHEESE STRAWS

INGREDIENTS—

180 grams flour (6 ozs).
120 grams cheese (4 ozs).
90 grams butter (3 ozs).
Salt spoon salt.

1 yolk of egg.
Little cold water.
Salt spoon cayenne.

METHOD—

1. Sift flour and salt.
2. Rub butter in with finger tips.
3. Add grated cheese, cayenne, beaten yolk and little water, mix to a stiff paste.
4. Turn on to a lightly floured board, knead lightly.
5. Roll out in strips 10 cms (4 in) wide, trim edge and cut in straws 1 cm (1/3 inch) thick.
6. Cut a few rings.
7. Cook in a very moderate oven until a pale brown for 7 to 10 minutes.
8. Serve bundle of straws in each ring.

OYSTER PATTIES

INGREDIENTS—

Rough Puff pastry.
2 doz. oysters, or
  1 small tin.
60 grams butter (2 ozs).
30 grams flour (1 oz).

½ cup oyster liquor.
½ cup milk.
1 tablespoon cream.
Salt, cayenne and
  parsley. Lemon.

METHOD—

1. Make pastry, roll out 1 cm (½ in.) thick, stamp in rounds, then mark with small cutter to half their depth.
2. Glaze and cook in hot oven for 10 to 15 minutes.
3. Melt butter, add flour, mix well. Add a little grated rind and teaspoon of juice of lemon, salt, cayenne, milk and oyster liquor. Stir over heat until it boils and cook gently a few minutes.
4. Remove from stove, add oysters, teaspoon of finely chopped parsley and cream.
5. Remove lids from patty cases and fill them with mixture, piling high in centre, put lids on.
6. Serve hot, garnished with sprigs of parsley.

CHEESE PASTRY

INGREDIENTS—

120 grams flour or flour
  and breadcrumbs (4 ozs).
45 grams butter (1½ ozs).
Cayenne.

3 tablespoons grated cheese.
Yolk of 1 egg.
Cold water.
Pinch salt.

METHOD—

1. Sift flour, cayenne and salt.
2. Add butter and rub in with finger tips. Add grated cheese.
3. Mix to a stiff paste with yolk of egg and little cold water.
4. Knead lightly, roll out and cut into desired shapes.
5. Bake in a moderate oven until pale brown, about 10 minutes.

Note—This pastry is used for biscuits, etc., for the foundation of savouries.

CROUTONS

1. Croutons may be made of fried or toasted bread, cut into various shapes.
2. Bread should be about 2 days old before using for croutons.

BREAD CASES

INGREDIENTS—

Thinly sliced day old
  bread.

Butter or substitute.

METHOD—

1. Soften butter, put a thick layer inside patty tins.
2. Cut bread into rounds to fit patty tins. Press rounds in firmly.
3. Brush bread with melted butter.
4. Bake in a low heat oven until dry and lightly browned.
   Bread cases may be stored and reheated when required.
   Use any suitable savoury filling.

CHEESE AIGRETTES

INGREDIENTS—

120 grams flour (4 ozs).
30 grams butter (1 oz).
½ cup water.

90 grams cheese (3 ozs).
2 eggs.
Cayenne and salt.

Cheese Aigrettes — Continued.

METHOD—

1. Boil butter and water.
2. Add sifted flour and salt, remove from heat and beat well.
3. Add cheese then eggs one at a time. Beat well.
4. Drop in small pieces into hot fat, cook gently until well puffed and a light brown.
5. Drain on kitchen paper, serve sprinkled with grated cheese.

MACARONI CHEESE

INGREDIENTS—

120 grams macaroni (4 ozs).
60 grams butter (2 ozs).
120 grams grated cheese (4 ozs).
1 tablespoon flour.

Breadcrumbs
2 cups milk.
Salt, cayenne and made mustard (¼ teaspoon).

METHOD—

1. Boil macaroni till soft then drain.
2. Make white sauce with butter, flour and milk.
3. Add macaroni, half cheese, seasoning, mustard.
4. Pour into greased pie dish, sprinkle with bread-crumbs, remainder of cheese and little butter on top.
5. Bake in a moderate oven until a pale brown.

Note—Pieces of ham or bacon may be added to mixture.

CHEESE BISCUITS

INGREDIENTS—

60 grams butter (2 ozs).
2 tablespoons flour.
2 tablespoons fine breadcrumbs.

2 tablespoons grated cheese.
Cayenne to taste.
¼ teaspoon celery salt.

METHOD—

1. Sift flour and salt.
2. Add other ingredients. Mix well and work together with fingers.
3. Roll out and cut into shape.
4. Bake in a slow oven until a pale brown, about 10 minutes.

Note—This mixture may be used for Cheese Straws.

ASPARAGUS MORNAY

INGREDIENTS—

1 tin asparagus pieces.
2 hard boiled eggs.
Melted butter sauce (page 125).

120 grams cheese, grated (4 ozs).
Fine breadcrumbs (dried)
Butter.

METHOD—

1. Drain liquid off asparagus and arrange in a buttered pyrex dish.
2. Arrange slices of egg on asparagus.
3. Make sauce, add half the cheese, pour over the asparagus and egg. Mix.
4. Sprinkle remainder of cheese and some breadcrumbs on top. Add a few small lumps of butter.
5. Bake in moderate oven till lightly browned.

Note 1—SWEET CORN may be used in the same way.

Note 2—A small cup of cooked rice may be added to the mixture.

Note 3—Mornay mixtures are enriched by the addition of cream.

WELSH RAREBIT

INGREDIENTS--

120 grams dry cheese (4 ozs).
2 tablespoons milk.
Pinch cayenne pepper.

¼ teaspoon made mustard.
1 teaspoon butter.
1 or 2 slices of hot buttered toast.

METHOD—

1. Grate cheese and place in saucepan, with milk, seasoning and butter.
2. Stir over heat until the mixture is perfectly smooth and beginning to thicken.
3. Pour mixture on to buttered toast, brown under griller and serve at once.

Note—The yolk of an egg may be added at the last. The egg makes it richer and prevents the cheese hardening so quickly.

SOUFFLE

INGREDIENTS—

3 eggs.
1 tablespoon flour.
2½ cups milk.

30 grams butter (1 oz).
Salt and pepper.

Flavouring . . . 1 large cup of one of the following: cooked fish (flaked), cooked meat (minced), cheese (grated).

METHOD—

1. Make a sauce with butter, flour and milk. Add beaten egg yolks, salt and pepper.
2. Stir in flavouring. Cool a little then fold in stiffly beaten egg whites.
3. Pour mixture into a well buttered oven dish, bake in a moderate oven for ½ an hour until well risen and brown.
4. Serve immediately.

BUBBLE BREAD

INGREDIENTS—

2 cups self-raising
  flour
1½ tablespoons butter.
Pinch salt.

¼ teaspoon cayenne.
4 tablespoons grated
  cheese.
Cold water.

METHOD—

1. Sift flour, salt, cayenne.
2. Rub butter and cheese into flour.
3. Mix to a stiff dough with cold water.
4. Roll out very thinly.
5. Cut into fingers or squares, bake in a slow oven till golden brown, about 10 minutes.

Note—Plain flour may be used instead of self-raising flour. Cheese may be omitted — use an extra tablespoon of butter.

SPICED GRAPE FRUIT

INGREDIENTS—

2 grapefruits.
2 level tablespoons
  sugar.

1 level teaspoon
  cinnamon.
4 tablespoons sherry.

Spiced Grape Fruit — Continued.

METHOD—
1. Cut grape fruit in halves. Cut fruit away from inside skin and cut across sections.
2. Sprinkle with sugar and cinnamon.
   Pour a tablespoon of sherry on each portion.
3. Place under griller until quite hot.
4. Top with cherry in centre and garnish with mint.

Spiced grape fruit should be served at the beginning of a dinner or lunch.

SANDWICHES

1. When uncut loaf of bread is used, cut just above lower hard crust and leave attached to end of loaf. This provides a firm base for slicing thinly.
2. To economise in quantity of butter and to facilitate spreading, prepare the following mixture.:—
   240 grams butter (8 ozs). ½ cup boiling water.
   Cut butter into small pieces, add boiling water. Beat well. A rotary beater or mix master is most suitable.
   This quantity will spread 2 large sandwich loaves.

SUITABLE FILLINGS
1. Sliced, skinned tomato with sprinkling of sugar and salt.
   Additions to above — grated cheese, sliced gherkin, mayonnaise, thinly sliced onion, finely chopped chives, finely chopped mint.
2. Cooked tomato and finely chopped onion, ¼ teaspoon herbs, salt and pepper. Stir in a beaten egg, heat slowly till thickened.
3. Salmon and thinly sliced cucumber.
4. Cheese with chutney, gherkins, pickle, onion, banana or dates.
5. Sardines and hot sauce.
6. Cooked brains with chopped mint or walnuts.
7. Preserved ginger and mayonnaise.
8. Celery (finely sliced) apple and dates.
9. Green peas (cooked) with chopped mint and a little cream or mayonnaise.
10. Cream cheese, smoked oysters and lemon juice.

Sandwich Fillings — Continued.

11. Hard boiled egg (have 1 egg softboiled) with curry powder, chopped parsley or chives, tomato sauce.
12. Thinly sliced or minced cooked meats of various kinds with flavourings e.g. mustard.
13. Meat, vegetable and fish pastes.
14. Asparagus. Mash and drain before spreading.

Note—A thick rich white sauce may form the base to which various ingredients may be added. Suitable additions — fish, minced meat, oysters, grated cheese, hard boiled egg, asparagus.

FILLINGS FOR SAVOURIES

Select suitable fillings from list under sandwiches.

Suitable garnishes — olives, cocktail onions, capsicum, nuts, dainty sprigs of parsley or mint, small thin wedges of lemon or orange, fancy shapes of cheese.

BOTTLING FRUIT

METHOD—

1. Use prime fruit in full season.
2. Have in readiness clean, dry jars, sound rubbers, perfectly fitting lids and a quantity of boiled water or syrup (cold).
3. *Syrup*—2 cups sugar to 4 cups of water. Bring to boil. Strain, if necessary and allow to cool.
4. Wash and prepare fruit. Use stainless steel knife.
   Apples and **pears,** peel thinly. **Quinces** peel thickly. Cut these fruits into halves or quarters, remove cores.
   Peaches — dip in boiling water to loosen skin. Cut in halves, remove stones.
   Apricots and **nectarines** — cut in halves, remove stones.
   Plums — cut in halves, remove stones or bottle whole.
   Berry fruits are bottled whole.

   Note—When preparing apples, quinces, pears and peaches drop pieces into cold water to prevent discoloration.
5. Fit rubbers on jars.
6. Pack prepared fruit neatly into empty jars, filling as full as possible.
7. Pour over boiled water or syrup, slowly, allowing liquid to sink well down, and avoid air bubbles. Fill to brim. Attach lids securely.
8. Stand bottles in boiler on a slab of wood or in a steriliser with cold water reaching half way up the bottles (no packing required). Bottles must not touch.
9. *Slow Method*—Bring water very slowly almost to simmering point. Maintain at even temperature about 2 hours. Slow cooking gives better colour, less broken fruit and clearer syrup.
10. Lift jars on to board or cloth. Tighten screw tops, or leave clips on jars until next day.
    Perfect sealing of jars is essential.
11. *Cooking before bottling* — Make syrup. Prepare fruit and bottles. Warm in oven. Put fruit into boiling syrup and simmer until tender. Pack fruit in jars. Re-heat syrup; pour in on fruit while hot, filling jars to the brim. Fasten lids on tightly while jars are hot.
12. *Oven Method* — Follow instructions given in Nos. 6 and 7. Stand jars in slow oven, on board or asbestos mat until fruit is cooked. Try with a skewer. Fill jars to brim with some boiling syrup. Fasten lids on tightly.

Bottling Fruit — Continued.

Reason for Fruit Rising in Jars—
   (a) Imperfect packing.
   (b) A sudden rise in temperature.
   (c) Too great heat.
   (d) Too heavy a syrup.
   (e) Over ripe fruit.
   If water is used for bottling, the fruit will keep, but must be sweetened before using.

BOTTLING VEGETABLES

METHOD—
   1. French beans, carrots, parsnips, asparagus, cauliflower, tomatoes and peas, if quite fresh are suitable for bottling.
   2. Choose best quality young vegetables.
   3. Have in readiness clean, hot jars, fresh rubbers, sound lids, boiling water and salt.
   4. Prepare vegetables as for ordinary cooking. Boil about 5 minutes or until just beginning to feel tender.
   5. Strain. Pack in hot jars.
   6. Fill to brim with boiling salted water.
   7. Adjust rubbers and covers exactly.
   8. Stand in steriliser or pan with warm water half way up. Add a handful of salt to water in steriliser to increase heat.
   9. Bring to boil. Boil ½ hour.
   10. Remove from steriliser. Screw tightly or see that clips are in place.
   11. Leave 24 to 48 hours and sterilise a second time.
   12. Tighten screw top. If clips are used, leave on for 36 hours.

Note—Re-Bottling Fruit and Vegetables. The jars which are capable of being hermetically sealed give the greatest success. They are so constructed as to form a vacuum during the heating process. The inside air is driven off, whilst the pressure of the heavier air outside prevents the lid from lifting, ensuring that the contents are air-tight.

Home Fruit Drying

Fruit contains fruit juices and fruit sugars, and, when ripe, contains a large amount of moisture. The sugar acts as a preservative, but the moisture must be driven off by evaporation. This can be done in four ways.

1. By sun-drying.
2. Drying in a heated oven.
3. By hanging in a warm, dry place.
4. By a process of dehydration.
   - (a) The first three methods are by far the most useful and successful for small quantities of fruit in home.
   - (b) *General Requirements*—Racks or trays or frames covered with hessian. A preserving pan or clean boiler, an improvised fumigating chamber, a wire basket.
   - (c) *Materials*—Sulphur and caustic soda.
   - (d) *Choice of Fruit*—Full ripe fruit, unblemished and clean.
   - (e) *Preparation of Fruit*—Fruits dried whole are figs, grapes (in small bunches). Apricots, peaches, plums (prunes), are cut in two and the stones removed. Apples, pears and quinces are peeled and cut into sections or sliced.
   - (f) *Processes*—

Lye should be mixed in an enamel, china, earthenware or copper vessel. Avoid using a tin vessel.

1. For figs, grapes and stone fruit have ready a pan of boiling lye (30 grams (1 oz) of caustic soda to 4½ litres (1 gal.) of water).
2. Place prepared fruit in a basket and dip quickly in and out of the boiling lye three times, counting 1, 2, 3, out, 1, 2, 3, out, 1, 2, 3; out.
3. Place separately on trays. Place trays in sunshine or dry by any of the first three methods.
4. Take care to cover when atmosphere is damp.
5. The time varies with size of fruit, weather conditions, different kinds of fruit.
6. Dry evenly.
8. Stack in heaps. Store in calico bags or boxes lined with grease-proof paper.

Fruits such as apples, pears and quinces prepare by peeling, coring and slicing. Do not dip these in lye solution, but fumigate by exposing to sulphur fumes for ¼ to ½ an hour, then drying in the same way as stone fruit.

Home Fruit Drying — Continued.

SULPHURING

(a) Use 480 grams (1 lb) of sulphur to each 2.83 cubic metres (100 cubic feet) of space in a box 1.37 metres (4½ feet) x 1.37 metres (4½ feet) x 1.37 metres (4½ feet). The box should contain trays about 15cms (6 ins.) apart, allowing air spaces front and back for fumes to circulate. A circular hole for the flue should be made in the centre of the floor of box protected by an iron tube to fit.

(b) Prepare a clean metal drum by cutting a circular hole in the centre of one of the long sides into which the flue of the box should fit. Cut out part of front, like the bars of a grate to admit air and make sulphur burn. Make sliding door at one end.

PROCESS—

Place box containing trays of fruit in position. Place sulphur on small dish, put into drum under flue, light with red hot coals. Close door securely. The draught of air will prevent fumes.

JAMS and JELLIES

Most fruits contain a jellying property, which is called "Pectin". This is found in fruit when it is ripening, but not in over-ripe fruit. Pectin begins to change into sugar when the fruit is ripe. It is the presence of pectin which enables jam to "jell' or set. Fruit, therefore, should be just under ripe when used for jam or jelly.

The best colour and flavour is produced in jam when it is at that stage.

Sugar is the preservative.

360 grams (¾ lb) to 480 grams (1 lb) of fruit is used.

The following notes apply generally to jam-making, but individual recipes show slight variations with regard to special fruits.

1. Use a thick sound preserving pan or saucepan. To prevent fruit sticking, grease bottom of pan with butter and put in three marbles.
2. Use jars or bottles with wide necks.
3. Rub bloom off fruit. Wash if necessary.
4. Cut stone fruit in two, and remove stone.
5. The addition of a little water gives clearness to jam and helps to prevent burning before juices begin to flow. Citrus fruits require a large amount of water.
6. Cook till fruit is tender before adding sugar. Stir at intervals.
7. Fast boiling after sugar is added gives best results. The jam is clearer and evaporation is quicker. Slow cooking spoils colour.
8. Test for "jell point" by cooling a little on a saucer. If it sets jam is cooked.
   Begin testing after 30 minutes boiling.
9. Heat jars before filling to prevent cracking and exclude the air.
10. Bottle while hot.
11. Paper is better for covering than tin lids.
12. Cut rounds of paper 2½ cms (1 inch) bigger than rim of bottle. Make a few slits round edges so they will overlap when pasted down. Brush paper with milk or flour paste. Cellophane may be used.
13. Jam should be neatly labelled and dated.

JELLY MAKING

In jelly making just under-ripe fruit gives the best results. The fruit must be perfectly clean, utensils and straining cloth clean, sugar free from specks. A chair inverted on a table with a clean tea towel tied at four corners to the legs make a good frame for draining. Place a basin under cloth to catch juice. Pour boiling water through cloth before using.

METHOD—

1. Wash fruit, cut apples, quinces into 4 or 6 pieces without removing skin. Grapes, cape gooseberries crush a little.
2. Put fruit into pan with sufficient water to well cover fruit.
3. Bring to boil and boil gently until soft, stirring occasionally.
4. Strain. Allow to drain without touching the pulp or the juice will become clouded.
5. Measure strained liquid, return to rinsed pan.
6. Heat again and add sugar to measure. 1 cup of liquid to 1 cup of sugar.
7. Boil quickly until it jells. This will be in about 20 minutes. Remove scum.
8. Test for "jell point". Pour slowly into heated jars while hot. Avoid bubbles.
9. Cover with paper or cellophane.

MARMALADE JELLY

INGREDIENTS—

6 oranges, 1 lemon or half and half.
Water.
Sugar (to measure).

METHOD—

1. Cut off about 1-3rd of the skins, coloured part only. shred finely. Keep separate.
2. Cut fruit up roughly (skins, seeds and pulp).
3. Place all in preserving pan and just cover with water.
4. Boil until quite tender.
5. Strain through prepared cloth.
6. Boil shredded skins separately until tender in a little water. Strain.
7. Measure fruit juice and add 1 cup of sugar to each cup of liquid. Bring to boil. Add shredded skins.
8. Boil until it reaches "jell" point.
9. Pour into hot jars. Cover and label when cold.

ORANGE JELLY (Preserve)

INGREDIENTS—

    6 oranges.   Water.

    1 lemon.   Sugar (to measure).

METHOD—

1. Wipe fruit.
2. Cut up roughly, using skins, seeds and pulp.
3. Cover well with water.
4. Boil until tender. Strain through prepared cloth.
5. Measure liquid. Add 1 cup of sugar to each cup of liquid.
6. Boil until it reaches "jell" point.
7. Pour into hot jars. Cover and label when cold.

LEMON JELLY

Make in the same way as for Orange Jelly, using all lemons.

CAPE GOOSEBERRY JELLY

METHOD—

1. Remove shells. Wash berries.
2. Cover well with water.
3. Boil until well broken down.
4. Strain through a prepared cloth.
5. Measure liquid. Add 1 cup of sugar to each cup of liquid.
6. Boil until it reaches "jell" point.
7. Pour into hot jars. Cover and label when cold.

APPLE JELLY

INGREDIENTS—

    3 kilograms of apples   Water.

      (6½ lbs).   Sugar (to measure).

    Juice of 1 lemon.   Sprigs of mint.

METHOD—

1. Wash or wipe apples. Cut up roughly. Put in large pan.
2. Cover with water.
3. Boil until tender and beginning to pulp. Strain through prepared cloth. Add lemon juice and mint.
4. Measure liquid. Add 1 cup of sugar to each cup of liquid.
5. Boil until it reaches "jell" point. Remove mint.
6. Pour into hot jars.
7. Cover and label when cold.

GUAVA JELLY

INGREDIENTS—

2¼ litres red guava
  (2 quarts).

2 lemons.
Sugar to measure.

METHOD—

1. Remove tops from guavas.
2. Cut up fruit. Put into preserving pan. Well cover with water.
3. Simmer for 2 hours. Strain.
4. Measure fruit juice and allow 1 cup sugar to each cup of juice.
5. Boil until "jell" point is reached.
6. Bottle at once in hot jars.
7. Cover and label when cold

QUINCE JELLY (No. 1)

METHOD—

1. Remove bloom and stalks from quinces.
2. Cut up rather small. Expose seed pods well.
3. Cover with plenty of water.
4. Cook steadily until soft and beginning to pulp.
5. Strain through prepared cloth.
6. Measure liquid. Add 1 cup sugar to each cup of liquid.
7. Boil until it reaches "jell" point.
8. Pour into hot jars.
9. Cover and label when cold.

QUINCE JELLY (No. 2)

INGREDIENTS—

6 large quinces (green).
3½ litres water (6 pints)

2 kilograms sugar
  (4 lbs 6 ozs).

METHOD—

1. Wipe quinces, cut off tops. Stand in a preserving pan with sugar and water.
2. Bring to boil and boil quickly till jell point is reached (about 2½ hours).
3. Drain off jelly and bottle in hot jars.
4. The fruit may be used for dessert.

LEMON AND MELON JELLY

INGREDIENTS—

5 kilograms melon (11 lbs)   Water.
8 lemons.   Sugar (to measure).

METHOD—

1. Cut up whole of the melon. Cover with water.
2. Cut up lemons roughly. Cover with boiling water in separate basin.
3. Next day boil all together until soft. Strain.
4. Measure. Allow 1 cup sugar to each cup liquid.
5. Boil until it reaches "jell" point.
6. Bottle at once. Cover and label when cold.

MARMALADE

INGREDIENTS—

6 large oranges.   4 litres of cold water
1 lemon.   (7 pints).
Sugar (to measure).

METHOD—

1. Wipe fruit.
2. Cut oranges and lemon in very thin slices, removing seeds. Cover with water and leave until next day.
3. Boil until skins are tender.
4. Measure and allow 1 cup sugar to each cup of fruit and liquid.
5. Boil until it reaches "jell point".
6. Pour into hot jars. Cover and label when cold.

Note—Use Seville oranges for a bitter marmalade.

Lemon Marmalade—Use all lemons and proceed in the same way.

CUMQUAT MARMALADE

METHOD—

1. Wash and wipe fruit.
2. Slice thinly. Remove seeds.
3. Put fruit into bowl. Cover with water. Stand over night.
4. Simmer fruit until tender and clear.
5. Measure fruit and water.
6. Add sugar (1 cup sugar to each cup fruit).
7. Add juice of ½ lemon to each cup fruit.
8. Boil quickly to jell point.
9. Bottle in hot jars. Cover and label when cold.

GRAPE FRUIT MARMALADE

METHOD—

1. Wipe fruit. Cut finely straight through.
2. Measure 1 cup of cut up fruit to
     2 cups water.
3. Boil until skin is tender. Test between fingers.
4. Measure again. Allow cup of sugar to each cup fruit and
     liquid.
5. Boil until it jells.
6. Pour into hot jars. Cover and label when cold.

DRIED APRICOT JAM

INGREDIENTS—

1 kilogram and 500 grams
   dried apricots
   (3 lbs 5 ozs).
3½ litres of water
   (3 quarts).

3 kilograms sugar
   (6lbs 10 ozs).
½ teaspoon essence almond.
60 grams blanched almonds
   (2 ozs).

METHOD—

1. Wash apricots. Soak overnight in the water.
2. Boil until soft. Stir frequently.
3. Add sugar and boil 1 hour or until setting point is reached.
4. Remove from stove. Add essence and split almonds.
5. Pour into hot jars. Cover and label when cold.

PLUM JAM

INGREDIENTS—

4 kilograms plums
   (8 lbs. 13 ozs).
1½ cups water.

3 kilograms sugar
   (6 lbs 10 ozs).

METHOD—

1. Wash plums. Cut up.
2. Add water and boil until soft.
3. Add sugar and boil to "jell" point.
4. Bottle at once in hot jars. Cover and label when cold.

Note—Remove stones if necessary.

LOQUAT JAM

METHOD—
1. Wash loquats. Split. Take out stones.
2. Put fruit into pan. Cover with water. Leave over night.
3. Boil until fruit is tender.
4. Measure fruit and liquid and allow ¾ cup sugar to each 1 cup of fruit.
5. Boil till a rich colour and syrup jells.
6. Bottle, cover, label when cold.

PASSION FRUIT JAM

INGREDIENTS—

2 kilograms fruit (ripe and smooth) (4 lbs 6 ozs).   Sugar (to measure).

METHOD—
1. Wipe or wash fruit.
2. Cut in two and scoop out pulp.
3. Cover skins with water and boil until inner part is tender.
4. Scoop out inside of skins and add to pulp.
5. Allow 1 cup of sugar to each cup of pulp.
6. Boil until it reaches "jell" point.
7. Pour into hot jars. Cover and label when cold.

CAPE GOOSEBERRY JAM

INGREDIENTS—

3 kilograms gooseberries (without shucks) (6 lbs. 10 ozs).
2½ cups water.

2 kilograms & 250 grams sugar (4 lbs 15 ozs).
2 lemons.

METHOD—
1. Wash berries, put in pan with juice of lemons and water. Cook till tender.
2. Add sugar and cook to "jell point".
3. Allow to cool slightly before bottling. Stir occasionally to keep berries through liquid.
4. Pour into hot jars. If fruit rises, stir with a long skewer.
5. Cover and label when cold.

Note—Cape gooseberries and melon make a very nice jam.

APRICOT JAM

INGREDIENTS—

4 kilograms apricots
  (8 lbs 13 ozs).
1 cup water.

3 kilograms sugar
  (6 lbs 10 ozs).

METHOD—

1. Wash, stone and cut up apricots, put into a large pan.
2. Crack 1-3rd of stones and add kernels to fruit.
3. Add water and boil until soft.
4. Add sugar and boil to "jell" point, stirring constantly.
5. Bottle in hot jars. Cover and label when cold.

FIG JAM

INGREDIENTS—

4 kilograms figs
  (8 lbs 13 ozs).
2 lemons.

3 kilograms sugar
  (6 lbs 10 ozs).

METHOD—

1. Wash figs. Cut up roughly, removing stalks.
2. Sprinkle over 2 cups of the sugar. Stand over night.
3. Add juice of lemons and skins (not cut up).
4. Boil until tender. Add rest of sugar, stir frequently.
5. Boil until a golden brown colour and at "jell" point. Remove
     lemon skins.
6. Bottle in hot jars. Cover and label when cold.

Note—Fig and satsuma plum in equal quantities make a good
   jam.

GRAPE JAM

INGREDIENTS—

4 kilograms grapes
  (8 lbs 13 ozs).
Juice of 2 lemons.

3 kilograms sugar
  (6 lbs 10 ozs).

METHOD—

1. Pluck grapes off bunches. Wash.
2. Put grapes in pan; press well. Add lemon juice.
3. When juice gathers, boil fruit until tender.
4. Add sugar. Remove seeds as they rise.
5. Boil until "jell" point is reached.
6. Bottle in hot jars. Cover and label when cold.

GRAPE AND APPLE JAM

INGREDIENTS—

3 kilograms grapes
(6 lbs 10 ozs).
1 kilogram apples
(2 lbs 3 ozs).

3 kilograms sugar
(6 lbs 10 ozs).
Juice of 2 lemons.

METHOD—

1. Wash fruit. Pluck grapes off bunches, slit or press.
2. Slice apples thinly leaving skin on. Discard cores.
3. Put fruit and lemon juice in pan. Cook gently until juice gathers, then boil until fruit is tender.
4. Add sugar. Boil until jam reaches "jell" point.
5. Stand for a little while, stir to bring seeds to top, skim off.
6. Bottle in warm jars. Cover and label when cold.

MOCK GINGER CONSERVE

INGREDIENTS—

4 kilograms melon
(weigh after cutting)
(8 lbs 13 ozs).
4 kilograms sugar
(8 lbs 13 ozs).
4½ litres water (1 gall.).

15 grams tartaric acid
(½ oz).
360 grams green ginger
(12 ozs).
150 grams lime
(unslaked) (5 ozs).

METHOD—

1. Soak lime in 2/3 of cold water overnight.
2. Next day cut melon into cubes, removing skin and seeds.
3. Strain lime. Pour lime water over the melon. Stand all night. Drain well.
4. Put into preserving pan with sugar and ginger (scraped and cut in thin slices).
5. Add acid and remaining one third of cold water.
6. Boil until a pretty golden colour (about 6 hours).
7. Bottle. Cover and label when cold.

Note—Do not use for at least 6 weeks.

QUINCE JAM

INGREDIENTS—

4 kilograms quinces
(8 lbs 13 ozs).
Water.

3 kilograms sugar
(6 lbs 10 ozs).

Quince Jam — Continued.
METHOD—
1. Wipe or wash quinces. Peel and core.
2. Put peel and seeds into saucepan. Cover barely with cold water. Boil until soft.
3. Strain liquid into preserving pan. Add fruit cut small.
4. Boil until quite tender, add sugar and boil until bright red colour and at "jell point".
5. Bottle in hot jars. Cover and label when cold.

MELON AND ORANGE JAM

INGREDIENTS—

4 kilograms melon (cut up) (8 lbs 13 ozs).
3 oranges.

3 kilograms sugar (6 lbs 10 ozs).

METHOD—
1. Cut melon into slices, seed, peel and cut up.
2. Weigh and place in a large bowl.
3. Peel oranges and shred skins finely. Cut fruit in thin slices, removing seeds.
4. Add to the melon and sprinkle over about 1 quarter of sugar. Stand over night.
5. Boil until melon is tender.
6. Add remainder of sugar and boil to "jell" point.
7. Bottle in hot jars. Cover and label when cold.

MELON AND LEMON JAM

Make as for Melon and Orange Jam, using lemons instead of oranges. The addition of 120 grams (4 ozs) of green ginger improves the flavour.

MELON AND DRIED APRICOT JAM

INGREDIENTS—

1 kilogram dried apricots (2 lbs 3 ozs).
2½ litres of water (2 quarts).
3 kilograms melon (6 lbs 10 ozs).

4 kilograms sugar (8 lbs 13 ozs).
1 teaspoon almond essence.
60 grams blanched almonds (2 ozs).

Melon and Dried Apricot Jam — Continued.

METHOD—

1. Wash apricots, soak over night in the water.
2. Cut melon into cubes, put in preserving pan, sprinkle with 2 cups of sugar, stand over night.
3. Boil melon until it begins to be tender, add apricots and water, boil till all fruit is tender.
4. Add remainder of sugar, boil for about 1 hour or until jam jells when tested.
5. Add essence and split almonds, bottle, cover and label when cold.

*Note—*Frequent stirring is necessary.

MELON AND GINGER JAM

INGREDIENTS—

4 kilograms and 500 grams melon (10 lbs).

3 kilograms and 175 grams sugar (7 lbs).

3 lemons.

240 grams preserved ginger (8 ozs).

½ level teaspoon cayenne (optional).

METHOD—

1. Slice, skin, seed and cut melon into squares.
2. Weigh and place melon in bowl with 1 quarter of sugar. Stand over night.
3. Add sliced ginger, cayenne, lemon juice and skins in halves.
4. Bring to boil. Cook till tender.
5. Add rest of sugar, boil until a golden colour and "jell" point.
6. Remove lemon skins.
7. Bottle in hot jars. Cover and label when cold.

PEAR GINGER CONSERVE

INGREDIENTS—

3 kilograms pears (6 lbs 10 ozs).

240 grams preserved ginger (8 ozs).

2 kilograms sugar (4 lbs 6 ozs).

1½ cups water.

Pear Ginger Conserve — Continued.

METHOD—
1. Peel and quarter pears. Add ginger cut in cubes.
2. Add sugar and water. Stand 24 hours.
3. Boil until a deep red colour.
4. Bottle in hot jars. Cover and label when cold.

*Note—*Make apple ginger by same recipe.

APPLE MARMALADE

INGREDIENTS—

1 kilogram of apples
  (2 lbs 3 ozs).
9 cups water.

1 kilogram lemons
  (2 lbs 3 ozs).
Sugar (to measure).

METHOD—
1. Peel lemons, shred skins finely. Cut lemons into thin slices, removing seeds.
2. Soak 24 hours in the water.
3. Peel, core and cut apples. Soak with lemons another 24 hours.
4. Boil without sugar until lemon skins are tender.
5. Measure fruit and liquid. Allow ¾ cup of sugar to each cup of liquid.
6. Add sugar and boil to "jell" point.
7. Pour into hot jars. Cover and label when cold.

QUINCE HONEY

INGREDIENTS—

5 large quinces.
2½ cups water

2 kilograms and 270 grams
sugar (5 lbs).

METHOD—
1. Peel, core and mince quinces.
2. Boil sugar and water to a syrup.
3. Drop quinces into boiling syrup.
4. Boil 20 minutes or until a nice pink colour.
5. Bottle in hot jars. Cover and label when cold.

PANCAKE BATTER

4oz Plain Flour or S.R.
Large pinch Salt
1 Standard Egg
½ Pint Milk
1 Tbls melted Butter or Marg.

1. Sift flour & salt in bowl.
2. Beat in unbeaten egg, to smooth, creamy batter, half the milk and butter.
3. Stir in remaining milk as required.

YORKSHIRE PUDD

2 oz butter or Marg
Make as for Pancakes.

TMENT CENTRE

uropathic Treatment

Telephone:
Harrogate 521164

ess.

aking over my Harrogate **Practice** on
ull-time in Scarborough.

ed Osteopath with a very caring personality.

ew premises —
ogate.   Tel. 521164. (The same).

$0\frac{1}{2}$ years.

ND.MRN.DO.MRO.

TOMATO JAM

INGREDIENTS—

4 kilograms and 500 grams
tomatoes (10 lbs).
1 kilogram sugar
(2 lbs 3 ozs).

2 tablespoons golden
syrup.
Juice of 2 lemons.

METHOD—

1. Skin tomatoes by first dipping them in boiling water.
2. Cut up tomatoes, boil to reduce liquid.
3. Add sugar, golden syrup, lemon juice. Boil quickly until jam jells when tested.
4. Bottle in hot jars. Cover and label when cold.

Note—This jam need a lot of boiling, owing to large quantity of water in tomatoes.

FIG PRESERVE

INGREDIENTS—

5 kilograms and 500 grams
figs (12 lbs 2 ozs).
3 kilograms and 630 grams
sugar (8 lbs).

1 cup water.
5 cups vinegar.
240 grams green ginger
(8 ozs).

METHOD—

1. Boil sugar, vinegar and water.
2. Cut stems off figs.
3. Put whole figs into vinegar, etc., also ginger tied in muslin.
4. Boil two hours. Remove ginger.
5. Bottle in hot jars. Cover and label when cold.

PULPED FRUIT JAM

INGREDIENTS—

Allow equal quantities of sugar and pulp.

METHOD—

1. Bring pulp to boil.
2. Add sugar.
3. Finish as other jams.

STRAWBERRY JAM

INGREDIENTS—

2 kilograms strawberries
(4 lbs 6 ozs).

1 kilogram and 500 grams
sugar (3 lbs 5 ozs).

METHOD—

1. Top and wash berries.
2. Sprinkle with half the sugar and leave over night.
3. Bring to boil. Add remainder of sugar.
4. Boil quickly until setting point.
5. Bottle in hot jars. Cover and label when cold.

MOCK STRAWBERRY JAM

INGREDIENTS—

3 kilograms plums
(satsuma) (6 lbs 10 ozs)
3 kilograms figs
(6 lbs 10 ozs).

4 kilograms and 500 grams
sugar (10 lbs.)
2 lemons.
2½ cups water.

METHOD—

1. Wash plums, halve and remove stones.
2. Put into large pan with water. Bring to boil.
3. Top and cut figs into halves. Add to plums. Boil until tender.
4. Add lemon juice and sugar.
5. Cook to setting point. Test.
6. Bottle in hot jars. Cover and label when cold.

PICKLES, Etc.

GREEN TOMATO PICKLE

INGREDIENTS—

2 kilograms and 750 grams green tomatoes (6 lbs).
1 kilogram and 375 grams onions (3 lbs).
1.75 litres vinegar (good quality) (3 pints)
360 grams treacle (12 ozs)
2 tablespoons mustard.

2 tablespoons flour.
1 tablespoon curry powder.
1 large teaspoon mixed spice.
2 dozen cloves.
½ level teaspoon cayenne
Salt.

METHOD—

1. Slice tomatoes and onions. Place in bowl, sprinkle well with salt; stand 12 hours.
2. Blend flour, mustard, cayenne, curry and spice with some of the vinegar.
3. Put into pan with rest of vinegar and treacle.
4. Strain water off tomatoes and onions. Add to vinegar etc.
5. Simmer for ¾ of an hour.
6. Bottle and cork when cold.

CAULIFLOWER PICKLE

INGREDIENTS—

1 medium cauliflower.
1.75 litres vinegar Good quality (3 pints).
3 tablespoons flour.
4 tablespoons mustard.

¼ teaspoon cayenne.
1 teaspoon curry.
240 grams sugar (8 ozs).
1 dessertspoon turmeric.

METHOD—

1. Cut cauliflower into small pieces. Sprinkle with salt and stand over night.
2. Bring vinegar to boil. Blend other ingredients with cold water and add. Boil 5 minutes.
3. Strain cauliflower and add it to vinegar etc.
4. Simmer gently about 15 minutes until tender but not soft.
5. Bottle and cork tightly or cover with wax when cold.

APPLE CHUTNEY (Cooked)

INGREDIENTS—

2 kilograms and 750 grams apples (6 lbs).
1 kilogram onions (2 lbs 3 ozs).
850 millilitres vinegar (1½ pints).
480 grams sugar (1 lb 1 oz).

480 grams raisins (1 lb 1 oz).
30 grams ground ginger (1 oz).
30 grams mixed spice (1 oz).
½ level teaspoon cayenne.
1 tablespoon salt.

METHOD—

1. Core and cut apples without peeling, chop raisins, peel and slice onions.
2. Boil apples and onions with vinegar and sugar until soft.
3. Allow to get cold. Add other ingredients. Mix well.
4. Bottle and cover with wax when cold.
5. Keep at least a month before using.

APPLE CHUTNEY (Uncooked)

INGREDIENTS—

1 kilogram apples (2 lbs 3 ozs).
1 kilogram raisins (2 lbs 3 ozs).
1 kilogram sugar (2 lbs 3 ozs).

850 millilitres vinegar (1½ pints).
15 grams garlic (½ oz).
1 level tablespoon salt.
½ level teaspoon cayenne.

METHOD—

1. Peel and core apples. Chop finely.
2. Wash, seed and chop raisins.
3. Chop garlic very finely.
4. Mix all ingredients in a bowl. Leave 3 days, stirring occasionally.
5. Bottle and cork or cover with wax.

TOMATO CHUTNEY

INGREDIENTS — SECTION 1

5 kilograms and 500 grams tomatoes (12 lbs 2 ozs).
120 grams shallots (4 ozs).
120 grams garlic (4 ozs).
15 grams each of mace, allspice, cloves (½ oz).

7 grams chillies (¼ oz).
90 grams salt (3 ozs).
7 grams pepper (¼ oz).
180 grams sugar (6 ozs).
30 grams ground ginger (1 oz).

METHOD—

1. Skin and cut up tomatoes, shallots and garlic.
2. Tie mace, cloves and allspice in a muslin bag.
3. Put all ingredients in section in a pan, boil for 2 hours, stirring frequently.

INGREDIENTS—SECTION 2

2 kilograms and 750 grams apples (peeled and sliced) (6 lbs).
480 grams sultanas (1 lb).

l kilogram sugar (2 lbs 3 ozs).
1.75 litres vinegar (3 pints).

METHOD—

Put all ingredients in another pan, boil till tender, stirring frequently.

Combine the two sections, boil for a few minutes.

Bottle and cork or cover with wax when cold.

LOQUAT CHUTNEY

INGREDIENTS—

2 kilograms and 750 grams loquats (after topping stoning) (6 lbs).
1 litre vinegar (1¾ pints)
1 kilogram and 800 grams sugar (4 lbs.)
480 grams seeded raisins and sultanas, mixed (1 lb).
3 level tablespoons salt.

2 level tablespoons ground ginger.
2 level teaspoons all spice or mixed spice.
½ level teaspoon cayenne pepper.
12 pepper corns.
12 cloves.
60 grams garlic — chopped or minced (2 ozs).

Loquat Chutney — Continued.

METHOD—

1. Chop or mince loquats, including skins.
2. Boil loquats and raisins in vinegar for 15 minutes.
3. Add sugar, boil for 15 minutes.
4. Add spices, etc. and boil until thick and brown.
5. Bottle while hot in hot jars.

PLUM SAUCE

INGREDIENTS—

2 kilograms and 750 grams satsuma plums (6 lbs).
1 kilogram and 360 grams sugar (3 lbs).
1.75 litres vinegar good quality (3 pints).
½ level teaspoon cayenne.

1 dessertspoon salt.
1 dessertspoon mixed spice.
1 dessertspoon cloves.
1 dessertspoon whole ginger (bruised).

METHOD—

1. Boil all ingredients together until stones separate.
2. Rub through strainer and bottle when cold.

TOMATO SAUCE (To Bottle)

INGREDIENTS—

4 kilograms and 540 grams tomatoes (10 lbs).
680 grams green apples (1lb 8 oz).
850 millilitres vinegar (1½ pints).
500 grams onions (1 lb 2 ozs).
1 level tablespoon white pepper.

1 level teaspoon cayenne.
15 grams cloves (½ oz).
15 grams whole ginger (½ oz).
15 grams whole allspice (½ oz).
30 grams garlic (1 oz).
120 grams salt (4 ozs).
1 kilogram sugar (2 lb 3 ozs).

METHOD—

1. Core apples, cut up tomatoes, apples and onions roughly.
2. Put into preserving pan. Add sugar, vinegar and spices.
3. Stir well and bring to boil. Boil 1 hour. Stir constantly.
4. Rub through strainer, bottle, cork and seal.

Note—For a mild sauce, decrease the amount of pepper and cayenne.

MUSHROOM KETCHUP

INGREDIENTS—

3 kilograms 170 grams
mushrooms (7 lbs).
120 grams salt. (4 ozs).

Allspice, ginger, mace,
whole pepper
(to measure).

METHOD—

1. Wash mushrooms and break into earthenware vessels. Sprinkle with salt and stand in a warm place about 14 hours.
2. Strain and measure liquid.
3. To each litre (1¾ pints) allow the following:—

    7 grams allspice (¼ oz), 7 grams ginger (¼ oz), 2 blades of mace, 30 grams whole pepper (1 oz).

4. Add spices to mushroom liquid. Boil for 30 minutes.
5. Strain, cool and bottle. Cork tightly.

PICKLED GRAPES

INGREDIENTS—

3 kilograms and 630 grams
grapes (large) (8 lbs).
1 litre vinegar
(1¾ pints).
120 grams sugar (4 ozs).
1 tablespoon cloves.

1 tablespoon whole spice.
1 level tablespoon white
pepper.
1 tablespoon whole ginger.
1 level tablespoon salt.

METHOD—

1. Fruit should be ripe but sound.
2. Cut grapes off bunches, leaving tiny piece of stalk on each grape. Wash and dry well.
3. Pack fruit in jars, shaking them well down.
4. Boil vinegar, spices, sugar and salt for 3 minutes and, when cold, pour over grapes.
5. Leave one week, drain off vinegar, bring to boil, cool and pour over grapes.
6. Cork tightly.

PICKLED RED CABBAGE

INGREDIENTS—

2 firm red cabbages
1 litre vinegar (1¾ pints)
240 grams sugar (8 ozs).
15 grams whole ginger
   (½ oz).

15 grams whole spice
   (½ oz).
15 grams peppercorns
   (½ oz).
10 cloves.

METHOD—

1. Cut cabbages in quarters. Remove hard stalks and decayed leaves. Wash.
2. Shred finely with a sharp knife.
3. Sprinkle shredded cabbage well with salt. Set aside in covered bowl 24 hours.
4. Strain and shake cabbage. Pack in jars.
5. Boil vinegar, sugar and spices for a few minutes. Strain and cool.
6. Pour vinegar over cabbage. See that cabbage is covered.
7. Cork tightly. The pickle is ready for use in one week.

PICKLED ONIONS

INGREDIENTS

1 kilogram pickling onions
   (2¼ lbs.)
750 mls. vinegar (3 metric cups).
240 grams sugar (8 ozs.)
30 grams peppercorns (1 oz.)

12 cloves
1 dessertspoon salt.
30 grams whole spice (1 oz.).
1 level teaspoon ground
   ginger.

METHOD—

1. Peel onions, wash and dry well. Pack tightly in jars.
2. Boil vinegar, spices, salt and sugar gently for 10 minutes, allow to cool.
3. Pour vinegar etc. over onions, covering well.
4. Cover jars. Keep for one month before using.

PICKLED PLUMS

INGREDIENTS—

2 kilograms and 750 grams
  plums (6 lbs).
3 cups sugar.
7 grams mace (¼ oz).
7 grams whole pepper
  (¼ oz).

1 litre vinegar,
  good quality (1¾ pints)
30 grams cloves (1 oz).
Stick of cinnamon.
15 grams whole allspice
  (½ oz).

METHOD—

1. Boil vinegar and flavourings 15 minutes. Strain over plums
   and stand 3 days.
2. Put into preserving pan and boil a few minutes.
3. Cool, bottle and cork tightly.

PICKLED FIGS

INGREDIENTS—

2 kilograms and 750 grams
  figs (6 lbs).
1 litre vinegar
  (1¾ pints).
240 grams sugar (8 ozs).
1 tablespoon salt.

Pinch cayenne.
1 tablespoon cloves.
1 tablespoon whole
  ginger.
½ tablespoon peppercorns.
½ tablespoon whole spice.

METHOD—

1. Wash and dry figs.
2. Put other ingredients in all together and boil ten minutes.
3. Drop figs into mixture. Leave 3 days.
4. Drain off vinegar and bring to boil.
5. Put figs in jars. Pour on vinegar.
6. Allow to stand five weeks before using.
7. Slightly under-ripe figs are best.

CANDIED PEEL

INGREDIENTS—

6 orange (or lemon) rinds.
6 cups sugar.

Salt.
3 cups water.

Candied Peel — Continued.

METHOD—
1. Soak rinds in slightly salted water for 3 days. Drain and rinse.
2. Boil slowly in fresh water until tender.
3. Make a syrup by boiling the sugar and 3 cups of water together for 5 minutes, keeping the pan uncovered.
4. Put rinds into a basin and cover with syrup. Leave for 2 days.
5. Strain off syrup and boil up again. Put in rinds. Boil until semi-transparent (about 20 minutes).
6. Take out rinds. Lay them on flat tins. Put a little of the syrup in the centre of each piece. Sprinkle with castor sugar. Dry a little in a cool oven.

MELON PICKLE

INGREDIENTS—

1 kilogram and 360 grams melon (3 lbs).
1 kilogram onions (2 lbs 3 ozs).
1 cup white sugar.
½ cup brown sugar.
2 dessertspoons salt.
1 teaspoon mixed spice.

1 dessertspoon turmeric.
1 dessertspoon mustard.
2 dessertspoons flour.
Vinegar.
½ level teaspoon cayenne or 7 grams chillies (¼ oz).

METHOD—
1. Cut up melon, removing skin and seeds. Barely cover with vinegar, stand overnight.
2. Add sliced onions, sugars, salt, mixed spice, cayenne.
3. Boil until melon and onion are tender.
4. Blend turmeric, mustard and flour with a little cold water.
5. Add to mixture, stir over heat until boiling.
6. Bottle and seal.

TO COVER PICKLES IN JARS

When jars have cooled, pour melted white wax on top of pickles. This keeps pickles moist.

TO PRESERVE OLIVES

Olives for preserving should be gathered before ripening. The object of pickling is to remove bitterness and preserve colour by impregnating with brine.

Place olives in lye composed of one part of quick-lime to six of ashes of young wood (sifted).

Leave for 12 hours then put into fresh water which is renewed every 24 hours for seven days.

Strain and put in a brine of common salt dissolved in water to which aromatic herbs are added. Should keep for 12 months.

SPICED PINEAPPLE

INGREDIENTS—

1 large can pineapple pieces
¾ cup pineapple syrup
¾ cup vinegar
1½ cups sugar
¼ teaspoon salt
8 cloves
10 centimetres stick cinnamon (4 inches)

METHOD—

1. Drain pineapple pieces reserving syrup.
2. Put syrup, vinegar, sugar, salt, cloves and cinnamon in a saucepan, boil for ten minutes.
3. Add pineapple, bring to boil.
4. When cold, bottle and store in refrigerator.
5. Serve with roast pork, any seasoned meat or poultry.

SALADS

FRUIT SALAD

Any kind of fruit in season may be used for salad, but no special flavour should predominate.

The following fruits are suitable — Orange, peach, nectarine, apples, passion fruit, apricot, mulberry, pineapple, strawberry, grapes, pear, banana.

METHOD—

1. Prepare fruit and slice thinly. Apples and other hard fruits should be chopped finely or grated.
2. Arrange fruits in layers in glass dish. Sprinkle each layer with castor sugar and squeeze over a little lemon juice to bring out the flavour. Add passion fruit pulp.
3. Let stand ½ hour.
4. Serve with cream, custard or icecream.

Note

1. Boiled custard is an economical substitute for cream.
2. Almonds may be blanched, chopped and sprinkled between the layers if liked.
3. Preserved fruit may be substituted for fresh.
4. Fruit should be cut up with stainless knife.

VEGETABLE SALADS

Vegetable salads may be made from raw or cooked vegetables.

Fruits such as oranges, pineapple and apples may be added.

Hard boiled eggs, small pieces of chicken, prawns, cheese, nuts, dates and raisins may be included.

Choice, fresh vegetables should be used.

Salads should be prepared near meal time or prepared earlier, covered and placed in refrigerator.

Suitable Raw Vegetables

Lettuce, cabbage, water cress, celery, cucumber, tomatoes, carrots, white onions, shallots, radishes, parsley, mint, chives, capsicums.

Vegetable Salads — Continued.

Suitable Cooked Vegetables

Potatoes, carrots, young white turnips, green peas, beetroot (cooked and pickled), lima, haricot or red beans, sweet corn, rice.

Vegetable salads are usually accompanied by a salad dressing.

PREPARATION

LETTUCE—

Discard coarse, outer leaves. Retain outer leaves which are tender.

Pull number of   leaves required off stem.

Wash thoroughly and drain off water. If leaves are limp soak in cold water until crisp. Long soaking reduces vitamin and mineral content.

CABBAGE —

Same as for lettuce.

WATER CRESS —

Wash very thoroughly. Make crisp if necessary.

CELERY —

Cut stalks into convenient lengths, wash thoroughly.

To curl celery, slit finely down stalk, soak in cold water until celery curls.

CUCUMBER —

Wash and dry. If skin is not tough, slice thinly leaving skin on. If skin is tough, peel off then run prongs of a fork down flesh. Cut in slices.

CARROT —

Scrape if necessary, wash and dry. Grate carrot or cut in fine match strips. Carrot may be cut in very thin slices then cut as for curled celery. Attractive shapes may be cut from carrots.

WHITE ONIONS —

Peel, then slice thinly or chop finely.

SHALLOTS —

Trim and wash.

RADISHES —

Top and tail, scrape if necessary. Radishes may be cut into fancy shapes. Slit into radishes, soak in cold water to open up cuts.

CAPSICUMS —

Wash and dry thoroughly. Cut in thin slices or small pieces. Reject seed centre.

Vegetable Salads — Continued.

TOMATOES —
    Wash and dry. Slice thinly or cut in wedges. If preferred, tomatoes may be skinned by dropping into boiling water. Remove skin as soon as it loosens.
PARSLEY AND MINT —
    Wash thoroughly, pick off dainty sprigs or chop finely.
CHIVES —
    Trim, wash and dry. Slice finely.

COOKED VEGETABLE

POTOES, CARROTS, WHITE TURNIP —
    Cut in dice.
BEETROOT —
    Slice or cut in dice
BEANS —
    Lima etc. must be soaked and boiled till tender but not broken.
SWEET CORN —
    Must be cooked till tender.

COOKED VEGETABLE SALAD

INGREDIENTS—

2 or 3 potatoes.	1 pickled beetroot.
1 cup cooked peas.	1 egg (hard boiled).
1 carrot.	Salt and pepper.
1 small turnip.	

METHOD—

1. Cook vegetables carefully. Cut into small dice.
2. Mix lightly. Season. Pile in glass dish.
3. Garnish with finely chopped parsley and grated yolk of egg.
4. Serve with melted butter or salad dressing.

RAW VEGETABLE SALAD

INGREDIENTS—

1 carrot.	1 cup dates or 3 table-
½ turnip.	spoons chopped nuts.
2 apples.	1 tablespoon sugar.
1 small onion.	1 teaspoon salt.
3 pieces celery.	Sliced banana
Juice of ½ lemon.	if liked.

Raw Vegetable Salad — Continued.

METHOD—

1. Peel vegetables, grate or mince finely.
2. Arrange in layers in glass dish, sprinkling lemon juice, salt and sugar between layers.
3. Spread chopped dates or nuts on top.
4. Serve with salad dressing or cream.

POTATO SALAD

INGREDIENTS—

500 grams cooked potatoes (1 lb 2 ozs).
1 white onion.
2 tablespoons of chopped mint.

1 hard boiled egg.
½ cup of salad cream dressing, or French dressing, salt, pepper.

METHOD—

1. Cut potatoes into cubes.
2. Put potato in basin, add chopped onion, mint and seasoning. Toss with two forks.
3. Add dressing. Mix well.
4. Put into dish, serve very cold.
5. Garnish with sliced egg or green peas (cooked).

*Note—*Basin may be rubbed with garlic if liked.

MIXED LETTUCE SALAD

1. Choose a large flat dish.
2. Arrange small lettuce leaves or pieces of torn lettuce leaves on dish.
3. Arrange additional pieces of food attractively. These may be tomatoes, radishes, celery, carrot, cucumber, capsicum, gherkins, hard boiled egg, chicken, prawns, orange, pineapple, apple, slices of ham (rolled).
4. Serve salad dressing separately.

TOSSED SALAD

INGREDIENTS—

Lettuce and French dressing.

1. Wash lettuce, make crisp. Drain well and dry without bruising leaves.
2. Tear lettuce into medium pieces.
3. Just before serving, sprinkle lettuce with French dressing. Toss lightly with salad servers.

COLE SLAW

INGREDIENTS—

4 cups finely shredded cabbage.
1 level teaspoon salt.
1 teaspoon grated onion.
6 tablespoons cream.

½ cup celery (sliced)
1 tablespoon sugar.
1 tablespoon vinegar.
1 tablespoon salad dressing with mustard.

METHOD—

1. Mix all ingredients except cabbage, together.
2. Pour over cabbage, toss lightly in a bowl.

BEAN SALAD

INGREDIENTS—

2 cups cooked and drained red, lima or haricot beans or mixed.
¼ cup shredded celery.
3 chopped pickled onions, cucumber or cauliflower.

1 small onion, minced or chopped.
2 hard boiled eggs (chopped).
1 level teaspoon salt.

Mix lightly with ½ cup salad dressing.

Serve on lettuce leaves or in a salad bowl. Sprinkle with grated cheese.

RICE SALAD

INGREDIENTS—

2 cups cooked rice.
½ cup sultanas.
½ cup grated carrot.

¼ cup chopped chives.
¼ cup drained sweetcorn
   kernels.
½ cup chopped capsicum.

METHOD—

Mix lightly with salad dressing or French dressing.

BOILED SALAD DRESSING (1)

INGREDIENTS—

3 eggs.
1 teaspoon mustard.
½ teaspoon salt.
3 tablespoons sugar.
Cayenne to taste
   (optional).

2 tablespoons melted
   butter.
1 cup milk or cream.
½ cup vinegar or lemon
   juice.

METHOD—

1. Beat eggs, add milk and melted butter.
2. Mix mustard, salt, sugar, cayenne with vinegar. Add gradually
   to eggs, etc.
3. Put mixture in a double saucepan, stir over heat till mixture
   resembles custard.
4. When cold, bottle. This dressing keeps well.

SALAD DRESSING (2)

INGREDIENTS—

1 egg.
2 tablespoons condensed
   milk.
2 saltspoons salt, pepper.

2 tablespoons lemon juice
   or vinegar.
1 teaspoon melted butter.
1 saltspoon mixed mustard.

METHOD—

1. Separate white from yolk of egg.
2. Add to yolk the milk. Blend well.
3. Add seasonings and melted butter and mustard.
4. Add vinegar or lemon juice gradually, stirring and blending all
   the time.
5. Stir in stiffly beaten white of egg.

Note—The mixture should be of the consistency of cream. If too
   thick add some fresh milk.

SALAD DRESSING (3)

INGREDIENTS—

1 teaspoon melted butter.
1 saltspoon salt, pepper.
Pinch of cayenne.
1 saltspoon mustard.

3 tablespoons condensed
   milk.
4 tablespoons vinegar.
1 tablespoon fresh milk.

METHOD—

1. Melt butter, add mustard, seasoning and condensed milk. Mix
   well.
2. Add vinegar gradually, stirring all the time.
3. Add the fresh milk.

Olive oil may be used instead of butter in each recipe.

MELTED BUTTER

INGREDIENTS—

2 tablespoons butter
Pinch cayenne.

1 teaspoon lemon juice.

METHOD—

Melt and skim well.

BEETROOT PICKLING VINEGAR

Mix 1 cup vinegar, 2 tablespoons sugar, 5 cloves
   and 5 peppercorns. Boil for 5 minutes. Pour
   over cooked beetroot.

FRENCH DRESSING

INGREDIENTS—

1 tablespoon sugar.
1 teaspoon paprika.
¼ teaspoon pepper.
½ teaspoon salt.
1 teaspoon mustard.

1 clove garlic or
   1 teaspoon onion juice
   (optional).
¾ cup salad or olive oil.
¼ cup vinegar.

METHOD—

1. Mix dry ingredients together with vinegar.
2. Add oil, put in jar, cover securely, shake well. Before using
   shake until oil and vinegar mix.

INVALID COOKING

GENERAL RULES

1. Food for the sick should be light, nourishing and easily digested.
2. Vary the food as much as possible. Use only freshest ingredients.
3. Prepare only small quantities and so avoid waste.
4. Do not over sweeten or over flavour food.
5. Two Golden Rules are —
   (a) Give little food at a time and give it often.
   (b) Serve it as daintily as possible.
6. Never leave food in the sick room.
7. Do not present the same food a second time.
8. Remove every particle of fat from soups, broths or beef tea.
9. Serve meals punctually and carefully. Note the amount taken.
10. Serve hot foods very hot. Cold foods very cold.
11. Avoid alcoholic drinks unless ordered by doctor.
12. Perfect cleanliness is necessary in preparation of food.

LEMONADE

INGREDIENTS—

1 lemon.
1 tablespoon sugar.

2½ cups of boiling water.

METHOD—

1. Peel lemon thinly, putting rind and sugar in jug.
2. Add boiling water. Cover. Stand till cold, add lemon juice.
3. Strain. Chill.

MILK ARROWROOT

INGREDIENTS—

1 teaspoon of arrowroot.
1 cup milk.

1 teaspoon sugar.
Pinch of salt.

Milk Arrowroot — Continued.

METHOD—

1. Blend arrowroot with a little cold milk.
2. Boil remainder of milk and pour on the arrowroot, stirring all the time.
3. Add sugar and salt.
4. Serve in cup with saucer.

Note—If cornflour is used instead of arrowroot, it must be returned to the saucepan, brought to boil. Boil 3 minutes.

WATER ARROWROOT

INGREDIENTS—

1 teaspoon arrowroot.
1 cup boiling water.
1 teaspoon sugar.

½ teaspoon butter or lemon juice.

METHOD—

Make by same method as milk arrowroot, adding sugar and butter before serving.

EGG FLIP

INGREDIENTS—

1 fresh egg.
¾ cup milk.

1 teaspoon sugar.

METHOD—

1. Beat egg and sugar thoroughly.
2. Add milk.
3. Strain into tumbler and serve.
4. Nutmeg may be grated on top.

THICK BARLEY WATER

INGREDIENTS—

1 tablespoon pearl barley.
½ rind of small lemon.
Sweeten to taste.

1 litre of water (1¾ pints).

Thick Barley Water — Continued.

METHOD—

1. Wash barley and put on to boil in 1 cup of water.
2. When it comes to boil, pour away water.
3. Add remainder of water and pinch of salt and simmer gently for 2 hours.
4. Strain barley water on to sugar and lemon rind.
5. Allow to cool, stirring occasionally to prevent jellying.
6. Remove lemon rind before serving.

THIN BARLEY WATER

Make as for thick barley water, boiling only 20 minutes.

GRUEL

INGREDIENTS—

1 tablespoon oatmeal   Pinch of salt.
  or substitute.   2 cups of milk.

METHOD—

1. Mix all ingredients together and allow to stand for ½ hour.
2. Strain through muslin, pressing out as much liquid as possible.
3. Put liquid into saucepan and stir till boiling.
4. Sweeten to taste.
5. Serve in a cup with saucer.
6. If allowed, a little nutmeg and butter may be added.

STANDARD BEEF TEA

INGREDIENTS—

240 grams gravy beef   2½ cups water.
  (8 ozs).   ½ teaspoon salt.

METHOD—

1. Remove fat and skin. Mince meat finely.
2. Put into jar with water and salt. Let stand 1 hour to extract red juice. Stir occasionally.
3. Cover jar closely and stand in saucepan of water. Heat slowly but do not boil.
4. Strain and press out as much of juice as possible.
5. Serve hot with fingers of toast.

LEMON SPONGE

INGREDIENTS—

2 level dessertspoons
gelatine
2 cups water including
lemon juice.

2 lemons
3 level tablespoons
sugar.
2 eggs, whites only.

METHOD—

1. Soak gelatine in 1 tablespoon of water.
2. Put in saucepan, water and lemon juice, sugar and thin strips of lemon rind. Bring to boil.
3. Add gelatine, stir till dissolved. Strain.
4. Leave to cool.
5. Gradually stir in well beaten white of egg. Beat until cold and thick.
6. Turn into wet mould.
7. When set, turn into glass dish, serve with whipped cream or custard.

SIBERIAN CREAM

INGREDIENTS—

1¼ cups milk.
1 tablespoon sugar.
2 eggs.
2 tablespoons water.

1 level dessertspoon
gelatine.
3 drops vanilla or
lemon essence.

METHOD—

1. Soak gelatine in two tablespoons cold water ten minutes and dissolve.
2. Beat yolks of eggs well. Gradually pour on hot milk. Stir well. Add ½ tablespoon sugar.
3. Return to saucepan. Stir over heat till custard thickens. Cool slightly. Add dissolved gelatine.
4. When cold, stir in well beaten whites of egg, to which has been added ½ tablespoon sugar. Beat well.
5. Turn into wet mould to set.
6. Serve in glass dish with cream.

STEAMED FISH

METHOD No. 1—

1. Fillet fish, place between two buttered plates.
2. Place over a saucepan of boiling water, steam gently for 10 to 15 minutes.

METHOD No. 2—

1. Scale and clean fish, leave head on, but remove the eyes.
2. Curl fish by drawing the tail through the mouth.
3. Place fish in greased basin, cover with greased paper.
4. Stand basin in a saucepan with a little boiling water; steam gently for 15 to 20 minutes.
5. This method is suitable for a long fish, such as garfish or whiting.
6. Steamed fish may be masked with a good white sauce and garnished with lemon, parsley and yolk of hard boiled egg (rubbed through fine strainer).

FRICASSEE OF BRAINS

INGREDIENTS—

1 set brains.	¼ teaspoon salt.
1 dessertspoon flour.	Slice lemon rind.
½ teaspoon butter.	Parsley.
¾ cup milk.	Sippets of toast.

METHOD—

1. Soak brains in salted water and remove skin.
2. Blanch and strain.
3. Make white sauce. Add lemon rind. Cook 3 minutes.
4. Put brains into sauce. Simmer gently for 10 minutes. Remove lemon rind.
5. Serve on hot dish with sippets of toast.
6. Garnish with parsley (sprigs or chopped).
7. Mashed potatoes may also be served with brains.

FRIED BRAINS

INGREDIENTS—

1 set brains.	Breadcrumbs.
Salt.	Parsley.
1 egg.	Dripping.

Fried Brain — Continued.

METHOD—

1. Soak brains in salty water. Skin.
2. Blanch and strain.
3. Dip in beaten egg, then crumbs.
4. Deep fry a golden brown.
5. Drain on kitchen paper.
6. Serve hot. Garnish with parsley.

Note—Fried or grilled bacon may be served with brains.

FRICASEE OF CHICKEN

INGREDIENTS—

Remains of cold chicken.	1 cup milk.
1 level tablespoon butter.	¼ cup cream.
1 dessertspoon flour.	Salt and pepper to taste.

METHOD—

1. Make white sauce with butter, flour and milk.
2. Remove from stove, add cream, salt and pepper.
3. Allow to cool.
4. Add chicken (cut into neat pieces). Reheat together.
5. Garnish with chopped parsley, and ham if allowed.

CHICKEN CREAM

INGREDIENTS—

Breast or leg of cold chicken.	Salt and pepper.
	Nutmeg.
Breadcrumbs.	1 egg.
½ cup cream or milk.	

METHOD—

1. Mince chicken.
2. Beat yolk of egg well. Add cream, salt and pepper, nutmeg, breadcrumbs and chicken. Mix thoroughly.
3. Add stiffly beaten white of egg and mix well.
4. Turn into greased mould, cover with greased paper.
5. Steam gently until set.
6. Serve with mashed potatoes and green peas.

BOILED CHICKEN

METHOD—

1. Prepare chicken.
2. Put into hot water with salt.
3. Simmer gently until tender from ¼ to 1 hour.
4. Serve with parsley or egg sauce.

STEAMED EGG

METHOD—

1. Grease breakfast cup with butter. Cover finely with chopped parsley.
2. Whip white of egg lightly. Add pinch salt. Put into cup.
3. Slip yolk into centre of cup.
4. Cover with greased paper.
5. Steam 2½ to 3 minutes. Serve on hot buttered toast.

WHITE WINE WHEY

INGREDIENTS—

1 wine glass of sherry   1¼ cups of milk.
  or white wine.

METHOD—

1. Bring the milk to boiling point.
2. Pour in wine and let it boil for 1 minute.
3. Let stand until curd settles.
4. Take off stove and strain through muslin.
5. Sweeten to taste.

STEAMED CUSTARD

INGREDIENTS—

1 egg.   Milk.
1 teaspoon sugar.

METHOD—

1. Beat egg and sugar in a cup.
2. Fill up cup with milk.
3. Grate a little nutmeg on top.
4. Cover with greased paper.
5. Stand in saucepan with water halfway up the cup. Heat slowly, leave in hot water until custard sets (about 15 minutes). Do not allow water to boil.

BAKED APPLES

METHOD—

1. Wipe and core apples. Half-way down apple cut round skin.
2. Fill centre with sugar, honey or golden syrup. Add clove or a pinch of cinnamon, and 1 teaspoon of butter.
3. Place apples in greased oven dish. Add a tablespoon of water to each apple.
4. Bake in moderate oven till tender.
5. Serve hot or cold with cream or custard.

BEVERAGES

LEMON SYRUP (No. 1)

INGREDIENTS—

2½ cups lemon juice
(strained).

2 cups sugar.

METHOD—

1. Put lemon juice and sugar in saucepan and heat until sugar is dissolved.
2. Bottle and keep in a cool place.

LEMON SYRUP (No. 2)

INGREDIENTS—

1 kilogram sugar
(2 lbs 3 ozs).
1 litre water (1¾ pints).

1 large teaspoon acetic acid.
Essence lemon.

METHOD—

1. Boil sugar and water, add acid.
2. When cool add essence of lemon to taste.
3. Bottle and cork tightly.

RASPBERRY SYRUP

Same as above, substituting raspberry essence for lemon. Add cochineal.

GINGER SYRUP

INGREDIENTS—

1 kilogram sugar
(2 lbs 3 ozs).
1 litre water (1¾ pints).
20 bird's eye chillies
1 level teaspoon citric acid.

Colour with caramel
(see page 261)
30 grams ginger (bruised)
(1 oz).
½ level teaspoon cream of tartar.

METHOD—

1. Boil water and sugar together with chillies and ginger about 15 minutes. Stir in citric acid and cream of tartar.
2. Strain. Colour with caramel.

MULBERRY SYRUP

INGREDIENTS—

2 kilograms mulberries
(4 lbs 6 ozs).

1 litre vinegar (1¾ pints).
Sugar to measure.

METHOD—

1. Prepare fruit, stand in vinegar for two days.
2. Strain, add 720 grams (1½ lbs.) sugar to each pint of juice
   and vinegar.
3. Boil mixture for 3 minutes.
4. Bottle when cold.

Note—This syrup will keep indefinitely. Other berry fruits may
   be used.

GINGER BEER

INGREDIENTS—

240 grams bruised ginger
(8 ozs).
1 kilogram and 360 grams
white sugar (3 lbs).

2 lemons.
5 litres of water
(9 pints).
1 teaspoon yeast.

METHOD—

1. Put ginger, sliced lemons, sugar and water into pan. Bring to
   boil. Boil 10 minutes. Strain.
2. Cool off, then add 1 teaspoonful yeast. Stir well.
3. Bottle. Cork securely. Tie corks to neck of bottle.

This should be ready for use in 48 hours.

HOP BEER

INGREDIENTS—

9 litres water
(2 gallons).
Handful of raisins,
or barley.
1 kilogram sugar
(2 lbs 3 ozs).
1 tablespoon cream of
tartar.

60 grams hops (2 ozs).
1 tablespoon tartaric
acid.
4 tablespoons bruised ginger or 240 grams (½ lb)
whole ginger.
Egg shell and white of
1 egg.

Hop Beer — Continued.

METHOD—

1. Boil water, hops, raisins and ginger 2 hours.
2. Remove from heat, strain and cool.
3. Add sugar, egg shell, white of egg and acids. Allow to stand till next day. Remove egg shell.
4. Add 2 tablespoons of caramel if a dark colour is desired.
5. Bottle and cork tightly.

Note—If the hop beer is not working at once add 1 teaspoon of flour and leave in open vessel a few hours, then bottle.

PASSION FRUIT SYRUP

INGREDIENTS—

8 passion fruit.	2½ cups boiling water.
2 cups sugar.	2 teaspoons citric acid.

METHOD—

1. Scoop out passion fruit.
2. Make a syrup by boiling sugar and water together. Stir in citric acid.
3. Pour syrup on to fruit.
4. Allow to stand ½ hour, strain and bottle to overflow.
5. Stand bottle in saucepan of water. Bring to boil to sterilise.
6. Boil 15 minutes. Cork and seal. This syrup will not keep indefinitely.

GRAPE CORDIAL

INGREDIENTS—

4 kilograms and 500 grams grapes (10 lbs).	1 kilogram sugar (2 lbs 3 ozs).
2¼ litres water (2 quarts)	

METHOD—

1. Place grapes in large pan. Partly crush. Add water. Boil 10 minutes.
2. Put in a straining bag. Drain overnight.
3. Return to pan, add sugar; boil hard 10 minutes.
4. Pour into heated bottles. Fill well, cork and seal.

To Use—1/3rd of tumbler of fruit juice to ½ of water.

Note—Other fruits, such as loganberry, may be prepared in the same way.

FRUIT CUP

INGREDIENTS—

4 bottles lemonade.
2 bottles ginger ale
(dry).
3 lemons.
3 oranges.
2 slices of pineapple.
30 grams cherries (1 oz).

4 passion fruit.
1 banana.
Few strawberries.
4 tablespoons of diced
fruit (apple, peach,
pear, etc).
2 tablespoons sugar.

METHOD—

1. Slice one orange and lemon into bowl.
2. Add passion fruit, diced fruit, pineapple, sliced banana and juice of remaining oranges, and lemons.
3. Sprinkle with sugar, bruise fruit slightly; allow to stand about 1 hour.
4. Add lemonade, ginger ale, and serve immediately.

*Note—*Amount of liquid (lemonade and ginger ale) should be approximately 4 litres (7 pints).

CONFECTIONERY

TOFFEE

INGREDIENTS—

2 cups sugar.
Level teaspoon cream of
tartar.

1 cup water.
Flavouring.

METHOD—

1. Put sugar, water and cream of tartar into saucepan. Bring to boil slowly.
2. Wipe down inside of pan with wet brush.
3. Boil quickly, without stirring, until the toffee reaches "large crack".
4. Remove from heat, add essence.
5. Pour into greased tins and when nearly set mark into desired shapes.
6. When cold wrap in wax paper and store in airtight tins.

Note—"The Large Crack"—Test by dropping a small quantity of toffee into very cold water. It should be short, brittle and break clean when bitten.

BUTTER ALMONDS

METHOD—

1. Make toffee as above.
2. Remove from stove, add essence of lemon and 60 grams (2 ozs) of butter. Mix well.
3. Put in teaspoon heaps over blanched almonds, placed on a greased slab or dish.
4. When cold wrap in wax paper and store in airtight tins or jars.

UNCOOKED FONDANT

INGREDIENTS—

1 kilogram icing sugar
(2 lbs 3 ozs).
1 white of egg.
Juice of half a lemon.

Dessertspoon hot water.
1 tablespoon glucose
(optional).

Uncooked Fondant — Continued.

METHOD—
1. Sift icing sugar into basin.
2. Add white of egg, lemon juice, warmed glucose and hot water.
3. Beat thoroughly.
4. Cover with damp cloth until ready to use.
5. This fondant may be coloured, flavoured and used as fillings for endless sweets.

NEAPOLITAN SQUARES

METHOD—
1. Prepare three coloured fondants of different flavours.
2. Roll each out about ½ cm (¼ inch) thick.
3. Put one piece on top of other. Press together.
4. Brush with white of egg. Sprinkle with almonds and angelica.
5. Next day cut in small cubes.
6. Wrap in wax paper.
7. Store in air tight jars.

DATE FONDANT

METHOD—
1. Make fondant and flavour with vanilla.
2. Stone date and fill cavity with fondant.
3. Press into a neat shape and spread out to dry and set.

TURKISH DELIGHT

INGREDIENTS—

30 grams gelatine (1 oz).
1¼ cups water.
480 grams sugar (1 lb).

1 lemon.
Colouring.
Icing sugar.

METHOD—
1. Soak gelatine in little cold water. Then dissolve over heat.
2. Put sugar, water and strip of lemon rind into saucepan and bring to boil.
3. Add dissolved gelatine.
4. Boil 15 to 20 minutes.
5. Add lemon juice and colouring. Strain into wet dish.
6. When cold and set, turn on paper well sprinkled with icing sugar. Cut in neat cubes and coat each well with icing sugar.
7. Store in air-tight boxes.

COCONUT ICE

INGREDIENTS—

3 cups sugar.
Level teaspoon cream of
  tartar.
½ cup dessicated coconut.

1 cup water.
Essence.
1 tablespoon glucose
  (optional).

METHOD—

1. Put sugar, water, glucose and cream of tartar into saucepan
   and boil to "soft ball".
2. Pour into a wet basin, cool slightly, then work with a wooden
   spoon. Gradually add the flavouring and coconut. When it
   begins to thicken pour quickly into a frame lined with
   wax paper.
3. Repeat recipe. Colour and pour over white. Whack well with
   hand. This is important.
4. When set and cold lift off frame. Cut slab of ice into blocks.
5. Wrap in wax paper and store in air-tight jars.

SOFT BALL—Test by dropping a small quantity into very cold
  water. It should mould into a soft ball between the fingers.

PEPPERMINT CREAMS

INGREDIENTS—

480 grams icing sugar
  (1 lb).
1 white of egg.

1 dessertspoon water.
Oil of peppermint.

METHOD—

1. Sift icing sugar into basin.
2. Add white of egg and water and beat well with wooden
   spoon.
3. Add sufficient peppermint to flavour to taste.
4. Turn onto a board covered with icing sugar and knead until
   smooth.
5. Roll and stamp into rounds.
6. Stand on wax paper to dry.
7. Store in air-tight jars.

SHERRY BALLS

INGREDIENTS—

1 packet milk arrowroot
  biscuits.
240 grams icing sugar
  (8 ozs).
1 cup mixed fruit.

1 tablespoon sherry.
Vanilla to taste.
1 tablespoon cocoa.
240 grams butter (8 ozs).
Coconut.

METHOD—

1. Crush biscuits with rolling pin.
2. Melt butter.
3. Mix all dry ingredients, pour over butter, sherry and vanilla.
     Mix well.
4. Roll into balls, roll in coconut.

APRICOT BALLS

INGREDIENTS—

240 grams dried apricots
  (8 ozs).
½ tin condensed milk
  (sweetened).

120 grams coconut (4 ozs).
60 grams chopped nuts
  (2 ozs).

METHOD—

1. Mince apricots. Add coconut, nuts and condensed milk. Mix
     well.
2. Roll into small balls, coat with icing sugar or coconut.

RUM BALLS

INGREDIENTS—

4 cups cake or biscuit
  crumbs.
2 tablespoons icing sugar.
2 tablespoons cocoa.
240 grams butter (8 ozs).

2 tablespoons condensed
  milk.
2 tablespoons rum.
2 drops almond essence.
4 drops vanilla.

METHOD—

1. Melt butter in a saucepan.
2. Stir in cocoa and sugar, heat until both are dissolved.
3. Remove saucepan ⁄ from heat, stir in rum, essences, and
     condensed milk.
4. Pour mixture over crumbs, mix well.
5. Roll into small balls, toss in chocolate cake topping.

Note—Keep in refrigerator during hot weather.

MARSHMALLOWS

INGREDIENTS—

3 dessertspoons gelatine.
1¼ cups hot water.
240 grams sugar (8 ozs).
pinch of salt.

¼ level teaspoon cream of
   tartar.
1 dessertspoon lemon
   juice.
Colouring if liked.

METHOD—

1. Boil water, sugar, gelatine and cream of tartar until mixture forms a thread when a teaspoonful is dropped in cold water. Stir and leave to cool.
2. Add lemon juice, salt and colouring. Beat until thick.
3. Pour into slightly greased dish and leave for 24 hours.
4. Cut into squares, roll in a mixture of 3 parts icing sugar and 1 part cornflour.

WHITE CHRISTMAS

INGREDIENTS—

1 cup powdered milk
1 cup coconut
1 cup icing sugar
1 cup mixed fruit

½ cup chopped nuts
1½ cups rice bubbles
Vanilla
240 grams copha (8 ozs)

METHOD—

1. Mix all dry ingredients and vanilla.
2. Melt copha, add to dry ingredients, mix well.
3. Form into balls or press in flat tin, then cut into squares when firm.
4. Keep in cool place.

BACON CURING

Weight of pig should be not more than 50 kilograms (110 lbs).

METHOD—

1. Cut off head, divide in two and clean thoroughly, cutting away all bony matter from nostrils.
2. Put the heads in strong salt water for two days to allow bleeding.
3. Cut sides across between third and fourth rib to form shoulder, and across at bottom of ribs to form ham. Remove the ribs.
4. Run a steel down the bones as close as possible in the ham and shoulder, and down hocks where feet have been cut off, and pack in fine salt, packing it in well with steel.
5. Place hams, shoulders and sides in prepared brine for two days to allow bleeding. Drain well.

BRINE RECIPE

36 litres of rain water (8 gallons).

8 kilograms salt (17 lbs).

1 kilogram brown sugar (2 lbs 3 ozs).

2 tablespoons saltpetre.

METHOD—

6. Boil for 1 hour and skim frothy matter rising to surface. Strain into clean barrel.

    Note—It is well to make this brine the day before so that it will be quite cool.

7. Weight the hams, etc., down so that the brine completely covers them.
8. Put fly-proof cover over barrel. A chaff bag placed across barrel with hoop to tighten it down makes a good cheap cover.

Note—The head, trotters and tongue, may be put in this brine after the hams, etc., are taken out and allowed to remain there for two weeks, when they will be ready for use.

Brine Recipe — Continued.

9. Now prepare the following mixture, which has to be rubbed in for three days, and sprinkled for eleven more days, turning the meat in rotation:—

5 kilograms and 440 grams fine salt (12 lbs)	480 grams all-spice (powdered) (1 lb).
1 kilogram and 800 grams brown sugar (4 lbs).	240 grams mustard (8 ozs).
	30 grams saltpetre (1 oz).

Do not be afraid to use the mixture freely and make more if required.

10. Place skin sides down one day then reverse next day. Cover well from flies. Put heavy weight on meat, as pressing squeezes out the moisture.
11. After curing, meat may be washed, dried and smoked.

SMOKING

Smoking takes about 3 days. An effective smoke house is an old iron tank. Hang the meat on wires. Sawdust makes a good, thick smoke.

MISCELLANEOUS
SELF-RAISING FLOUR

INGREDIENTS—

1 kilogram plain flour
   (2 lbs 3 ozs).
4 level teaspoons
   bi-carobonate of soda.

10 level teaspoons
   cream of tartar.

METHOD—

1. Crush soda, cream of tartar, add to flour.
2. Sift three times.
3. Keep in air-tight tin.

BAKING POWDER

INGREDIENTS—

60 grams bi-carbonate of
   soda (2 ozs).
30 grams ground rice (1 oz)

150 grams cream of tartar
   (5 ozs).

METHOD—

1. Roll bi-carbonate of soda thoroughly. Add cream of tartar.
   Roll again. Add ground rice. Roll again.
2. Sift mixture 3 times.
3. Put away in air-tight tins or screw top bottles.

TO RENDER FAT

METHOD—

1. Cut up suet and uncooked fat. Take care to remove meat.
2. Put into saucepan with a little water. Simmer until fat is
   extracted.
3. Strain off fat. When set, remove any water.

Note—This may be done in slow oven without water.

TO CLARIFY DRIPPING

METHOD—

1. Put dripping into saucepan with water to cover.
2. Bring slowly to the boil. Simmer 10 minutes. Skim well.
   Strain into a bowl.
3. When cold and set remove fat and scrape under side. Put into
   saucepan and heat to evaporate any water.

CARAMEL

INGREDIENTS—

240 grams sugar (8 ozs).   Water.

METHOD—

1. Put sugar with 4 tablespoons of the water into saucepan. Cook till brown.
2. Add sufficient water to make the consistency of honey.
3. Cool and bottle.

BREAD CRUMBS (DRIED)

METHOD—

1. Cut off brown crusts.
2. Brown bread evenly in a slow oven.
3. Roll out, sift and bottle for use.

HARD-BOILED EGGS

1. Place eggs in boiling water. Boil 10 to 15 minutes.
2. Crack shell, put into cold water till cooled (this prevents eggs discolouring).

Note—Eggs from refrigerator should be started in cold water.

TO CHOP PARSLEY

1. Wash parsley and remove from stalks.
2. Dry well.
3. Gather parsley as tightly as possible, in the fingers. Cut with sharp edge of knife, keeping point on board.
4. Turn parsley and cut opposite way.
5. Chop finely, keeping point of knife on board all the time.

TO CHOP MINT

Same as for parsley.

When chopping mint for mint sauce, sprinkle sugar on mint before chopping.

TO CHOP SUET

Suet should have skin removed before attempting to chop and should also be sprinkled with flour.

Cut first in flakes, then chop.

(Suet may be stored in flour).

GARNISHING

1. To garnish is to decorate food after dishing.
2. A garnish should be light, dainty and not overdone.
3. The garnish should be prepared before serving so that the food will not become cold.
4. All green garnishes must be fresh and stiff.
5. When lemon is used it should be cut in thin slices.
6. Steamed fish may be garnished with sprigs of parsley, lemon, yolk of egg (hard-boiled).
7. Fried fish may garnished with lemon and sprigs of parsley.
8. Fried meat dishes may be garnished with parsley.
9. Cold meat may be garnished with parsley, shredded lettuce, slices of tomato, dainty celery tops.
10. Sandwiches may be garnished with shredded lettuce or parsley and mint sprigs.
11. Olives, gherkins, small nasturtium leaves, cress, beetroot, hard-boiled egg and mint make effective garnishes for salads and savouries.

Notes

Notes

Notes

Notes

Notes

Notes

Notes

Notes